The Hard Road to Renewal

The Hard Road to Renewal

Thatcherism and the Crisis of the Left

STUART HALL

VERSO

London · New York

(In association with Marxism Today)

This edition published by Verso 1988 in association with Marxism Today
© 1988 Stuart Hall
All rights reserved

Verso
UK: 6 Meard Street, London W1V 3HR
USA: 29 West 35th Street, New Yorks, NY 10001-2291

Verso is the imprint of New Left Books

British Library Cataloguing in Publication Data
Hall, Stuart *1932-*
    The hard road to renewal: Thatcherism
    and the crisis of the left.
    1. Great Britain. Socialism
    I. Title
    335'.00941

    ISBN 0-86091-199-3
    ISBN 0-86091-915-3 Pbk

US Library of Congress Cataloging in Publication data
Hall, Stuart.
    The hard road to renewal.

    Includes index.
    1. Conservative Party (Great Britain) 2. Labour
Party (Great Britain) 3. Great Britain—Politics and
government—1979-   I. Title.
JN1129.C7H28 1988 324.24104   88-20574
ISBN 0-86091-199-3
ISBN 0-86091-915-3 (pbk.)

Typeset by Leaper & Gard Ltd, Bristol, England
Printed in Great Britain by Bookcraft (Bath) Ltd

Contents

Acknowledgements

For permission to reprint material first published elsewhere, I should like to thank the following: *Marxism Today* and *The New Socialist*, where many of these articles first appeared; Macmillans and my collaborators and co-authors, Charles Critcher, Tony Jefferson, John Clarke and Brian Roberts for the extract from *Policing The Crisis*; Lawrence and Wishart for 'Popular–Democratic vs Authoritarian Populism' from *Marxism and Democracy*; Hutchinsons and the Centre for Contemporary Cultural Studies for the extract from *Crises of the British State*; Merlin Press for 'The Battle for Socialist Ideas in the 1980s' from *The Socialist Register 1982*; Polity Press for 'The Crisis of Labourism' From *The Future of the Left*; Bill Schwarz and Martin Jacques for allowing me to reprint articles which were jointly authored.

I am indebted to colleagues and friends too numerous to mention by name for many of the ideas which have been incorporated in an unacknowledged form here – although it goes without saying that they are not responsible for the use and misuse I have made of them. I would like to thank everyone at the Centre for Cultural Studies, especially the 'Policing the Crisis' collective, with whom some of the earliest formulations of these problems were first debated; all those who participated in the 'Populism, Discourse and Political Ideologies' research seminar organized and funded by the Open University; Neil Belton, for first suggesting that these articles should be collected into a single volume; Kevin Davey, for the extensive editorial work and careful judgement required to pull the project together; Catherine Hall, for love and friendship over more than twenty years, but especially for teaching me the centrality of feminism and sexual politics to the renewal of socialism; James Souter for, among many other things, providing a critical sounding-board for many of the ideas developed here and for sharing my sense of outrage at the contempt with which Thatcherism has treated ordinary people, black and white; and Martin Jacques, who as editor of *Marxism Today*, was the instigator of many of these articles and their constant and critical interlocutor.

The book is dedicated to my children, Rebecca and Jesse, who spent their adolescence under the shadow of 'Iron Times' – in the hope of better things to come.

Stuart Hall, May 1988

Introduction:
Thatcherism and the
Crisis of the Left

These articles represent an attempt to define the character and significance of the political project of 'Thatcherism' and the crisis of the left
which it has precipitated. They were written at different times over the
decade 1978 to 1988. This conjuncture has a unique and specific
character, and has proved to be a historic turning-point in postwar
British political and cultural life. The essays have the dubious distinction
of having helped to launch the word which has dominated the period –
'Thatcherism' – into our political vocabulary. 'The Great Moving Right
Show', first published in December 1978, was one of the earliest articles
to analyse Thatcherism in terms of this historic shift.

Initially conceived as a series of interventions, these articles are of
necessity somewhat polemical and were designed to have a cutting edge in
relation to other positions in an ongoing debate. But despite their
ephemeral nature, they do propose a distinctive 'reading' of the period
and engage a number of longer-running themes. For these reasons they
have seemed worth preserving in a more permanent form. Inevitably,
they contain many repetitions and though every effort has been made to
cut out the most glaring of these, some have had to be retained for the
sake of coherence of argument.

The essays in Part One foreground the analysis of Thatcherism; those
in Part Three concentrate on the crisis of the left. This neat arrangement, with its apparently simple chronology, is somewhat deceptive. In
fact, the two themes are interrelated throughout – two sides of the same
coin. For example, the growing contradictions of Labour governments

1

of the 1960s and 1970s, the 'crisis of authority' of 1968–72, the onset of recession in the mid-1970s, and the turn towards a Labourist version of 'monetarist realism' not only provide the narrative contexts for the rise of Thatcherism but are shown, analytically, to have formed the terrain on which Thatcherism specifically first grounded itself, the contradictions which it worked to its advantage, the 'enemy within' against which it defined its project. The rising fortunes of Thatcherism were tied to the tail of Labour's fading ones. At the other end of the story, the failure since then of Labour, and of the left more generally, to comprehend what Thatcherism really represents – the decisive break with the postwar consensus, the profound reshaping of social life which it has set in motion – provides the measure of the left's historic incapacity so far to meet the challenge of Thatcherism on equal terms.

The main storylines are therefore 'framed' by a set of wider concerns and histories, which are more directly referenced in the short middle section of the book, entitled 'Questions of Theory'. Thus, Thatcherism's economic strategy is set against the relative decline and comparative 'backwardness' of the British economy and the state. Its restructuring of society is contextualized within certain emergent 'sociological' tendencies which are beginning to be decisive for the next phase of capitalism's development as a global system. Politically, Thatcherism is related to the recomposition and 'fragmentation' of the historic relations of representation between classes and parties; the shifting boundaries between state and civil society, 'public' and 'private'; the emergence of new arenas of contestation, new sites of social antagonism, new social movements, and new social subjects and political identities in contemporary society.

Ideologically, Thatcherism is seen as forging new discursive articulations between the liberal discourses of the 'free market' and economic man and the organic conservative themes of tradition, family and nation, respectability, patriarchalism and order. Its reworking of these different repertoires of 'Englishness' constantly repositions both individual subjects and 'the people' as a whole – their needs, experiences, aspirations, pleasures and desires – contesting space in terms of shifting social, sexual and ethnic identities, against the background of a crisis of national identity and culture precipitated by the unresolved psychic trauma of the 'end of empire'. Culturally, the project of Thatcherism is defined as a form of 'regressive modernization' – the attempt to 'educate' and discipline the society into a particularly regressive version of modernity by, paradoxically, dragging it backwards through an equally regressive version of the past.

The narrative offered here often appears to be governed by immediate questions of tactics, strategy and the rhythms of electoral politics.

In fact, 'politics' is always used with a broader, more expanded, meaning. Power is never merely repressive but, in Foucault's sense, always productive. The contrast is drawn between the narrow, corporate and electoralist conception of politics, which largely dominates official Labour thinking and strategy; and the expanded, multifaceted and hegemonic conception of politics as a 'war of position' with which (however instinctively and intuitively) Thatcherism always works. Politics is understood here in terms of the different modalities of power (cultural, moral and intellectual, as well as economic and political); the 'play' of power within and between different sites, which is only at certain moments condensed into 'party' or electoral terms in relation to the state; the interplay between what Gramsci identified as the 'two moments' of Machiavelli's Centaur – 'force and consent, authority and hegemony, violence and civilization': in short, politics in Gramsci's sense – as 'the various levels of the relations of force' in society.

The so-called 'overemphasis' on politics and ideology has been one of the main criticisms levelled at this work over the years.[1] One effect of this foregrounding is certainly to undercut any claim the essays might otherwise have had to represent a comprehensive analysis of Thatcherism. For instance, they provide no substantive assessment of Thatcherism's economic policy, though in fairness they cannot be said to neglect the economic dimension. I do not give sufficient attention to the issues of defence and foreign policy, war and peace. Thatcherism has many other aspects, crucial to any comprehensive account, which these essays do not address. However, the decision to focus on politics and ideology was the result of a deliberate strategy; if necessary, to 'bend the stick' in this direction, in order to make a more general point about the need to develop a theoretical and political language on the left which rigorously avoids the temptations to economism, reductionism or teleological forms of argument.

In very general terms, and with many honourable exceptions, political analysis on the left seems pitifully thin, and ideological analysis is, if anything, in a worse state. As conventionally practised, both lack any sense of the specificity or real effectivity of what we might call the political and ideological instances in the shaping of contemporary developments. This is not because the left is stupid but because, in both its orthodox Marxist and economistic variants, it tends to hold to a very reductionist conception of politics and ideology where, 'in the last instance' (whenever that is), both are determined by, and so can be 'read off' against, some (often ill-defined) notion of 'economic' or 'class' determination. This now looks less and less like the sign of active and ongoing theoretical work likely to break new ground and tell us things we did not already know, and more and more like a confirmation of the correctness of what we always, anyway, believed to be true: the product of a sort of self-confirming circularity, theoretical whistling in the wind. It is partly the product of the inherited habits of a low-flying economism masquerading as 'materialism', or the search for some philosophical guarantee that the law of history will, like Minerva's owl, take wing at five minutes to midnight, rescuing us from the vicissitudes of the present. If Thatcherism has done nothing else, it has surely destroyed for good these fatal consolations.

I believe these positions are theoretically untenable and also that they constitute a major blockage to political analysis and strategy on the left. These essays are therefore, for better or worse, predicated on the end of the conventional wisdom that there is a simple, irreversible correspondence between the economic and the political, or that classes, constituted as homogeneous entities at the economic or 'mode of production' level, are ever transposed in their already unified form onto the 'theatre' of political and ideological struggle. They therefore insist that political and ideological questions be addressed in their full specificity, without reduction.

Many critics have read this as tantamount to 'abandoning class analysis'.[2] At one level, the charge seems beside the point. Nothing in these essays suggests that British society or Thatcherism could be analysed without the concept of class. However, the real question is not whether to use 'class', but what the term actually means and what it can – and cannot – deliver. In some quite obvious and undeniable ways, the whole point of Thatcherism is to clear the way for capitalist market solutions, to restore both the prerogatives of ownership and profitability and the political conditions for capital to operate more effectively, and to construct around its imperatives a supportive culture suffused from end to end by its ethos and values. Thatcherism knows no measure of the good life other than 'value for money'. It understands no other compelling force or motive in the definition of civilization than the forces of the 'free market', which it is busy dressing up in the pharisaic cloak of biblical hypocrisy. Of the present New Utilitarians we can say what Marx once remarked of Jeremy Bentham: he 'takes the modern shopkeeper, especially the English shopkeeper, as the normal man. Whatever is useful to this queer normal man, and to his world, is absolutely useful. This yard-measure, then, he applies to past, present and future.' Does anyone seriously doubt that this 'profits' the industrial and business classes of society, whom Thatcherism has now erected into the sacred bearers of 'the enterprise culture', keepers of the moral conscience and guardians, inter alia, of our education system?

On the other hand, the effectivity of Thatcherism has rested precisely on its ability to articulate different social and economic interests within this political project. It is therefore a complicated matter to say in any precise sense which class interests are represented by Thatcherism (multinational capital 'lived' through the prism of petty-bourgeois ideology?) since it is precisely class interests which, in the process of their 're-presentation', are being politically and ideologically redefined.

The fact is that a profound reshaping of the classes of contemporary British society is underway at the present time. It is perhaps as far-reaching as that 'remaking' at the turn of the century which created the institutional culture and political agendas of Labour and the labour movement, and set the terms of modern, mass-democratic politics as we know them today. (Bill Schwarz and I discuss the ways in which the conjuncture of the 1880s–1930s was formative for the present moment in 'State and Society, 1880–1930').[3] This recomposition is transforming the material basis, the occupational boundaries, the gender and ethnic composition, the political cultures and the social imagery of 'class'. It has made even more problematic something which the left should always have been more scrupulous about – the sliding of the word across a range of different, sometimes incompatible, meanings and discursive contexts. Thatcherism is both constituted by, and constitutive of, those changes. The left, however, has not yet really begun to grasp how radically these recompositions are displacing its historic perspectives.

Ralph Miliband, in his critique of 'The New Revisionism', acknowledges in much the same terms as I do here that 'an accelerated process of recomposition' is going on and that class 'recomposition' is not in the least synonymous with disappearance.[4] Nevertheless, he restates his belief that there is no good reason to suppose that 'this recomposed working class is less capable of developing the commitments and "class consciousness" which socialists have always hoped to see emerge'. My view is that this entails a much more careful and evidenced argument than the simple reiteration that, since this is what Marx said and we have thought, it is and will ever be so. The argument would also have to address the failure of the classic scenarios and forms of 'commitment and class-consciousness' to emerge in anything like the predicted manner, not just in the last decade in Britain, but also in much of the twentieth century since the 'proletarian moment' before and after the First World War, and across the industrialized capitalist countries of Western Europe and North America. This failure cannot be attributed to the weaknesses of the Labour and other social democratic parties alone, and it must surely problematize for any materialist analysis the orthodox ways of thinking the relationship between what, for shorthand purposes, we may call 'the economic', 'the political' and 'the ideological'.

In addition, Miliband's unproblematic assignment of the new social movements to their position in and with the working class and his dismissive treatment of any conflicts of consciousness, identity and practice (between, say, being a woman, or a black, worker) as 'a matter of the greatest importance' but not therefore to be taken as 'an accurate representation of reality' seems to evade all the really difficult, concrete questions of strategy and organization which face us in the present conjuncture. For these and other reasons, what has passed for the conventional 'class analysis' of politics and ideology is no longer adequate on its own to explain the precise disposition of social forces or the new sites of social antagonism which characterize our increasingly divided, but also our increasingly diversified social world.

This is why the question of Thatcherism and 'the popular', which cannot be immediately reread either in terms of a simple class model or in terms of votes or public opinion polls, plays such an important part in my analysis. Thatcherism's 'populism' signals its unexpected ability to harness to its project certain popular discontents, to cut across and between the different divisions in society and to connect with certain aspects of popular experience. Ideologically, though it has certainly not totally won the hearts and minds of the majority of ordinary people, it is clearly not simply an 'external' force, operating on but having no roots in the internal 'logics' of their thinking and experience. Certain ways of thinking, feeling and calculating characteristic of Thatcherism have entered as a material and ideological force into the daily lives of ordinary people. We underestimate the degree to which Thatcherism has succeeded in representing itself as 'on the side of the little people against the big battalions'. Ideologically, it has made itself, to some degree, not only one of 'Them', but, more disconcertingly, part of 'Us'; it has aligned itself with 'what some of the people really want', while at the same time continuing to dominate them through the power bloc.

That Thatcherism is in any serious sense 'popular' or has made any inroads into popular consciousness is, of course, an idea which is often resisted – paradoxically, as much by psephologists and poll analysts of a centrist persuasion as by left critics of 'the new revisionism'. This question cannot be settled by simply 'looking at the facts': in the end it is a matter of political analysis and judgement. But I do not find either the conception of an eternal and impermeable consciousness of 'the' working class, nor the underlying scenario of the present conjuncture implied by it at all convincing. We know that consciousness is contradictory (think of working-class racism) and that these contradictions *can* be articulated by quite different political strategies because they have a material and social basis and are not simply the chimeras of 'false consciousness'. This means that a politics which depends on 'the' working class being, essentially and eternally, either entirely 'Thatcherite' or entirely the revolutionary subject-in-waiting is simply inadequate. It is no longer telling us what we most need to know.

Many of these essays, therefore, have tried to understand in a less mystified way precisely what the specific character of Thatcherism's 'populism' is. (I discuss the theoretical distinction between a 'populist' and a 'popular' rupture in 'Popular-Democratic vs Authoritarian Populism'.)[5] The linkages between Thatcherism's strategic interventions in popular life, the reactionary character of its social project (socially and sexually regressive, patriarchal and racist) and its directive and disciplinary exercise of state power, constitute the contradictory and overdetermined formation for which I coined the term, 'authoritarian populism'. The meaning and genealogy of this concept are discussed in 'Authoritarian Populism: a Reply to Jessop et al.

Many of the concepts which I use to think the 'specificity of the political' in relation to the present crisis I owe to my reading of Gramsci. They flow from Gramsci's sustained polemic against economism and what he called the positive effects of 'the introduction of the concept of distinction into a philosophy of praxis'. I acknowledge some measure of my indebtedness in 'Popular-Democratic vs Authoritarian Populism', in 'Gramsci and Us', and in several other places in the collection. I have deliberately used the Gramscian term 'hegemony' in order to foreclose any falling back on the mechanical notion that Thatcherism is merely another name for the exercise of the same, old, familiar class domination by the same, old, familiar ruling class. 'Hegemony' implies: the struggle to contest and dis-organize an existing political formation; the taking of the 'leading position' (on however minority a basis) over a number of different spheres of society at once – economy, civil society, intellectual and moral life, culture; the conduct of a wide and differentiated type of struggle; the winning of a strategic measure of popular consent; and, thus, the securing of a social authority sufficiently deep to conform society into a new historic project. It should never be mistaken for a finished or settled project. It is always contested, always trying to secure itself, always 'in process'. Thus, I do not argue that Thatcherism is now and will be forever 'hegemonic'. I contrast, not Thatcherism's 'hegemony', but its hegemonic project and strategy, with both the economic-corporatist politics of Labourism and the all-or-nothing, class-against-class scenarios of the 'war of manoeuvre' which still dominate the political imagination of the left.

I also use 'historical bloc' instead of 'ruling class' to suggest Thatcherism's complex and heterogeneous social composition of power and domination. I give much greater weight than orthodox analyses to social contradictions other than those of class, to social forces which do not have a clear class designation and social antagonisms which have a different history and trajectory within contemporary societies. There is no space to elaborate further on this conceptual apparatus but it is essential to acknowledge its influence and theoretical effects.

The object to which this analysis is addressed is, in part, cultural: and, as Thatcherism has developed and changed over the years, I have come, if anything, to pay greater, not less, attention to its cultural roots and to the cultural terrain. Arenas of contestation which may appear, to a more orthodox or conventional reading, to be 'marginal' to the main question, acquire in the perspective of an analysis of 'hegemony', an absolute centrality: questions about moral conduct, about gender and sexuality, about race and ethnicity, about ecological and environmental issues, about cultural and national identity. Thatcherism's search for 'the enemies within'; its operations across the different lines of division and identi-fication in social life; its construction of the respectable, patriarchal, entrepreneurial subject with 'his' orthodox tastes, inclinations, prefer-ences, opinions and prejudices as the stable subjective bedrock and guarantee of its purchase on our subjective worlds; its rooting of itself inside a particularly narrow, ethnocentric and exclusivist conception of 'national identity'; and its constant attempts to expel symbolically one sector of society after another from the imaginary community of the nation – these are as central to Thatcherism's hegemonic project as the privatization programme or the assault on local democracy (which is of course often precisely attacked in their name: what else is the 'loony left'?). The left cannot hope to contest the ground of Thatcherism with-out attending to these cultural questions, without conducting a 'politics' of the subjective moment, of identity, and without a conception of the subjects of its project, those who it is making socialism *for* and *with*.

To a significant extent, Thatcherism is about the remaking of common sense: its aim is to become the 'common sense of the age'. Common sense shapes out ordinary, practical, everyday calculation and appears as natural as the air we breathe. It is simply 'taken for granted' in practice and thought, and forms the starting-point (never examined or questioned) from which every conversation begins, the premises on which every television programme is predicated. The hope of every ideology is to naturalize itself out of History into Nature, and thus to become invisible, to operate unconsciously. It is Mrs Thatcher's natural idiom of speech and thought – some would say her only idiom. But common sense, however natural it appears, always has a structure, a set of histories which are traces of the past as well as intimations of a future philosophy. However fragmentary, contradictory and episodic, common sense is, as Gramsci says, 'not without its consequences' since 'it holds together a specific social group, it influences moral conduct and the direction of will'.[6]

Another criticism often made is that I 'place too much emphasis on the role of ideology in the social process'[7] and assume that Thatcherism has 'an ideological homogeneity in the conception and pursuit of policies which does not exist'.[8] Certainly, Thatcherism is not only an ideological phenomenon. However, questions of ideology and culture play a key role in any analysis from the 'hegemonic' perspective and cannot be regarded as secondary or dependent factors. No social or political force can hope to create a new type of society or raise the masses to a new level of civilization without first becoming the leading cultural force and in that way providing the organizing nucleus of a wide-ranging set of new conceptions. Ideology has its own modality, its own ways of working and its own forms of struggle. These have real effects in society which cannot be reduced to, nor explained as, merely the secondary or reflexive effects of some factor which is primary or more determining. All economic and political processes have ideological 'conditions of existence' and, as Gramsci constantly reminded us, 'popular beliefs ... are themselves material forces'.[9] In several places in this collection (for example, in 'The Culture Gap') I have tried to suggest how damaging has been Labour's failure to establish itself as a leading cultural force in civil society, popular culture and urban life.

The analysis offered here contests the idea that each class has its own, fixed, paradigmatic ideology and that ideological struggle consists of the clash between fully constituted and self-sufficient 'world views'. I adopt instead a *discursive* conception of ideology – ideology (like language) is conceptualized in terms of the articulation of elements. As Volosinov remarked, the ideological sign is always multi-accentual, and Janus-faced – that is, it can be discursively rearticulated to construct new meanings, connect with different social practices, and position social subjects differently. 'Differently oriented accents intersect in every ideological sign'. As different currents constantly struggle within the same ideological field, what must be studied is the way in which they contest, often around the same idea or concept. The question is, as Gramsci put it, 'how these currents are born, how they are diffused and why in the process of diffusion they fracture along certain lines and in certain directions.'[10] We have seen over the last decade precisely such an intense and prolonged contestation within the same ideological terrain over some of the leading ideas which shape practical consciousness and influence our political practice and allegiances – those of 'freedom', 'choice', 'the people', 'the public good'; and what constitutes, and who can and cannot claim, 'Englishness'. Ideologies therefore matter profoundly because, when they become 'organic' to historical development and to the life of society, they acquire 'a validity which is psychological; they organize human masses and create the terrain on which men [sic] move, acquire consciousness of their position, struggle, etc'.[11]

It follows from this that ideology always consists, internally, of the articulation of different discursive elements; and externally that discursive articulations can position the same individuals or groups differently. Given that disarticulation–rearticulation is the primary form in which ideological transformations are achieved, I do not believe that organic ideologies are logically consistent or homogeneous; just as I do not believe the subjects of ideology are unified and integral 'selves' assigned to one political position. In fact, they are fractured, always 'in process' and 'strangely composite'. It is because Thatcherism knows this that it understands why the ideological terrain of struggle is so crucial. This is why it believes that the conceptions which organize the mass of the people are worth struggling over, and that social subjects *can* be 'won' to a new conception of themselves and society.

Thus, from 'The Great Moving Right Show' onwards, I have tried to show how Thatcherism articulates and condenses different, often contradictory, discourses within the same ideological formation. It presupposes, not the installation of an already-formed and integral conception of the world, but the *process of formation* by which 'a multiplicity of dispersed wills, with heterogeneous aims, are welded together'. I do not believe that just anything can be articulated with anything else and, in that sense, I stop short before what is sometimes called a 'fully discursive' position. All discourse has 'conditions of existence' which, although they cannot fix or guarantee particular outcomes, set limits or constraints on the process of articulation itself. Historical formations, which consist of previous but powerfully forged articulations, may not be guaranteed forever in place by some abstract historical law, but they *are* deeply resistant to change, and do establish lines of tendency and boundaries which give to the fields of politics and ideology the 'open structure' of a formation and not simply the slide into an infinite and neverending plurality.

Nevertheless, ideology does not obey the logic of rational discourse. Nor does it consist of closed systems, although it has 'logics' of its own. Like other symbolic or discursive formations, it is connective across different positions, between apparently dissimilar, sometimes contradictory, ideas. Its 'unity' is always in quotation marks and always complex, a suturing together of elements which have no necessary or eternal 'belongingness'. It is always, in that sense, organized around arbitrary and not natural closures. For this way of conceptualizing the ideological ruptures of our times, I am much indebted to recent debates in poststructuralist theory and the work of Ernesto Laclau, especially *Politics and Ideology in Marxist Theory*.[12] However, for reasons too briefly indicated above, I do not always follow to their logical conclusion the extension of those arguments he and Chantal Mouffe have made in their challenging and provocative book, *Hegemony and Socialist Strategy.*[13] I am much more in agreement with their reformulations – for example, concerning the relations between discursive and non-discursive elements in their conception of discourse – in a recent reply to criticism from Norman Geras.[14]

I have spent more time in this brief introduction trying to set out the essential starting-points in my analysis of Thatcherism than I have given to the crisis of the left: but that is because, analytically, the two cannot be separated. I have come to a particular view about at least the elements of a strategy of renewal on the left because I think I understand what constitutes Thatcherism as not simply a worthy opponent of the left, but in some deeper way its nemesis, the force that is capable in this historical moment of unhingeing it from below. Thus, what I say about the crisis of the left is a sort of mirror-image of what I say about Thatcherism. The only way of genuinely contesting a hegemonic form of politics is to develop a counter-hegemonic strategy. But this cannot, in my view, be done if we go on thinking the same things we have always thought and doing the same things we have always done – only more so, harder, and with more 'conviction'. It means a qualitative change: not the recovery of 'lost ground' but the redefinition, under present conditions, of what the whole project of socialism now means.

My position on the prospects for rethinking and realignment has often been described as 'pessimistic'. And in certain respects it is: not because it is impossible, or utopian, but because the left is not convinced that it cannot continue in the old way. In many of its leading echelons, it does not possess a hegemonic conception of political strategy or a sense of arrival at a historic turning-point. It is good at defending the immensely valuable things it has accomplished. But it is not good at conceiving of itself as a force capable of reshaping society or civilization. Paradoxically, the 'party' of history and change seems paralysed by the movement of history and terrified of change. Orthodoxy is its way of warding off evil spirits and guarding against what Miliband calls 'the sharp dilution of radical commitments'.[15] This is a concern we ought to take seriously, but it must not be used as an excuse to postpone the radical re-examination of left conventional wisdom.

Of course, 'rethinking' of a kind is now in progress in Labour Party circles and it would be churlish to predict that nothing new will come of it. But the signs are not propitious. It is held on an extremely tight reign within the party leadership, which has closed itself off from the many currents of thinking and new ideas circulating in that big wide world beyond Walworth Road which the leadership has nervously failed to recruit. It is not structured and organized around any broad political agenda, which might release intellectual energies in surprising places or capture the public imagination. The one thing which is unlikely to be effective in either the short or the long run is a pragmatic adaptation to Thatcherite ground for the purposes of short term electoral advantage. However, what seems to be at stake here, as Gramsci once remarked, 'is rotation in governmental office ... not the foundation and organization of a new political society and even less a new type of civil society'.[16]

The rethinking process cannot be engaged at the level of 'policies' without first formulating a number of strategic questions. Can Labour create the material conditions for a society which is socially just and individually prosperous, and can it sketch how we are to bear the social costs of the transition to a new economic order which alone can guarantee this goal, without the Thatcherite consequences of gross inequality, unemployment, poverty, regional decline and the destruction of human communities? What now is the conception of 'the public', of 'the social good', indeed, of 'society' to set against Mrs Thatcher's assertion that 'there is no "society"', only individuals and their families'? For without such a conception (neither a retreat to the old collectivism nor a whoring after the new individualism) we cannot create the popular will for those levels of public taxation or for the redistribution of wealth, property and power necessary to restore the crumbling fabric of society. What does the commitment to 'choice' really mean in terms of the balance between market and planning – and what variety of forms of democratic participation are to be brought concretely to bear against the inevitable drift of Labour towards new corporatist and statist forms of regulation? What do we mean by an expanded and democratized 'civil society' which is not simply driven by blind will or coordinated by the vicious vagaries of 'market forces'? What does 'diversity' mean for this new conception of civil society and how are the rights as well as the vulnerabilities of minorities to be protected in such a society. How is our deeply socially and sexually conservative culture to be 'reeducated' towards a more open and tolerant moral regime?

The questions are endless – but one thing unifies them all. They are hard, searching, difficult questions. They take us to the root of things – to core values and commitments, to the outer limits of our capacities to reimagine the future. They need to be boldly and starkly outlined, in such a way as to connect with, capture and transform the social imaginary. They are an alternative agenda for 'modernity'. They cannot be addressed in that tone of bland reassurance so characteristic of contemporary 'Walworth-Road-speak' – as if, with a little tinkering here and there, and without disturbing anyone too much, we can stealthily slip unnoticed into the New Age.

When the GLC addressed itself, in a massively popular campaign, to the question of reducing the fares on public transport and subsidizing cheaper travel through public subsidy, it did so not only in terms of pence in the pocket but also in terms of an alternative vision: a 'fare's fair' society – a conception of all sorts of ordinary people, with different tastes, purposes, destinations, desires (choice, diversity) nevertheless enabled by a system of public intervention in the pricing, provision and consumption of a social need (public good), to enlarge their freedoms to move about the city (social individuals), to see and experience new things, to go into places hitherto barred to them – because they were priced, or culturally defined, beyond their reach – in safety and comfort. The striking reduction in violence on the tubes and buses was not something which could have been administratively 'planned for' in this scenario; but it was a consequence positively aimed for, enunciated in the campaign, and achieved. There is a lesson here somewhere for those who have turned their backs so decisively and dismissively on the whole GLC experience to learn. It has to do, in part, with how to construct the social imaginary in ways which enable us to see ourselves transformed in the mirror of politics, and thus to become its 'new subjects'. But we have only to think of the speed and manifest relief with which Labour took on board the 'loony left' slogan to understand the deep resistances to this whole form and conception of popular politics – and not only in the leadership of the party.

In the face of these many resistances to the painful and difficult task of radical renewal, I have tried to show, in an indicative way, that however shocking and 'scandalous' it appears, the left has everything to gain from ruthlessly exposing its most cherished shibboleths and sacred taboos to the searching light cast by what Marx called 'the real movement of history'. Indeed, it is in this sense – and not in the religious expectation that every one of his specific prophecies of the nineteenth century could be true for the end of the twentieth – that Marx remains a significant and revolutionary thinker. In this risk-taking venture I hold – against the odds – to the formula which Gramsci appropriated from Romain Rolland: 'pessimism of the intellect, optimism of the will'. Ralph Miliband has declared this 'an exceedingly bad slogan for socialists' because what it really implies, he says, is that 'defeat is more likely than success ... but that we must nevertheless strive towards it, against all odds, in a mood of resolute despair'.[17] I beg leave to disagree. What it means is that every commitment to the construction of a new political will must be grounded, if it is to be concrete and strategic, in an analysis of the present which is neither ritualistic nor celebratory and which avoids the spurious oscillations of optimism and pessimism, or the triumphalism which so often pass for thought on the traditional left. Ritual and celebration are for the religious. They are for keeping the spirits up; for consolidating and consoling the faithful; and for anathematizing the heretics. They inhibit advance, while keeping the spirit of sectarian rectitude alive and well. There is no alternative to making anew the 'revolution of our times' or sinking slowly into historical irrelevance. I believe, with Gramsci, that we must first attend 'violently' to things as they are, without illusions or false hopes, if we are to transcend the present.

At least implicitly, this book therefore has a 'project', a strategy if not a programme or set of policies (which always, in my view, follow, and cannot precede a new conception of politics). I have tried (for example in 'The Crisis of Labourism') to analyse the dominant political culture of Labour which constitutes so profound a barrier to this process of renewal. In 'Realignment for What?', I have suggested what any regrouping of forces committed to this project of renewal would be like, and how far this is from a conventional shuffling of the existing forces of the right, centre and left – how deeply it cuts across these conventional and now outdated divisions. In 'The Battle for Socialist Ideas' and 'Learning from Thatcherism', I have addressed the question of how, and over what issues, the ideological struggle could be engaged so as to construct around this project a new social bloc which has learned to live positively with difference and diversity, rather than suppress it. I have in several places criticized the Fabian and statist legacies on the left which have stood for so long in the path of popular mobilization or democratization. In 'The State – Socialism's Old Caretaker', I try to confront some of the dilemmas implicit in the left's shift of emphasis from the state back to the democratization of civil society. In 'The Culture Gap' and elsewhere, I take on the centrality of the questions of culture and the politics of identity. These essays do not add up to 'a programme' which can be enshrined in some policy document or shunted mechanically through the formal bureaucracies of the left. But I believe they do begin to stake out in very provisional form some of the key questions for what we might call the 'agenda of renewal'.

I offer them within the framework of a simple but radical perspective on this process of renewal on the left – understood in its broadest, not its narrowest sense. Submit everything to the discipline of present reality, to our understanding of the forces which are really shaping and changing our world. As Laclau and Mouffe put it, 'accept in all their radical novelty, the transformations of the world we live in, neither to ignore them nor to distort them in order to make them compatible with outdated schemas'. Start 'from that full insertion in the present – in its struggles, its challenges, its dangers – to interrogate the past and to search within it for the genealogy of the present situation'. And from that starting point, begin to construct a possible alternative scenario, an alternative conception of 'modernity', an alternative future.[18] In this respect at least, far from occupying a different world from that of Thatcherism, we can only renew the project of the left by precisely occupying *the same world* that Thatcherism does, and building from that a *different* form of society. As Gramsci said, 'If one applies one's will to the creation of a new equilibrium among the forces which really exist and are operative ... one still moves on the terrain of effective reality, but does so in order to dominate and transcend it.... What "ought to be" is therefore concrete; indeed it is the only realistic ... interpretation of reality, it alone is history in the making and philosophy in the making, it alone is politics'.[19]

Notes

1. See, for example, the critique by Jessop, Bonnett, Bromley and Ling in 'Authoritarian Populism, Two Nations and Thatcherism' in *New Left Review* 147, 1984, and my reply reprinted in this volume, pp. 150–160.
2. A question posed, for example, by Ellen Meiksins Wood in *The Retreat from Class*, London 1986, and assumed to be already proven by many other critics.
3. Reprinted from Mary Langan and Bill Schwarz, eds, *Crises of the British State 1880–1930*, London 1985.
4. R. Miliband, 'The New Revisionism in Britain', *New Left Review* 150, 1985, p. 9.
5. Reprinted from A. Hunt, ed., *Marxism and Democracy*, London 1980.
6. A. Gramsci, 'The Study of Philosophy' in *Selections from the Prison Notebooks*, London 1971.
7. See, for example, Ruth Levitas, *The Ideology of the New Right*, London 1986.
8. See, for example, Desmond King in *The New Right*, London 1987.
9. A. Gramsci, *Prison Notebooks*, p. 165.
10. *Ibid.*, p. 327.
11. *Ibid.*, p. 377.
12. E. Laclau, *Politics and Ideology in Marxist Theory*, London 1977.
13. E. Laclau and C. Mouffe, *Hegemony and Socialist Strategy*, London 1985.
14. See N. Geras, 'Post-Marxism?', *New Left Review* 163, 1987; and the response by E. Laclau and C. Mouffe, 'Post-Marxism without Apologies', *New Left Review* 166, 1987.
15. R. Miliband, 'The New Revisionism', p. 21.
16. A. Gramsci, *Prison Notebooks*, p. 170.
17. R. Miliband, 'The New Revisionism', p. 26.
18. E. Laclau and C. Mouffe, 'Post-Marxism without Apologies'.
19. A. Gramsci, *Prison Notebooks*, p. 172.

PART ONE

◆

The New Challenge of the Right

1

Living with the Crisis

with Charles Critcher, Tony Jefferson, John Clarke and Brian Roberts

We can identify four principal aspects of the 1972–6 conjuncture, which set the stage for the dénouement of Thatcherism: the political crisis; the economic crisis; the 'theatre' of ideological struggle; and the direct inter-pellation of the race issue into the crisis of British civil and political life. All four themes must be understood as unrolling within an organic conjuncture whose parameters are overdetermined by two factors: the rapid deteri-oration of Britain's economic position; and the maintenance of a poli-tical form of 'that exceptional state' which gradually emerged between 1968 and 1972 and which now appears, for 'the duration' at least, to be permanently installed.

The Heath return to corporate bargaining after 1972 was undertaken in the face of a massive political defeat. It was accepted with ill grace; and there is every sign that in Mr Heath's mind the final showdown had simply been postponed. Moreover, as the recession, following the world-wide 'crisis boom' of 1972–3, began to bite in earnest, the unemploy-ment figures rose, inflation graduated to riproaring Weimar Republic proportions, and the whole balance of world capitalism was thrown side-ways by the lurch in Arab oil prices. There was little left in the kitty with which to 'bargain'. Phase 1 of Mr Heath's strategy, therefore, imposed a six-month total freeze on wages; Phase 2 a limit of £1 plus 4 per cent. Phase 3, initiated in the autumn of 1973, with its 'relativities clauses' designed to allow the more militant sectors to 'catch up', was met by the revived strength and unity of the miners' claim. The showdown had arrived.

19

In response, Mr Heath unleashed an ideological onslaught. He pinpointed the unpatriotic action of the miners in timing their claim to coincide with the Arab oil embargo. They were 'holding the nation up to ransom'. The media at once seized on this lead – attacks on those who act against the 'national interest' no longer appeared to contravene the protocol on balanced and impartial news coverage. Between 1972 and the present, as the 'national interest' has become unequivocally identified with whatever policies the state is currently pursuing, the reality of the state has come to provide the raison d'être for the media. Once any group threatening this delicately poised strategy has been symbolically cast out of the body politic – through the mechanism of the moderates/extremist paradigm – the media have felt it quite legitimate to intervene, openly and vigorously, on the side of the 'centre'.

The phenomenon of the 'Red Scare' is, of course, well documented in British history, and its success has depended before now on a skilful orchestration of politicians and the press. But the virulence of its reappearance in this period is worth noting. In this period the press begins again its deep exploration to unearth the 'politically motivated men' in the miners' union; later (1974) it was to conspire in an organized hounding of the 'red menace' in the person of Mr McGahey, the Scottish miners' leader; later (1976) it was to project Mr Benn as the 'Lenin' of the Labour Party. Throughout the early period of the 'social contract', it was, again and again, openly to intervene to swing elections within the key unions from the 'extremist' to the 'moderate' pole; later it was mesmerized by the spectre of 'Marxism'. All good, objective, impartial stuff. On occasion, the press opened its feature columns to the sniffers-out of Communist subversion: the Institute for the Study of Conflict, the National Association for Freedom, the Aims of Industry Group, the Free Enterprise League, the 'Let's Work Together Campaign'. Later, it required no extreme prod to give front page treatment to every and any spokesman who could discern the presence of another 'totalitarian Marxist' inside the Labour Party.

Mr Heath then turned to his 'final solution' – one dictated entirely by the political motive of breaking the working class at its most united point. Its damaging economic consequences precipitated Britain's economic decline into 'slumpflation'. The miners had to be defeated, fuel saved; more important, the 'nation' had to be mobilized against the miners by projecting the crisis right into the heart of every British family. The economy was put on a three-day working 'emergency', and the country plunged into semi-darkness. In a wild swipe, the 'costs' of the miners' actions were thus generalized for the working class and the country as a whole, in the hope that this would open up internal splits in the ranks: bringing Labour and TUC pressure to bear on the NUM, and the pressure of women, having to make do on short-time wages, to bear against their striking men. The splits failed to materialize. When the NUM was finally pressured to a ballot, the vote in favour of a strike was 81 per cent. The 'crisis scare' failed to break that class solidarity which had been tempered in the two-year season of open class warfare with Heath Toryism. To the accompaniment of this fully mobilized 'Red Scare', 'Reds Under the Bed' campaign, Mr Heath called and lost the February election. The February 1974 election 'was more clearly a class confrontation than any previous election since the Second World War'.[1] It was also the most resounding victory, not for Labour (returned in a weak minority position, once Mr Heath could be persuaded to call in the removal men), but for the organized working class. It had brought the government to the ground.

The state of the political class struggle in the two years following can be briefly summarized by looking at three strands: first, the level of militancy sustained through the rest of 1974 in the wake of the miners' victory; second, the return to the social democratic management of the deepening capitalist crisis, principally through another variant of the mechanism of the 'social contract' (long mistitled, in a form which inconveniently called to mind its cosmetic aspects – a 'social compact'); third, the articulation of a fully fledged capitalist recession, with extremely high rates of inflation, a toppling currency, cuts in the social wage and in public spending, a savaging of living standards, and a sacrifice of the working class to capital: all managed by a Labour government with its centrist stoical face (Mr Callaghan) turned to the wall of its international creditors, and its belligerent face (Mr Healey) turned against his own ranks.

The 'social contract' was the latest form in which British social democracy attempted to preside over and ride out the contradictory effects of a declining capitalism. Like its predecessors, the 'social contract' was the Labourist version of that corporate bargain, organized within the capitalist state, and struck between the formal leadership of the labour movement (a Labour government in office), the formal representatives of the working class (the TUC) and – a silent and sceptical partner, in this phase – the representatives of capital itself. Once more, in this form, the crisis of capitalism was drawn directly on to the territory of the state. In the concessions, made in the 'contract's' early days, to 'bringing about a fundamental shift in the distribution of wealth', and in its recognition that the whole of the 'social wage' was now the area to be bargained over, the 'social contract' marked the relative strength and cohesiveness of working-class demands, and gave the unions some formal veto over government policies. That strength has since been systematically whittled away in the subsequent conditions of severe cuts in welfare and public expenditure, cuts which the working class has supported with ill grace, to some degree resisted, but – once again bemused and confused by the spectacle of being led into poverty and unemployment by its own side – failed to push to its limits.

This unstable social base to the present social contract has had contradictory consequences: formal commitments 'to the left' – just far enough to secure the 'consent' of left trade unionists like Scanlon of the AEUW and Jones of the TGWU, and to ensure some credibility to the press portrayal of the Labour Party as a party of 'irresponsible leftists'; just centrist enough to persuade the working class to be pushed and bullied by the Labour pragmatists into tolerating a dramatic rise in the rate of unemployment and a dynamic, staged lowering of working-class living standards. In this way, Labour has 'captured' for its management of the crisis, for capitalism, that measure of working-class and union support required to represent itself as the only 'credible party of government'; while the very presence of the unions so close to the centre of its unsteady equilibrium was quite enough to enable the government to be represented as 'in the pocket of the trade union barons', thereby legitimating the strike of capital investment at home and frightening the currency dealers abroad. A more unstable political 'resolution' can hardly be imagined.

The 'governor' of this stalemate position was the deep economic trough into which Britain has finally fallen. By 1975, the first synchronized worldwide recession of capitalism was in full swing – one manifesting the unusual form of productive slump coupled with soaring inflation. How far into recession world capitalism will fall is, still, an open guess. But its consequences for Britain are no longer in doubt. The 'weak reeds' in the capitalist partnership – Britain and Italy especially – have been severely damaged. The whole Keynesian apparatus for the control of recession is in tatters, with not even a minimum consensus amongst economists as to whether the money supply has anything or nothing to contribute to lowering the rate of inflation. At the same time, the attempt is in progress to transfer the costs on to the backs of the working class. This is no longer the description of an economy suffering endemic weaknesses. It is an economy being steadily battered down into poverty, managed by a government which is silently praying that it can effect the transfer of the crisis to the working class without arousing mass political resistance, and thus create that mirage of British social democratic governments – 'favourable investment conditions'. If it cuts too fast, the unions will be forced to bolt the 'social contract', and destroy social democracy's fragile social and political base; if it does not cut fast and hard, the international bankers will simply cut their credit short. If it raises taxes, the middle classes – now in a state of irritable, Thatcher-like arousal – will either emigrate en masse or begin, Chilean-style, to rattle their pressure-cooker lids; if it does not tax, the last remnants of the welfare state – and with them any hope of buying working-class compliance – will disappear. Britain in the 1970s is a country for whose crisis there are no viable capitalist solutions left, and where, as yet, there is no political base for an alternative socialist strategy. It is a nation locked in a deadly stalemate: a state of unstoppable capitalist decline.

This has had the deadliest and most profound ideological consequences. Although, under the guardianship of social democracy, Britain backed off a little from the 'law-and-order' state whose construction was well underway between 1972 and 1974, the exceptional form which the capitalist state assumed in that period has not been dismantled. The mobilization of the state apparatuses around the corrective and coercive poles has been coupled with a dramatic deterioration in the ideological climate generally, favouring a much tougher regime of social discipline: the latter being the form in which consent is won to this 'exceptional' state of affairs. Such an ideological thrust is difficult to delineate precisely, but it is not difficult to identify its principal thematics and mechanisms.

Between 1972 and 1974, the 'crisis' came finally to be appropriated – by governments in office, the repressive apparatuses of the state, the media and some articulate sectors of public opinion – as an interlocking set of planned or organized conspiracies. British society became little short of fixated by the idea of a conspiracy against 'the British way of life'. The collective psychological displacements which this fixation requires are almost too transparent to require analysis. To put it simply, 'the conspiracy' is the necessary and required form in which dissent, opposition or conflict has to be represented in a society which is, in fact, mesmerized by *consensus*. If society is defined as an entity in which all fundamental or structural class conflicts have been reconciled, and government is defined as the instrument of class reconciliation, and the state assumes the role of the organizer of conciliation and consent, and the class nature of the capitalist mode of production is presented as one which can, with goodwill, be 'harmonized' into a unity, then, clearly, conflict must arise because an evil minority of subversive and politically motivated men [sic] enter into a conspiracy to destroy by force what they cannot dismantle in any other way. How else can 'the crisis' be explained? Of course, this slow maturing of the spectre of conspiracy – like most dominant ideological paradigms – has material consequences. Its propagation makes legitimate the official repression of everything which threatens or is contrary to the logic of the state. Its premise, then, is the identification of the whole society with the state. The state has become the bureaucratic embodiment, the powerful organizing centre and expression of the disorganized consensus of the popular will. So, whatever the state does is *legitimate* (even if it is not 'right'); and *whoever threatens the consensus threatens the state*. This is a fateful collapse. On the back of this equation, the exceptional state prospers.

In the period between 1974 and the present, this conspiratorial world view – once the sole prerogative of the *East–West Digest*, Aims of Industry, the Economic League and other denizens of the far right – has become received doctrine. It surges into the correspondence columns of *The Times*, is weightily considered in *The Economist*, mulled over in Senior Common rooms, and debated in the House of Lords. Industrial news is systematically reported in such terms. Any industrial conflict is subject to being blackened – as the Chrysler dispute was by Mr Wilson – as the result of 'politico–industrial action'. Peers like Lord Chalfont are given the freedom of the air to fulminate against Communist 'maggots and termites' dedicated to smash democracy: a thesis supported by his proposition that in Britain all of Lenin's preconditions for revolution have already been fulfilled! Dr Miller, Director of North London Polytechnic, facing protests from students he dubs 'malignants', confesses, 'I sit in my office and itch for the ability to say, "Hang the Ringleaders".' The *Daily Telegraph*, now openly an organ of the far right, runs colour-supplement features tracing Communism's 'creeping, insidious, cancer-like growth', the 'treachery, deceit and violence of a small minority and ... foreign-directed subterfuge'. Public opinion is constantly and unremittingly *tutored* in social authoritarian postures by the method of sponsored 'moral panics': the skilfully elevated panic surrounding comprehensive education, falling standards and 'Reds' in the classrooms is one of the most effective and dramatic examples – an instance of how, through an apparently 'non-political' issue, the terrain of social consciousness is prepared for exactly that political dénouement required by the 'iron times' into which we are drifting.

Not surprisingly, it was – literally – under the banner of the conspiracy charge, an ancient and disreputable statute, retrieved and dusted off for the occasion, that the law was brought into the service of the restoration of 'law and order'. In 1971, some Sierra Leone students who occupied their Embassy were charged and convicted of conspiracy, appealed, and were denied by the Lord Chancellor, Lord Hailsham, in the infamous Karama decision (July 1973). This decision, which laid down a formidable precedent in a contested area, represented a piece of law-making by the court rather than by parliament and was unmistakably in keeping with a political rather than a legal chain of reasoning. As John Griffith observed: 'The power of the state, of the police, or organized society can now be harnessed to the suppression of minority groups whose protests had formerly been chargeable only in the civil courts.'[2] It perfectly embodied the Lord Chancellor, Lord Hailsham's, view that 'the war in Bangladesh, Cyprus, the Middle East, Black September, Black Power, the Angry Brigade, the Kennedy murders, Northern Ireland, bombs in Whitehall and the Old Bailey, the Welsh Language Society, the massacre in the Sudan, the mugging in the tube, gas strikes, hospital strikes, go-slows, sit-ins, the Icelandic cod war' were all 'standing or seeking to stand on different parts of the same slippery slope'.[3] The conspiratorial world view can hardly be more comprehensively stated.

Many others were thrust through the breach thus opened. The editors of *IT* were charged with 'conspiracy to outrage public decency' and the editors of *Oz* with 'conspiracy to corrupt public morals'. Mr Bennion and his Freedom Under the Law Ltd entered a private citizen's prosecution against Peter Hain for 'conspiracy to hinder and disrupt' the South African rugby team tour. The judge agreed that Hain had illegally interfered with the public's right in 'a matter of substantial, public concern – something of importance to citizens who are interested in the maintenance of law and order'. The Aldershot bombers and the Angry Brigade both had 'conspiracy' added to their charges. So did the Welsh Language Society protestors who did not, in fact, trespass on BBC property; so did the building workers who had so successfully adopted the 'flying-picket' tactic in the disputes of 1972–3.

The conspiracy charge was perfectly adapted to *generalizing* the mode of repressive control: enormously wide, its terms are highly ambiguous, designed to net whole groups of people whether directly involved in complicity or not. Convenient for the police in imputing guilt where hard evidence is scarce, it aimed to break the chains of solidarity and support, and deter others. It was directable against whole ways of life – or struggle.

One might have expected liberal pragmatists, like the police chief Sir Robert Mark, to have backed off from this overt recruitment of the law. But he continued to advance his charge – against considerable evidence – that acquittals were too high and that criminals were escaping through 'corrupt lawyers' practices'. He criticized trial by jury. He accused magistrates of 'effectively encouraging burglary and crime'; of failing to discourage hooliganism and violence through the punishments handed out; of 'being too lenient with violent demonstrators'. A period of rising political dissent is clearly a difficult one for the police to handle – and thus one in which the police can only defend themselves against the charge of colluding with repression by the most scrupulous drawing of lines. Instead, in this period, the police and Home Office clearly came to approve, if not to revel in, the steady blurring of distinctions. Emergency legislation like the anti-terrorist legislation drew the police into that ambiguous territory between suspicion and proof. A number of occasions revealed the steady drift towards the arming of the British Police Force. When the National Council for Civil Liberties remarked upon the striking erosion of civil liberties involved, they won the rebuke that the NCCL should be renamed the 'National Council for Criminal License'.

This collective conspiratorial paranoia is only the most overt side of the ideological polarization into which the country has fallen. Other themes ride high within its matrix of propositions. One is the charge that, despite all appearances, the country has fallen victim to the stealthy advance of socialist collectivism. This theme – with its attractive counterposing of the 'little man', the private citizen, against the anonymous, corporate tentacles of the swollen state – has won many converts. While it captures something of the authentic reality of an interventionist state under the conditions of monopoly capitalism, what is obscurely thematized within this populist sleight of hand is the slowly maturing assault on the welfare state and any tendency towards social equality. Long the target of covert ideological attack from the right, this is now also the space where social democracy, in conditions of economic recession, is itself obliged to make deep surgical incisions. Under the guise of monetarist orthodoxy, the attempt to dismantle the welfare state has now received the cloak of respectability. (Just exactly what capital will do without an enormous state edifice to ensure the social and political conditions of its survival remains to be seen.) A related theme is the charge that the government and indeed the whole society is now 'run by the trade unions' – a development of the theme, launched in Mr Heath's era, of the unions 'holding the nation up to ransom', which has now also entered public orthodoxy, and which is peculiarly pointed in a period where the survival of Labour depends exactly on the degree to which the unions are in *its* pocket.

A more powerful ideological thrust is to be found in the coordinated swing towards tougher *social discipline*, behind which a general turn to the right in civil and social life is being pioneered. For the first time since the New Conservatives swallowed 'Butskellism', there is an open, frontal attack on the whole idea of equality, a shameless advocacy of elitism, and a complete refurbishing of the competitive ethic. Sir Keith Joseph has not hesitated to give this its full philosophical justification. 'For self-interest is a prime motive in human behaviour ... any social arrangements for our epoch must contain, harmonize and harness individual and corporate egoisms if they are to succeed.... Surely we can accept ... that the least educated classes in the population should be less open to new ideas, more fixated on past experience...? Anyway, conservatism, like selfishness, is inherent in the human condition.' [4] The economic recession has provided the cover for a return to those 'aggressive' Tory themes of 'patriotism, the family, the breakdown of law, and the permissive society'. Sir Keith Joseph's defence of the small business entrepreneur ('He exercises imagination.... He takes risks ... he is sensitive to demand, which often means to people') and his Birmingham speech in defence of the traditional family of modest size, moderate habits, thrift and self-reliance, with its noxious assault on 'mothers, the under twenties in many cases, single parents, from classes 4 and 5', those 'least fitted to bring children into the world' who are now producing 'a third of all births', articulate a virulent and unapologetic propaganda for what are euphemistically called 'market values' but which few politicians would have risked uttering in public ten years ago.

These themes, in which the dismantling of the welfare state is strongly advanced, are cross-laced by the usual moral negatives – 'teenage pregnancies ... drunkenness, sexual offences, and crimes of sadism' – all of which can be laid at the door of the welfare philosophy, supported by 'bully boys of the left', cheered on by some university staffs, the 'cuckoos in our democratic nest'.[5] The undisguised effort here is to 'reverse the vast bulk of the accumulating detritus of socialism'. The sustained assault on 'welfare scroungers and layabouts' which has developed in the wake of this line of attack is quite consistent with it – a moral backlash against the vast masses of the unemployed reputed to be living on social security on the Costa Brava. It is evident, also, in the wide-ranging counter-offensive against moral pollution led by Mrs Whitehouse and others ('Let us take inspiration from that remarkable woman,' Sir Keith advised), cresting in the anti-abortion campaigns, to which Labour has itself partly capitulated.

Another arena in which the authoritarian mood is now much in evidence is that of public education. The backlash against progressive education is in full swing, with the William Tyndale school chosen as the site of Custer's last stand. Mr Boyson – Mrs Thatcher's second in command at Education – is, of course, one of the most articulate range-riders on this front, advancing the case for elite education and the voucher system, stimulating the panic surrounding classroom violence, vandalism, truancy and falling academic and literacy standards. The whole welfare state, he says, is destroying 'personal liberty, individual responsibility and moral growth' and 'sapping the collective moral fibre of our people as a nation'. These themes are skilfully orchestrated, at a high level, by the education Black Papers and manipulators of 'parent power' like Mr St John Stevas. Tory councils, meanwhile, are making stirring last stands to halt comprehensivization and defend the private education sector.

What lends political muscle to this steady drift into an active authoritarian 'social gospel' is the emergence, for the first time since the war, of an organized and articulate fraction of the radical right *within the leadership of the Conservative Party itself*. With the election of Mrs Thatcher and her entourage, this fraction no longer belongs to the Tory fringes and backbenches. It has been installed at its intellectual and political centre. Its principal alibi has been the doctrine of tight money, cuts in public expenditure and a return to the discipline of the free market, which is the main anti-inflation plank advanced by the monetarist doctrinaires who have clustered into the Thatcher camp:

> The more governments have intervened to remove economic decisions out of the market and into the political arena, the more they have set group against group, class against class and sectional interest against public interest. The politicization of so wide an area of the country's economic activities has set up strains which are threatening its social cohesion. In short, what the country is now confronted with is not a crisis of the market economy but a crisis of government interference with the market economy.[6]

This goes hand in hand with the defence of the small businessman, lower-middle-class respectability, self-reliance and self-discipline constantly propagated by Mrs Thatcher, Sir Keith Joseph, Mr Maude and the others at the helm of the Tory leadership. Its ideologues are vociferous elsewhere – in Mr Worsthorne's column in the *Sunday Telegraph*, in Mr Cosgrave's *Spectator* (now virtually a Thatcher housejournal) and in *The Economist*. It has its more populist ventriloquists in the Clean-Up Television, Anti-Abortion, Festival of Light campaigns, the National Association of Ratepayers Action Groups, the National Association for Freedom, the National Federation of the Self-Employed, the National Union of Small Shopkeepers, and the Voice of the Independent Centre lobbies, who give to the new authoritarianism of the right a considerable popular penetration.

It is one of the paradoxes of the extraordinary Heath interregnum that, in toying and playing, but only up to a point, with extremist alternatives, Mr Heath – an 'extremist' of the *moderate* sort, and probably ultimately a man of the Conservative middle-ground rather than the far right – nevertheless helped to let extremism out of the bag. He appears to have hoped to ride these dangerous forces through to a defeat of the working class, but then to stop short (in the interests of the more centrist Conservative forces, who were also part of his coalition) of a full elaboration of a moral-political programme of the petty-bourgeois right. The spectacle of a head-on collision with the working class – a collision he seemed doomed to lose – frightened away his centrist support in the Party and his industrialist support in business. But the consequence of his defeat, and the disintegration of the bizarre class alliance which he yoked together in 1970, was to release the genuinely extreme right into an independent life of its own. He and his supporters are now pilloried as unwitting contributors to the drift into 'creeping collectivism'. The Thatcher–Joseph–Maude leadership, in its breakaway to the right, has pulled those floating themes of extremism and conspiracy into an alternative political programme. It says something for the ability of British capital to recognize its own, long-term interests that it settled once more, after 1974, for a management of the crisis by its 'natural governors' – a social-democratic party. But it says something for the transformed ideological and political climate of the exceptional state that those half-formed spectres which once hovered on the edge of British politics have now been fully politicized and installed in the vanguard, as a viable basis for hegemony, by the 'other' party of capital, the Conservatives of the radical right. As the span of Labour's fragile base is eroded, this is the historical 'bloc' poised to inherit the next phase of the crisis. It is a conjuncture many would prefer to miss.

There is no doubt that, as recession sharpens the competitive instincts, so a petty-bourgeois civil ethic exerts a stronger appeal to the public at large. In the absence of a well-founded and sustained thrust to democratic education, some working-class parents will certainly be attracted by the promises of 'parent power' and private education, if by these means they can ensure that rapidly narrowing education opportunities will be channelled to their own children. The old petty bourgeoisie – the small shopkeeper, the clerical and black-coated worker, the small salariat and the small businessman – has certainly been squeezed by the growing power of the corporate enterprises, the state and the multinationals. The middle classes have taken a sharp drop in living standards, and may have to bear more before the crisis ends. Of course, these do not constitute on their own a viable bloc on which sustained political power from the right could be based. They provide the vociferous subalterns in such a class alliance – its political cutting-edge; but it is more difficult to see with what fractions of capital they could be combined as a way of 'settling the crisis' under the management of the radical right. But a reorganized capitalist interest, determined to drive through a radical economic solution to the crisis at the expense of the working class, operating – as has happened before in European history in this century – behind a rampant petty-bourgeois ideology, the ideology of 'a petty bourgeoisie in revolt',[7] *could* provide the basis for a formidable dénouement. This *regression* of capitalism to a petty-bourgeois ideology in conditions of political stalemate and economic stagnation is one of the features which makes the equilibrium on which the post-1970 capitalist state is poised an 'exceptional' moment.

It is now de rigueur to refer to 'the British crisis', often without specifying in what respects such a 'crisis' exists. It is necessary for us, then, to define how we understand the 'crisis' whose development we have been delineating. First, it is a crisis of and for British capitalism: the crisis, specifically, of an advanced industrial capitalist nation, seeking to stabilize itself in rapidly changing global and national conditions on an extremely weak, post-imperial economic base. It has become, progressively, also an aspect of the general economic recession of the capitalist system on a world scale. The reason for this global weakness of capitalism is beyond our scope. But we must note, historically, that postwar capitalism in general survived only at the cost of a major reconstruction of capital, labour and the labour process during the long boom upon which the extraction and realization of the surplus depends: that profound recomposition entailed in the shift to 'late' capitalism. All the capitalist economies of the world undertook this internal 'reconstruction' differently in the period immediately before and immediately after the Second World War; the comparative history of this period of capitalist reconstruction has yet to be written. Britain attempted such a deep transformation, too – on the basis, we suggest, of an extremely weak and vulnerable industrial and economic base; and this attempt to raise a backward industrial capitalist economy to the condition of an advanced productive one created, for a time, the hot-house economic climate and conditions popularly known and mistakenly experienced as 'affluence'. Its success was extremely limited and short-lived. Britain – in these late-capitalist terms – remains unevenly developed, permanently stuck in 'the transition'. The effects of this stalemate position, this uncompleted transition, have been experienced at every level of society in the period since.

Second, it is a crisis of the 'relations of social forces' – a crisis in the political field and in the political apparatuses. Here, the matter is again extremely complicated, and we must settle for a simplification. At the point where the political struggle issues into the 'theatre of politics', it has been experienced as a crisis of 'party', i.e. of both the ruling-class and the working-class parties. Politically, the key question has been what peculiar alliance of social forces, organized on the terrain of politics and the state in terms of a specific 'equilibrium' of forces and interests, is capable of providing hegemonic political leadership into and through 'the transition'.

The question of 'Party', in Gramsci's sense, is crucial here: not at the level of the parliamentary game, but at the more fundamental level of organized political interests, trajectories and forces. We have not been able precisely to delineate the succession of historical class alliances which have made their bid for power in this period, nor to provide detail on the basis of what kinds of concessions such alliances have been constructed. Once again, this history of parties and blocs (which is something very different from a history of the Conservative or the Labour Party as such, or of the interplay of parties in parliament) remains to be written. We can only note that there has indeed been a succession of such historically constructed 'blocs' since 1945. We need only think of the particular popular alliance which coalesced in the Labour landslide of 1945; of that which underpinned Macmillan's successful period of 'hegemonic rule' in the 1950s: of the quite distinctive alternative class alliances behind which Mr Wilson attempted to return to power in 1964 – 'workers by hand and brain' (including the revolutionaries in white coats and modern-minded managers of capital); and of the peculiar alliance which supported Mr Heath's return to power in 1970.

Without question, the most important feature of this level of the crisis, for our purposes, is the role of 'labourism' – specifically that of the Labour Party, but also the labourist cast of the organized institutions of the working class. Labourism has emerged as an alternative manager of the capitalist crisis. At the most fundamental political level – and shaping every feature of the political culture before it – the crisis of British capitalism *for* the working class has thus been, also, a crisis *of* the organized working class and the labour movement. This has had the most profound effect, not simply in terms of the massive struggle to incorporate the working classes into the capitalist state, as junior partners in the management of crisis, but also in terms of the consequent divisions within the class, the growth of sectional class consciousness, of economism, syndicalism and reformist opportunism. It has been of profound importance that the major strategies for dealing with the crisis and containing its political effects have been drawn in large measure *from the social-democratic repertoire*, not from that of the traditional party of the ruling class. The dislocations which this has produced in the development of the crisis, as well as the resistances to it and thus to the possible forms of its dissolution, have hardly begun to be calculated.

Third, it has been a crisis *of the state*. The entry into 'late capitalism' demands a thorough reconstruction of the capitalist state, an enlargement of its sphere, its apparatuses, and its relation to civil society. The state has come to perform new functions at several critical levels of society. It now has a decisive economic role, not indirectly but directly. It secures the conditions for the continued expansion of capital. It therefore assumes a major role in the economic management of capital. Therefore conflicts between the fundamental class forces, which hitherto formed up principally on the terrain of economic life and struggle, and only gradually, at points of extreme conflict 'escalating' up to the level of the state, are now immediately precipitated on the terrain of the state itself, where all the corporatist political bargains are struck. Needless to say this 'corporate' style of crisis management, in which the state plays an active and principal role on behalf of 'capital as a whole', and to which, increasingly, independent capitals are subscribed, represents a major shift in the whole economic and political order. Its ideological consequences – for example, the role which the state must now play in the mobilization of consent behind these particular crisis-management strategies, and thus in the general construction of consent and legitimacy – are also profound.

Fourth, it is a crisis in political legitimacy, in social authority, in leadership, and in the forms of class struggle and resistance. This crucially touches the questions of consent and of coercion. The construction of consent and the winning of legitimacy are, of course, the normal and natural mechanisms of the liberal and post-liberal capitalist state; and its institutions are peculiarly well adapted to the construction of consent by these means. But consent also has to do with the degree and manner of the 'social authority' which the particular alliance of social forces which is in power can effect or wield over subordinate groups. In short, it has to do with the concrete character of social hegemony. The degree of success in the exercise of hegemony – leadership based on consent, rather than on an excess of force – has to do, in part, precisely with success in the overall management of society; and this is more and more difficult as the economic conditions become more perilous. But it also has to do with the development of coherent and organized oppositional forces, of whatever kind, and the degree to which these are won over, neutralized, incorporated, defeated or contained: that is to say, it has to do with the containment of the class struggle. Here, the matter of periodization becomes imperative. It seems to us that, however uncertain and short-lived were the conditions which made it possible, a period of successful 'hegemony' was indeed brought about in the mid-1950s. But this consensus begins to come apart, at least in its natural and 'spontaneous' form, by the end of the 1950s. The state was then obliged to draw heavily on what we have described as the 'social-democratic' variant of consensus.

We must not allow ourselves to be confused by this. It matters profoundly that, in however 'reformist' a way, the capitalist crisis in the 1960s can only be managed at the 'expense' of recruiting the party of Labour to the seat of management.

Undoubtedly the fact of hegemony presupposes that account be taken of interests and the tendencies of groups over which hegemony is to be exercised, and that a certain compromise equilibrium be formed – in other words that the leading group should make sacrifices of an economic-corporate kind. But there is also no doubt that such sacrifices and such a compromise cannot touch the essential.[8]

It is, in any event, difficult to know whether this period can in any proper sense be characterized as one of hegemony. It is more akin to what we have characterized as 'managed dissensus'. Consent is won, grudgingly, at the expense only of successive ruptures and breakdowns, stops and starts, with the ideological mechanisms working at full throttle to conjure up out of the air a 'national interest' – on which consensus might once again come to rest – which cannot any longer be naturally or spontaneously represented. This is no longer a period of hegemony: it is the opening of a serious 'crisis in hegemony'. And here, of course, not only do the social contradictions begin to multiply in areas far beyond that of the economic and productive relations, but here, also, the varying forms of social resistance, class struggle and popular dissent begin to reappear. There is certainly no overall coherence to these forms of resistance – indeed, in their early manifestations, they resolutely refuse to assume an explicitly political form at all. The British crisis is, perhaps, peculiar precisely in terms of the massive *displacement* of political class struggle into new forms of social, moral and cultural protest and dissent, as well as in terms of the revival, after 1970, of a peculiarly intense kind of 'economism' – a defensive working-class syndicalism.

Nevertheless, in its varying and protean forms, official society – the state, the political leadership, the opinion leaders, the media, the guardians of order – *glimpses*, fitfully at first, then (1968 onwards) more and more clearly, the shape of *the enemy*. Crises must have their causes. The causes cannot be structural, public or rational, since they arise in the best, the most civilized, most peaceful and tolerant society on earth. So they must be secret, subversive, irrational, a plot. Plots must be smoked out. Stronger measures need to be taken – more than 'normal' opposition requires more than usual control. This is an extremely important moment: the point where, the repertoires of 'hegemony through consent' having been exhausted, the drift towards the routine use of the more repressive features of the state comes more and more prominently into play. Here the pendulum within the exercise of hegemony tilts, decisively, from where consent overrides coercion, to that condition in which coercion becomes, as it were, the natural and routine form in which consent is secured. This shift in the internal balance of hegemony – consent to coercion – is a response, within the state, to an increasing polarization of social forces (real and imagined). It is exactly how a 'crisis in hegemony' represents itself.

Control comes to be implemented progressively, in slow stages. It is differently imposed on the different 'trouble areas' which the crisis precipitates. Interestingly and significantly, it occurs at two levels – both above and below. Hence it assumes the form of a coercive management of conflict and struggle, which – paradoxically – also has popular 'consent' and has won legitimacy. We must not for a moment abandon the specific form in which the British state slides into an 'exceptional' posture. The simple slogans of 'fascism' are more than useless here – they cover up, conveniently, everything which it is most important to keep in view. A society where the state is abrogated through the seizure of state power, by, say, an armed coup, and in which the repressive forces openly take command and impose by fiat and the rule of the gun, official terror and torture, and where a repressive regime is installed (Chile and Brazil are examples), is quite different from a society in which each step towards a more authoritarian posture is accompanied by a powerful groundswell of popular legitimacy, and where the civil power and all the forms of the post-liberal state remain solidly intact and in command.

We have few theoretical and analytic tools, or comparative evidence, with which to characterize the slow development of such a state of legitimate coercion. In their absence, we have settled for a more simple, descriptive term: we have called it 'the drift into a law-and-order society'. It is clear, as we look across the water to the United States or to the erection of 'emergency laws' in one Western European country after another, that, despite its peculiarly British features, this is no idiosyncratic British development. The carrying of the law directly into the political arena has not, of course, gone uncontested – the intense working-class resistance leading to the defeat of the Industrial Relations Act and the political destruction of the Heath government marks, in this context, a development of profound significance. But, in many departments of social life, it has occurred steadily, if apparently haphazardly. The whole tenor of social and political life has been transformed by it. A distinctively new ideological climate has been precipitated.

Schematically, this movement – the 'social history of social reaction' – begins with the unresolved ambiguities and contradictions of affluence, of the postwar 'settlement'. It is experienced, first, as a diffuse social unease, as an unnaturally accelerated pace of social change, as an unhingeing of stable patterns and moral points of reference. It manifests itself, first, as an unlocated surge of social anxiety. This fastens on different phenomena: on the hedonistic culture of youth, on the disappearance of the traditional insignia of class, on the dangers of unbridled materialism, on change itself. Later, it appears to focus on more tangible targets: specifically, on the anti-social nature of youth movements, on the threat to British life by the black immigrant, and on the 'rising fever chart' of crime. Later still – as the major social upheavals of the counter-culture and the political student movements become more organized as social forces – it surges, in the form of a more focussed 'social anxiety', around these points of disturbance. It names what is wrong in general terms: it is the *permissiveness* of social life. Finally, as the crisis deepens, and as the forms of conflict and dissent assume a more clearly delineated class form, social anxiety also precipitates in its more political form. It is directed against the organized power of the working class; against political extremism; against trade-union blackmail; against the threat of anarchy, riot and terrorism. It becomes the reactionary pole in the ideological class struggle. Here, the anxieties of the public and the perceived threats to the state coincide and converge. The state comes to provide just that 'sense of direction' which the public feels society has lost. The anxieties of the many are orchestrated with the need for control of the few. The interest of 'all' finds its fitting armature only by submitting itself to the guardianship of those who lead. The state can now, publicly and legitimately, *campaign* against the 'extremes' on behalf and in defence of the silent majority – the 'moderates'. This is 'authoritarian populism'. The 'law-and-order' society has slipped into place.

Let us guard, once again, against our own conspiratorial reading of this process. Society is more polarized, in every part and feature, in the 1970s than it was in the 1950s. Conflicts, repressed and displaced at an earlier point in time, emerge into the open, and divide the nation. The 'crisis' is not a crisis, alone, in the heads of ruling-class conspirators; it is the form assumed by the social struggle in this period. What are important, however, are the distortions and inflections which are endemic to the ways in which this crisis, and the forces of resistance and opposition ranged against it, are ideologically perceived and represented by those in power, and how those misrecognitions come to form the basis for misconceptions of the crisis in popular consciousness.

It is then, finally, a crisis in and of ideology. The 'consensus' ideologies of the 1950s are clearly inadequate for a period of sharpening conflict and economic decline. In general, these ideologies, constructed around the key post-capitalist themes, give way to more embattled ideologies organized around the issues of national unity, national-cultural identity and 'national interest'. Not only is there, then, a break in the dominant ideological frameworks, but an enormous variety of oppositional and counter-ideologies develop, presenting challenges of varying force, coherence and effectiveness to the taken-for-granted orthodoxies. Such moments of ideological rupture and transformation are never smooth; the ideological 'work' required, shows through; so do the breaks and dislocations. Above all, there is the question of how the progressive polarization of society and the 'crisis' of capitalism come to be signified and interpreted within the framework of these competing ideological constructions.

It is of the utmost importance to analyse, precisely, the mechanisms through which the tilt in the crisis of hegemony from consent to coercion is publicly signified: how it wins legitimacy by appearing to be grounded and connected, not simply in myths, fears and speculations, but in the experience of ordinary people. The actual ideological passage into a 'law-and-order' society entails a process of a quite specific kind. Crucially, in the early years of our period, it is sustained by what we call a *displacement effect*: the connection between the crisis and the way it is appropriated in the social experience of the majority – social anxiety – passes through a series of false 'resolutions', primarily taking the shape of a succession of *moral panics*. It is as if each surge of social anxiety finds a temporary respite in the projection of fears on to and into certain compellingly anxiety-laden themes: in the discovery of demons, the identification of folk-devils, the mounting of moral campaigns, the expiation of prosecution and control – in *the moral-panic cycle*. None of these projected 'workings-through' of social anxiety succeeds for long. The 'trouble' about youth is not appeased by the Teddy Boys, 'mods' and 'rockers' sent down in court; it surfaces again, now about hooliganism, vandalism, long hair, drugs, promiscuous sex and so on. The fears about race are not expiated by a succession of panics about blacks, or catharsized by Powellite rhetoric, or calmed by tougher and tougher measures of control on the entry of immigrants. Up they rise again, now about 'the ghetto', or about black schools, or about the black unemployed, or about black crime. The same could be said for a whole number of 'moral panics' about similar areas of social concern throughout the 1960s – by no means excluding that perennial and continuing public panic, about crime itself. The first form which the 'experience of social crisis' assumes in public consciousness, then, is the *moral panic*.

The second stage is where particular moral panics converge and overlap: where the enemy becomes both many-faceted *and* 'one'; where the sale of drugs, the spread of pornography, the growth of the women's movement and the critique of the family are experienced and signified as the thin edges of that larger wedge: the threat to the state, the breakdown of social life itself, the coming of chaos, the onset of anarchy. Now the demons proliferate – but, more menacingly, they belong to the same subversive family. They are 'brothers under the skin'; they are 'part and parcel of the same thing'. This looks, on the surface, like a more concrete set of fears, because here social anxiety can cite a specific enemy, can name names. But, in fact, this naming of names is deceptive. For the enemy is lurking *everywhere*. He (or, increasingly, she) is 'behind everything'. This is the point where the crisis appears in its most abstract form: as a 'general conspiracy'. It is 'the crisis' – but in the disguise of Armageddon.

This is where the cycle of moral panics issues directly into a law-and-order society. For if the threat to society 'from below' is at the same time the subversion of the state from within, then only a general exercise of authority and discipline, only a very wide-ranging brief to the state to 'set things to right' – if necessary at the temporary expense of certain of those liberties which, in more relaxed times, we all enjoyed – is likely to succeed. In this form, a society famous for its tenacious grasp on certain well-earned rights of personal liberty and freedom, enshrined in the liberal state, screws itself up to the distasteful task of going through a period of 'iron times'. The sound of people nerving themselves to the distasteful but necessary exercise of 'more than usual law' to ensure, in a moment of crisis, 'more than usual order', is to be heard throughout the land. Mrs Thatcher puts it one way; Sir Keith Joseph puts it another; the Archbishop of Canterbury brings the authority of the Church to bear on it in still another way; there is a populist and a social-democratic variant of it as well. In these disparate voices we can hear the closure occurring – the interlocking mechanisms closing, the doors clanging shut. The society is battening itself down for 'the long haul' through a crisis. There is light at the end of the tunnel – but not much; and it is far off. Meanwhile, the state has won the right, and indeed inherited the duty, to move swiftly, to stamp fast and hard, to listen in, discreetly to survey, to saturate and swamp, to charge or to hold without charge, to act on suspicion, and to hustle and shoulder, in order to keep society on the straight and narrow. Democracy, that last back-stop against arbitrary power, is in retreat. It is suspended. The times are exceptional. The crisis is real. We are inside the 'law-and-order' state.

1978

Notes

1. I. Birchall, 'Class Struggle in Britain: Workers against the Tory Government, 1970–74', in *Radical America*, vol. 8, no. 5, 1974.
2. J. Griffith, 'Hailsham – Judge or Politician?', *New Statesman*, 1 February 1974.
3. Quoted, ibid.
4. Sir Keith Joseph, in *New Statesman*, 13 June 1975.
5. Sir Keith Joseph, in *Sunday Times*, 20 October 1974.
6. Centre for Policy Studies, *Why Britain Needs a Social Market Economy*, London 1975.
7. N. Poulantzas, 'Marxist Political Theory in Great Britain', *New Left Review* 43, 1967.
8. A. Gramsci, *Prison Notebooks*, London 1971, p. 161.

2

The Great Moving Right Show

No one seriously concerned with the development of left political strategies in the present situation can afford to ignore the 'swing to the right'
which is taking place. We may not yet fully understand its extent,
specific character, causes or effects. There is still some debate as to
whether it is likely to be short-lived or long-term, a movement of the
surface or something more deeply lodged in the body politic. But the
tendency is hard to deny. It no longer looks like a temporary swing of
the pendulum in political fortunes. Indeed, it would be wrong to identify
the rise of the radical right solely with the success in the political party
stakes of Mrs Thatcher and the hard-edged cronies she has borne with
her into high office inside the Conservative Party. Mrs Thatcher has
given the 'swing to the right' a powerful impetus and a distinctive
personal stamp, but the deeper movement which finds in her its personification has – when properly analysed – a much longer trajectory. It has
been well installed – a going concern – since the late 1960s. It has
developed through a number of different phases. First, the 'backlash'
against the revolutionary ferment of '1968' and all that. Then, the bold,
populist bid by Mr Powell – speaking over the heads of the party
factions to 'the people', helping to construct 'the people' in their most
patriotic, racist, constitutional disguise. Then – borrowing the clothes of
his opponent, in the best Tory tradition – Mr Heath: a politician
instinctively of the soft centre, but not averse, in the anxiety-ridden days
of the early 1970s to going to the country with a programme to restore
'Selsdon Man' – a close cousin of Neanderthal Man – to the centre of

British politics. It was this Heath version of the backlash – a chillingly reactionary spectre in its own way – which the miners and others stopped in its tracks. But they did not cut short the underlying movement.

There now seems little doubt that, as we moved through the 1970s, the popular mood shifted decisively against the left. This fact was mirrored in the decline of Mr Callaghan's government. As Labour lost parliamentary strength, so it has drifted deep into the ideological territory of the right, occupying with panache many of the positions only just evacuated by the right. It was Labour, not the Conservatives, which applied the surgical cut to the welfare state. And there was Mr Healey's not wholly unexpected conversion to orthodox monetarism and fiscal restraint – tutored by the IMF and the oil price. In this climate of austerity, Keynes has been decently buried; the right has re-established its monopoly over 'good ideas'; 'capitalism' and 'the free market' have come back into common usage as terms of positive approval.

And yet the full dimensions of this precipitation to the right still lack a proper analysis on the left. The crisis continues to be read by the left from within certain well-entrenched, largely unquestioned assumptions. Our illusions remain intact, even when they clearly no longer provide an adequate analytic framework. Certainly, there is no simple, one-to-one correspondence between a 'correct' analysis and an 'effective' politics. Nevertheless, the failure of analysis cannot be totally unrelated to the obvious lack of political perspective which now confronts the left.

In spite of this there are still some who welcome the crisis, arguing that 'worse means better'. The 'sharpening of contradictions', comrades, together with the rising tempo of the class struggle, will eventually guarantee the victory of progressive forces everywhere. Those who hold such a position may enjoy untroubled nights; but they have short political memories. They forget how frequently in recent history the 'sharpening of contradictions' has led to settlements and solutions which favoured capital and the extreme right rather than the reverse.

Then there are those who dismiss the advance of the right as 'mere ideology'. Ideology, as we know, is not 'real' and so cannot become a material factor, let alone a political force. We have only to wait until the *real* economic forces exert their absolute determinacy, and then all this ideological vapour will be blown away ... Yet another common response is an extension of this last position. It argues that the current 'swing to the right' is only the simple and general expression of every economic recession. On this view, there are no significant differences between the present and any other variant of Tory philosophy. 'Thatcherism', 'Baldwinism', etc. – each is only a name for the same phenomenon: the permanent, unchanging shape of reactionary ideas. What is the point of drawing fine distinctions?

Such arguments are especially characteristic of a certain hard-headed response from the 'hard' left. All this analysis, it is implied, is unnecessary. The committed will not waste time on such speculations, but get on with the job of 'engaging in the real struggle'. In fact, this last is a position which neglects everything that is specific and particular to this historical conjuncture. It is predicated on the view that a social formation is a simple structure, in which economic conditions will be immediately, transparently and indifferently translated on to the political and ideological stage. If you operate on the 'determining level', then all the other pieces of the puzzle will fall into place. The idea that we should define a conjuncture as the coming together of often distinct though related contradictions, moving according to different tempos, but condensed in the same historical moment, is foreign to this approach. The name of Lenin is frequently and reverently invoked in these circles. Yet the approach precisely neglects Lenin's graphic reminder that 1917 was 'an extremely unique historical situation', in which 'absolutely dissimilar currents, absolutely heterogeneous class interests, absolutely contrary political and social strivings have merged ... in a strikingly "harmonious" manner'. Above all, it takes for granted what needs to be explained – and is in no sense simple or obvious: namely, how a capitalist economic recession (economic), presided over by a social-democratic party with mass working-class support and organized depth in the trade unions (politically) is 'lived' by increasing numbers of people through the themes and representations (ideologically) of a virulent, emergent 'petty-bourgeois' ideology. These contradictory features of the present crisis are absorbed into some orthodox analyses only at considerable cost. The ideology of the radical right is less an 'expression' of economic recession than the recession's condition of existence. Ideological factors have effects on and for the social formation as a whole – including effects on the economic crisis itself and how it is likely to be politically resolved.

We also encounter variants of 'revolutionary optimism' as a counter to what is considered to be exaggerated 'revolutionary pessimism'. The left, it is said, will rise again, as it has done before. We should look for the points of resistance – the class struggle continues! Of course, in one sense, they are right. We must not underestimate the possibilities of struggle and resistance. We must look behind the surface phenomena. We must find the points of intervention. But, on the other hand, if we are to be effective, politically, it can only be on the basis of a serious analysis of things as they are, not as we would wish them to be. Gramsci once enjoined those who would be politically effective to turn their thoughts 'violently' towards the present *as it is.* Whistling in the dark is an occupational hazard not altogether unknown on the British left. Gramsci's slogan is old, but it contains the essence of the matter none the less: 'Pessimism of the intelligence, optimism of the will.'

Finally, there is the long-awaited threat of 'fascism'. There is a sense in which the appearance of organized fascism on the political stage seems to solve everything for the left. It confirms our best-worst suspicions, awakening familiar ghosts and spectres. Fascism and economic recession together seem to render transparent those connections which most of the time are opaque, hidden and displaced. Away with all those time-wasting theoretical speculations! The Marxist guarantees are all in place after all, standing to attention. Let us take to the streets. This is *not* an argument against taking to the streets. Indeed, the direct interventions against the rising fortunes of the National Front – local campaigns, anti-fascist work in the unions, trades councils, women's groups, the mobilization behind the Anti-Nazi League, the counter-demonstrations, above all Rock Against Racism (one of the timeliest and best constructed of cultural interventions, repaying serious and extended analysis) – constitute one of the few success stories of the conjuncture. But it *is* an argument against the satisfactions which sometimes flow from applying simplifying analytic schemes to complex events. What we have to explain is a move toward 'authoritarian populism' – an exceptional form of the capitalist state which, unlike classical fascism, has retained most (though not all) of the formal representative institutions in place, and which at the same time has been able to construct around itself an active popular consent. This undoubtedly represents a decisive shift in the balance of forces, and the National Front has played a 'walk-on' part in this drama. It has entailed a striking weakening of democratic forms and initiatives; but not their suspension. We miss precisely what is specific to this exceptional form of the crisis of the capitalist state by mere name-calling.

An Organic Crisis?

The swing to the right is part of what Gramsci called an 'organic' phenomenon:

> A crisis occurs, sometimes lasting for decades. This exceptional duration means that uncurable structural contradictions have revealed themselves ... and that, despite this, the political forces which are struggling to conserve and defend the existing structure itself are making efforts to cure them within certain limits, and to overcome them. These incessant and persistent efforts ... form the terrain of the conjunctural and it is upon this terrain that the forces of opposition organize.[2]

Gramsci insisted that we must get the 'organic' and 'conjunctural' aspects of a crisis into a proper relationship. What defines the 'conjunctural' – the immediate terrain of struggle – is not simply the given economic conditions, but precisely the 'incessant and persistent' efforts which are being made to defend and conserve the status quo. If the crisis is deep – 'organic' – these efforts cannot be merely defensive. They will be *formative*: aiming at a new balance of forces, the emergence of new elements, the attempt to put together a new 'historic bloc', new political configurations and 'philosophies', a profound restructuring of the state and the ideological discourses which construct the crisis and represent it as it is 'lived' as a practical reality: new programmes and policies, pointing to a new result, a new sort of 'settlement' – 'within certain limits'. These new elements do not 'emerge': they have to be constructed. Political and ideological work is required to disarticulate old formations, and to rework their elements into new ones. The 'swing to the right' is not a reflection of the crisis: it is itself a *response* to the crisis. In what follows I consider some aspects of that response, concentrating particularly on the neglected political and ideological dimensions.

Economic Crisis

We must first examine the precipitating conditions. These are the result of a set of discontinuous but related histories. In economic terms, Britain's structural industrial and economic weakness emerged in the immediate aftermath of the postwar boom. The 1960s were marked by the oscillations between recession and recovery, with a steady underlying deterioration. These effectively destroyed the last remnants of the 'radical programme' on the basis of which Wilson won power in 1964, and to which he tried to harness a new social bloc. By the end of the 1960s, the economy had dipped into full-scale recession – slumpflation – which sustained the exceptional 'Heath course' of 1971–4, and its head-on collisions with organized labour. By the mid-1970s, the economic parameters were dictated by a synchronization between capitalist recession on a global scale, and the crisis of capital accumulation specific to Britain – the weak link in the chain. Domestic politics have thus been dominated by crisis management and containment strategies: dovetailed through an increasingly interventionist state, intervening to secure the conditions of capitalist production and reproduction. The dominant strategy had a distinctively corporatist character – incorporating sections of the working class and unions into the bargain between state, capital and labour, the three 'interests'. Crisis management has drawn successively on different variants of the same basic repertoire: incomes policy, first by consent, then by imposition; wage restraint; social contracting. The 'natural' governor of this crisis has been the party of social democracy in power: Labour. This last factor has had profound effects in disorganizing and fragmenting working-class responses to the crisis itself.

At the ideological level, however, things have moved at a rather different tempo; in certain respects they predate the economic aspects. Many of the key themes of the radical right – law and order, the need for social discipline and authority in the face of a conspiracy by the enemies of the state, the onset of social anarchy, the 'enemy within', the dilution of British stock by alien black elements – had been well articulated before the full dimensions of the economic recession were revealed. They emerged in relation to the radical movements and political polarizations of the 1960s, for which '1968' must stand as a convenient, though inadequate, notation. Some of these themes got progressively translated to other fronts as the confrontation with organized labour, and militant resistance developed during the Heath interregnum. For the constitution of the principle thematics of the radical right, this must be seen as a formative moment.[3]

The Radical Right

The radical right does not therefore appear out of thin air. It has to be understood in direct relation to alternative political formations attempting to occupy and command the same space. It is engaged in a struggle for hegemony, within the dominant bloc, against both social democracy and the moderate wing of its own party. Not only is it operating in the same space: it is working directly on the contradictions within those competing positions. The strength of its intervention lies partly in the radicalism of its commitment to break the mould and not simply to rework the elements of the prevailing 'philosophies'. In doing so, it nevertheless takes the elements which are already constructed into place, dismantles them, reconstitutes them into a new logic, and articulates the space in a new way, polarizing it to the right.

This can be seen with respect to both the earlier competing positions. The Heath position was destroyed in the confrontation with organized labour. But it was also undermined by its internal contradictions. It failed to win the showdown with labour; it could not enlist popular support for this decisive encounter; in defeat, it returned to its 'natural' position in the political spectrum, engaging in its own version of corporatist bargaining. 'Thatcherism' therefore succeeds in this space by directly engaging the 'creeping socialism' and apologetic 'state collectivism' of the Heath wing. It thus centres on the very nerve of consensus politics, which dominated and stabilized the political scene for over a decade. To sustain its credibility as a party of government in a crisis of capital, 'Thatcherism' retains some lingering and ambivalent connections to this centre territory: Mr Prior is its voice – but *sotto voce*. On other grounds, it has won considerable space by the active destruction of consensus politics from the right. Of course, it aims for the construction of a national consensus of its own. What it destroys is that form of consensus in which social democracy was the principal tendency. This evacuation of centrist territory has unleashed political forces on the right which have been kept in rein for most of the postwar period.

The Contradictions within Social Democracy

But the contradictions within social democracy are the key to the whole rightward shift of the political spectrum. For if the destruction of the Heath 'party' secures hegemony for 'Thatcherism' over the right, it is the contradictory form of social democracy which has effectively disorganized the left and the working-class response to the crisis, and provided the terrain on which Thatcherism is working.

This contradiction can be put in simple terms: to win electoral power, social democracy must maximize its claims to be *the* political representative of the interests of the working class and organized labour. It is the party capable of (a) mastering the crises, while (b) defending – within the constraints imposed by capitalist recession – working-class interests. It is important here to remember that this version of social democracy – 'Labourism' – is not a homogeneous political entity but a complex political formation. It is not *the* expression of *the* working class 'in government', but the principal means of the political representation of the class. Representation here has to be understood as an active and formative relationship. It organizes the class, constituting it as a political force of a particular kind – a social-democratic political force – in the same moment as it is constituted. Everything depends on the means – the practices, the apparatuses and the 'philosophies' – by which the often dispersed and contradictory interests of a class are welded together into a coherent position which can be articulated and represented in the political and ideological theatres of struggle.

The expression of this representative relationship of class-to-party, in the present period, has depended decisively on the extensive set of corporatist bargains negotiated between Labour and the trade-union representatives of the class. This 'indissoluble link' is the practical basis for Labour's claim to be the natural governing party of the crisis. This is the contract it delivers. But, once in government, social democracy is committed to finding solutions to the crisis which are capable of winning support from key sections of capital, since its solutions are framed within the limits of capitalist survival. But this requires that the indissoluble link between party and class serves both to advance and to discipline the class and the organizations it represents. This is only possible if the class-to-party link can somehow be redefined or dismantled and if there can be substituted for it an alternative articulation: people-to-government. The rhetoric of 'national interest', which is the principal ideological form in which a succession of defeats has been imposed on the working class by social democracy in power, is exactly the site where this contradiction shows through and is being constantly reworked. But people-to-government dissects the field of struggle differently from class-to-party. It sets Labour, at key moments of struggle – from the strikes of 1966 right through to the 1979 5 per cent pay norm – by definition 'on the side of the nation' *against* 'sectional interests', 'irresponsible trade-union power', etc., i.e. against the class.

This is the terrain on which Mr Heath played such destructive games in the lead-through to the Industrial Relations Act and its aftermath, with his invocation of 'the great trade union of the nation' and the spectre of the greedy working class 'holding the nation to ransom'. 'Thatcherism', deploying the discourses of 'nation' and 'people' against 'class' and 'unions' with far greater vigour and populist appeal, has homed in on the same objective contradiction. Within this space is being constructed an assault, not on this or that piece of 'irresponsible bargaining' by a particular union, but on the very foundation of organized labour. Considerable numbers of people – including many trade unionists – find themselves reflected and set in place through this interpellation of 'nation' and 'people' at the centre of this mounting attack on the defensive organizations of the working class.

Anti-Collectivism

A closely related strand in the new philosophy of the radical right are the themes of anti-collectivism and anti-statism. 'Thatcherism' has given these elements of neo-liberal doctrine within conservative 'philosophy' an extensive rejuvenation. At the level of theoretical ideologies, anti-statism has been refurbished by the advance of monetarism as the most fashionable economic credo. Keynesianism was the lynch-pin of the theoretical ideologies of corporatist state intervention throughout the postwar period, assuming almost the status of a sacred orthodoxy or *doxa*. To have replaced it in some of the most powerful and influential apparatuses of government, in research and the universities, and restored in its place the possessive individualist and free-market nostrums of Hayek and Friedman is, in itself, a remarkable reversal. Ideological transformations, however, do not take place by magic. For years bodies like the Institute for Economic Affairs have been plugging away in the margins of the Conservative Party and the informed public debate on economic policy, refurbishing the gospel of Adam Smith and the free market, undermining the assumptions of neo-Keynesianism, planning and projecting how the 'competitive stimulus' could be applied again to one area after another of those sectors which, as they see it, have fallen into the corporatist abyss.

Gradually, in the more hospitable climate of the 1970s, these seeds began to bear fruit. First in the learned journals, then in the senior common rooms, and finally in informal exchanges between the 'new academics' and the more 'sensitive' senior civil servants, a monetarist version of neo-classical economics came to provide the accepted frame of reference for economic debate. The economic journalists helped to make this revolution in ideas acceptable in the media and the serious financial press – and thus, not long after, in the boardrooms of enterprises which everyone imagined had long since abandoned open competition for the safer waters of state capitalism.

Neither Keynesianism nor monetarism, however, win votes as such in the electoral marketplace. But, in the discourse of 'social market values', Thatcherism discovered a powerful means of translating economic doctrine into the language of experience, moral imperative and common sense, thus providing a 'philosophy' in the broader sense – an alternative *ethic* to that of the 'caring society'. This translation of a theoretical *ideology* into a populist *idiom* was a major political achievement: and the conversion of hard-faced economics into the language of compulsive *moralism* was, in many ways, the centrepiece of this transformation. 'Being British' became once again identified with the restoration of competition and profitability; with tight money and sound finance ('You can't pay yourself more than you earn!!') – the national economy projected on the model of the household budget. The essence of the British people was identified with self-reliance and personal responsibility, as against the image of the over-taxed individual, enervated by welfare-state 'coddling', his or her moral fibre irrevocably sapped by 'state handouts'. This assault, not just on welfare over-spending, but on the very principle and essence of collective social welfare – the centrepiece of consensus politics from the Butskell period onwards – was mounted, not through an analysis of which class of the deserving made most out of the welfare state, but through the emotive image of the 'scrounger': the new folk-devil.

To the elaboration of this populist language and the reconstruction of a 'free-market' ethic both the excessively high-minded Sir Keith Joseph and the excessively broad-bottomed Rhodes Boyson, both the 'disinterested' leader writers of *The Times, Telegraph* and *The Economist* and the ventriloquists of populist opinion in the *Mail,* the *Express,* the *Star* and the *Sun* lent their undivided attention. The colonization of the popular press was a critical victory in this struggle to define the common sense of the times. Here was undertaken the critical ideological work of constructing around 'Thatcherism' a populist common sense.

Thatcherite populism is a particularly rich mix. It combines the resonant themes of organic Toryism – nation, family, duty, authority, standards, traditionalism – with the aggressive themes of a revived neo-liberalism – self-interest, competitive individualism, anti-statism. Some of these elements had been secured in earlier times through the grand themes of one-Nation popular Conservatism: the means by which Toryism circumnavigated democracy, lodged itself in the hearts of the people and lived to form many another popular government. Other elements derived from the anachronistic vocabulary of political economy and possessive individualism. The latter had been absorbed into Conservative rhetoric only when the old Liberalism ceased to provide the Conservatives with a viable political base. The idea that 'freedom of the people equals the free market' has never been wholly banished from the Tory universe; but, despite Powellism, and Mr Heath in the 'Selsdon Man' phase, it has failed to achieve full ascendancy within the party in the postwar period, until recently. But now, in the wake of an era dominated by the social-democratic consensus, and a Conservatism tainted with distinct corporatist tendencies, 'Freedom/free market' is once again in the foreground of the conservative ideological repertoire. 'Free market – strong state': around this contradictory point, where neo-liberal political economy fused with organic Toryism, the authentic language of 'Thatcherism' has condensed. It began to be spoken in the mid-1970s – and, in its turn, to 'speak' – to define – the crisis: what it was and how to get out of it. The crisis has begun to be 'lived' in its terms. This is a new kind of taken-for-grantedness; a reactionary common sense, harnessed to the practices and solutions of the radical right and the class forces it now aspires to represent.

The Repertoire of Thatcherism

Only two aspects of this rich repertoire of anti-collectivism can be remarked on in the space available here. First, there is the way these discourses operated directly on popular elements in the traditional philosophies and practical ideologies of the dominated classes. These elements – as Ernesto Laclau and others have argued[4] – often express a contradiction between popular interests and the power bloc. But since the terms in which this contradiction is expressed have no intrinsic, necessary or fixed class meaning, they can be effectively recomposed as elements within very different discourses, positioning the popular classes in relation to the power bloc in different ways. When, in a crisis, the traditional alignments are disrupted, it is possible, on the very ground of this break, to construct the people into a populist political subject: *with*, not against, the power bloc; in alliance with new political forces in a great national crusade to 'make Britain "Great" once more'. The language of 'the people', unified behind a reforming drive to turn the tide of 'creeping collectivism', banish Keynesian illusions from the state apparatus and renovate the power bloc is a powerful one. Its radicalism connects with radical-popular sentiments; but it effectively turns them round, absorbs and neutralizes their popular thrust, and creates, in the place of a popular rupture, a *populist unity*. It brings into existence a new 'historic bloc' between certain sections of the dominant and dominated classes. We can see this construction of ideological cross-alliances between 'Thatcherism' and 'the people' actually going on in the very structure of Mrs Thatcher's own rhetoric: 'Don't talk to me about "them" and "us" in a company,' she once told the readers of *Woman's Own*: 'You're all "we" in a company. You survive as the company survives, prosper as the company prospers – everyone together. The future lies in cooperation and not confrontation.' This displaces an existing structure of oppositions – 'them' vs 'us'. It sets in its place an alternative set of equivalents: 'Them *and* us equals *we*'. Then it positions we – 'the people' – in a particular relation to capital: behind it, dominated by its imperatives (profitability, accumulation); yet at the same time, yoked to it, identified with it. 'You survive as the company survives'; presumably also, you collapse as it collapses ... Cooperation not confrontation! The process we are looking at here is very similar to that which Gramsci once described as *transformism*: the neutralization of some elements in an ideological formation and their absorption and passive appropriation into a new political configuration.

The second aspect is closely related to this process of transformism. For what we have so far described could well appear – and has often been described by the traditional left – as mere illusion, pure 'false consciousness': just a set of ideological con-tricks whose cover will be blown as soon as they are put to the stern test of material circumstances. But this reading greatly underestimates both the rational core on which these populist constructions are situated, and their real, not false, material basis. Specifically, such a reading neglects the materiality of the contradictions between 'the people' – popular needs, interests, desires and aspirations – on the one hand, and the actual, imposed structures of the interventionist state – the state of the monopoly phase of capitalist development – on the other. 'Thatcherism', far from simply conjuring demons out of the deep, operated directly on the real and manifestly contradictory experience of the popular classes under social-democratic corporatism.

It is important to understand why Labourist social democracy was vulnerable to the charge of 'statism' – and therefore why 'anti-statism' has proved so powerful a populist slogan: otherwise, we may confuse ourselves into believing that the headway which 'Thatcherism' is undoubtedly making among working people, committed Labour voters and some sectors of skilled labour, can be wholly attributed to 'false consciousness'. As we have seen, the project which social-democratic corporatism set itself was the containment and reform, not the trans-formation, of the crisis of British capitalism. What capital manifestly could no longer accomplish on its own, 'reformism' would have to do by harnessing capital to the state, using the state as representative of the 'general interest' to create the conditions for the effective resumption of capitalist accumulation and profitability. Social democracy had no other viable strategy, especially for 'big' capital (and 'big' capital had no viable alternative strategy for itself), which did not involve massive state regu-lation and support. Hence the state has become a massive presence, inscribed over every feature of social and economic life. But, as the recession bit more deeply, so the management of the crisis required Labour to discipline, limit and police the very classes it claimed to repre-sent – again, through the mediation of the state.

The best index of this problem was the incomes policy strategy, especially in its last and most confusing manifestation, the Social Contract. The Social Contract was one of those open-ended or double-sided ideological mechanisms into which each side could read quite contradictory meanings. To the left, it represented an attempt to use the corporatist bargaining of the state to graft certain powerful social and economic objectives on to the 'price' of limiting wage demands. To the Labour government, it clearly represented the only form in which social and economic discipline could be 'sold' to the trade union movement. The glaring discrepancies between the redistributive language of the Social Contract and its actual disciplinary character was the best index of how 'the state' under corporatist management came to be experi-enced as 'the enemy of the people'. This contradiction bit deeper and deeper into the Labour/trade union alliance until, with the revolt against incomes policies and in favour of 'collective bargaining', it undermined the credibility and raison d'être of Mr Callaghan's government itself.

The radical right welcomed this trade union revolt against 'state inter-ference in free collective bargaining' much in the manner of the prodigal son.

It would be easy to believe that Labourism has been trapped by the statist dilemma only recently and inadvertently. In fact, 'Labourism', or Labour socialism, has been marked from its origins by its Fabian–collectivist inheritance. The expansion of the state machine, under the management of state servants and experts, has often been defined in this tradition as synonymous with socialism itself. Labour has been willing to use this state to reform conditions for working people, provided this did not bite too deeply into the 'logic' of capitalist accumulation. But it has refused like the plague the mobilization of democratic power at the popular level. This has always been the site on which Labour has been brought back from the brink into its deep reverence for 'constitutiona-lism'. Nothing, indeed, so rattles the equanimity of Labour leaders as the spectacle of the popular classes on the move under their own steam, outside the range of 'responsible' guidance and leadership. The fact is that 'statism' is not foreign to the trajectory of Labour socialism: it is intrinsic to it. Corporatism is only the latest form in which this deep commitment to using the state on behalf of the people, but without popular mobilization, has manifested itself.

The radical right has capitalized on this fatal hesitancy, this deep weakness in Labour socialism. Mrs Thatcher is therefore guilty of exag-geration – but of no more than that – when she identifies state bureau-cracy and creeping collectivism with 'socialism', and 'socialism' with the spectre of 'actual existing socialism' under the East European regimes: and then counterposes to this fatal syllogism the sweet sound of 'Free-dom' which, of course, she and her New Model Conservative Party represent.

It is also the case that the actual experience which working people have had of the corporatist state has not been a powerful incentive to further support for increases in its scope. Whether in the growing dole queues or in the waiting-rooms of an over-burdened National Health Service, or suffering the indignities of Social Security, the corporatist state is increasingly experienced by them not as a benefice but as a powerful bureaucratic imposition *on* 'the people'. The state has been present to them, less as a welfare or redistributive agency, and more as the 'state of monopoly capital'. And since Labour has foregrounded the requirements of monopoly capital above all others, what is it that can be said to be 'false' in this consciousness?

Instead of confronting this contradiction at the heart of its strategy, Labourism has typically fallen back on reaffirming the neutral-benevolent definition of the state, as incarnator of the National Interest and above the struggle between the contending classes. It is precisely this abstract state which now appears transformed in the discourses of Thatcherism as the enemy. It is 'the state' which has overborrowed and overspent; fuelled inflation; fooled the people into thinking that there would always be more where the last handout came from; tried to assume the regulation of things like wages and prices which are best left to the hidden hand of market forces; above all, interfered, meddled, intervened, instructed, directed – against the essence, the Genius, of The British People. It is time, as she says, with conviction, 'to put people's destinies again in their own hands'.

Thus, in any polarization along the fissure between state and people, it is Labour which can be represented as undividedly part of the power bloc, enmeshed in the state apparatus, riddled with bureaucracy, in short, as 'with' the state; and Mrs Thatcher, grasping the torch of freedom with one hand, as someone who is undividedly out there, 'with the people'. It is the Labour Party which is committed to things as they are – and Mrs Thatcher who means to tear society up by the roots and radically reconstruct it! This is the process by which – as they say – the radical right has 'become popular'.

Education

We might turn to another area of successful colonization by the radical right: the sphere of education. Until very recently, the social-democratic goals of 'equality of opportunity' and 'remedying educational disadvantage' were dominant throughout the world of secondary education. The struggle over comprehensivization was its political signature. Contestation in this area has only gradually developed, through a series of strategic interventions. The 'Black Paper' group – at first no more than an elitist, education rump – has moved from very modest beginnings to the point where it could justly be claimed (and was) that its preoccupations set the agenda for the 'Great Debate' which the Labour government initiated in 1978. In the 1960s 'progressive' and 'community' education made considerable advances within state schools. Today, 'progressivism' is thoroughly discredited: the bodies of a whole series of well-publicized schools – William Tyndale and after, so to speak – lie strewn in its path. The panic over falling standards and working-class illiteracy, the fears concerning politically motivated teachers in the classroom, the scare stories about the 'violent' urban school, about the adulteration of standards through the immigrant intake, and so on, have successfully turned the tide in the education sphere towards themes and goals established by the forces of the right. The press –

especially those three popular ventriloquist voices of the radical right, the *Mail*, the *Sun* and the *Express*, have played here a quite pivotal role. They have publicized the 'examples' in a highly sensational form – and they have drawn the connections.

These connections and couplings are the key mechanisms of the process by which education as a field of struggle has been articulated to the right. There are long, deepseated resistances within the philosophy of state education to any attempt to measure schooling directly in terms of the needs and requirements of industry. That these were resistances often shot through with ambiguity is not so important for our purposes. However it arose, the reluctance to cash schooling in terms of its imme- diate value to capital was one on which campaigns could be mounted with some hope of professional administrative support. These defences have now been dismantled. Clear evidence is supposed to exist that standards are falling: the principal witnesses to this alarming trend are employers who complain about the quality of job applicants: this, in turn, must be having an effect on the efficiency and productivity of the nation – at a time when recession puts a premium on improving both. Once the often ill-founded elements were stitched together into this chain of reasoning, policies could begin to be changed by leading educationists of the political right, indirectly, even before they took charge at the DES. And why?

First, because the terrain on which the debate is being conducted has been so thoroughly reconstructed round this new 'logic' that the ground- swell for change is proving hard to resist. Second, because Labour itself has always been caught between competing goals in schooling: to improve the chances of working-class children and the worse-off in education, *and* to harness education to the economic and efficiency needs of the productive system. We can see now that this contradiction, even within the social-democratic educational programme, is another variant of what earlier we called the principal contradiction of social democracy in this period. The educational experts and spokesmen, the educational press, sections of the profession, the media, many educational interest groups and organizations have been operating exactly on the site of this dilemma and – in conditions of recession – carried the argument with the Labour government which in turn took the lead in promoting debates and policies designed to make this equation – 'success in education = meeting the needs of industry' – come true!

The 'Great Debate'

Thus the agenda for the 'great debate' was indeed set for social democracy by the social forces of the radical right. And the language of comprehensive education has been effectively displaced by the language of educational excellence. The Labour government, which initiated this 'great debate' was almost certainly still convinced that this is largely a non-political debate, as debates about education ought to be. 'Education should not be a political football,' Labour ministers solemnly declared – a slogan they should try selling to the public school headmasters' conference! And, lest it be thought that this is, after all, only a debate, we should be aware that a major restructuring of the educational state apparatuses is taking place. The Department of Education and Science (DES) is to be set somewhat to one side, and new apparatuses capable of realizing the equation in more immediate and practical forms have moved into a central position in the field: the Manpower Services Commission, the new TSA and 'Tops' retraining programmes, directly geared to the demands and movements of industry and to the silent reskilling and deskilling of the unemployed.

The restructuring of the state apparatus from above is one thing. But the active and positive support from parents – including many working-class ones – is another. As unemployment grows, working-class parents are obliged to take the competitive side of education more seriously: being skilled – even if it is only for particular places in dead-end, low-skill, routine labour – is better than being on the dole. If comprehensivization in the form in which it was offered is not going to deliver the goods, then working-class children may have to be content to be 'skilled' and 'classed' in any way they can. This is what Marx meant by the 'dull compulsion' of economic existence.

But it is also the case that, as the failure of social-democratic initiatives to turn the tide of educational disadvantage becomes more manifest, so the positive aspirations of working people for the education of their children can be rearticulated towards the support for a more conventional and traditional approach to the educational marketplace. This great exodus back to known and familiar territory, to tried pathways, to the traditional and the orthodox, to the safe territory of what is, is one of the strongest and deepest of common-sense sentiments: and, for that reason, one of the most resonant themes in the discourse of the radical right. In the 1960s, 'parent power' belonged with the radical movements, with Ivan Illich and 'deschooling'. In the 1970s and 1980s it was one of the strongest cards in the educational pack shuffled by Tory education spokespersons.

Law and Order

If education is an area where the right has won territory without having to win power, two other areas in the repertoire of the radical right – race and law and order – are ones where the right has traditionally assumed a leading role. We can be brief about them since they have gained considerable attention on the left in the recent period. They are chosen as examples here only to make a general point. On law and order, the themes – more policing, tougher sentencing, better family discipline, the rising crime rate as an index of social disintegration, the threat to 'ordinary people going about their private business' from thieves, muggers, etc., the wave of lawlessness and the loss of law-abidingness – are perennials of Conservative Party conferences, and the sources of many a populist campaign by moral entrepreneur groups and quoting editors. But if the work of the right in some areas has won support over into its camp, the law and order issues have scared people over. The language of law and order is sustained by a populist moralism. It is where the great syntax of 'good' versus 'evil', of civilized and uncivilized standards, of the choice between anarchy and order, constantly divides the world up and classifies it into its appointed stations. The play on 'values' and on moral issues in this area is what gives to the law-and-order crusade much of its grasp on popular morality and common sense conscience. But it also touches concretely the experience of crime and theft, of the loss of scarce property and the fears of unexpected attack in working-class areas and neighbourhoods; and, since it promulgates no other remedies for their underlying causes, it welds people to that 'need for authority' which has been so significant for the right in the construction of consent to its authoritarian programme.

Race constitutes another variant of the same process. In recent months questions of race, racism and relations between the races, as well as immigration, have been dominated by the dialectic between the radical-respectable and the radical-rough forces of the right. It was said about the 1960s and early 1970s that, after all, Mr Powell lost. This is true only if the shape of a whole conjuncture is to be measured by the career of a single individual. In another sense, there is an argument that 'Powellism' won: not only because his official eclipse was followed by legislating into effect much of what he proposed, but because of the magical connections and short-circuits which Powellism was able to establish between the themes of race and immigration control and the images of the nation, the British people and the destruction of 'our culture, our way of life'.

I have looked exclusively at some political–ideological dimensions of the emergence of the radical right, not to evoke wonder at its extent, but to try to identify what is specific to it, what marks its difference from other variants which have flourished since the war. The first is the complex but interlocked relationship of the right to the fortunes and fate of social democracy when the latter takes power in a period of economic recession, and tries to provide a solution 'within certain limits'. It is always the case that the right is what it is partly because of what the left is. The second is its popular success in neutralizing the contradiction between people and the state/power bloc and winning popular interpellations so decisively for the right. In short, the nature of its *populism*. But now it must be added that this is no rhetorical device or trick, for this populism is operating on genuine contradictions, it has a rational and material core. Its success and effectivity do not lie in its capacity to dupe unsuspecting folk but in the way it addresses real problems, real and lived experiences, real contradictions – and yet is able to represent them within a logic of discourse which pulls them systematically into line with policies and class strategies of the right. Finally – and this is not limited to this analysis, though it seems especially relevant – there is the evidence of just how ideological transformation and political restructuring of this order is actually accomplished. It works on the ground of already constitued social practices and lived ideologies. It wins space there by constantly drawing on these elements which have secured over time a traditional resonance and left their traces in popular inventories. At the same time, it changes the field of struggle by changing the place, the position, the relative weight of the condensations within any one discourse and constructing them according to an alternative logic. What shifts them is not 'thoughts' but a particular practice of social struggle: ideological and political class struggle. What makes these represent-ations popular is that they have a purchase on practice, they shape it, they are written into its materiality. What constitutes them as a danger is that they change the nature of the terrain itself on which struggles of different kinds are taking place; they have pertinent effects on these struggles. Their effect is to constitute a new balance of political forces. This is exactly the terrain on which the forces of opposition must organ-ize, if we are to transform it.

Notes

1. V.I. Lenin, 'Letters from Afar', No. 1, *Lenin Selected Works* Vol. 2, Moscow 1970.
2. A. Gramsci, *Prison Notebooks*, London 1971, p. 179.
3. A fuller analysis of this moment can be found in the chapters on the 'Exhaustion of Consent' and 'Towards the Exceptional State' in Hall, Clarke, Critcher, Jefferson and Roberts, *Policing the Crisis*, London 1978. Some of this material is reprinted in this volume, pp. 19–38.
4. See E. Laclau, *Politics and Ideology in Marxist Theory*, London 1977.

3

The 'Little Caesars' of Social Democracy

The left is clearly in some difficulty as to how to explain or respond to the new Social Democratic/Liberal regrouping in the 'centre'. The formation of the Council for Social Democracy (CSD) and of a Social-Democratic bloc in parliament, is, at one level, such a media-inspired and stimulated phenomenon, that it is hard to know how to make a realistic assessment of its electoral and political prospects. Its pragmatism, soul-searching 'good sense', the eminent 'reasonableness' of its leading figures, the agony of their hesitations, the renunciation of 'doctrinaire extremes', the rhetoric of 'novelty', are all calculated to project just that illusion of a viable centre, free of monetarist and Marxist 'dogma', dear to the centrist instincts of many sections of the press. Commentators like Peter Jenkins of the *Guardian* have been hoping and praying so long for this deliverance from the burden of socialism, that it is impossible to know any longer whether columns like his represent sober political analyses or just more self-fulfilling prophecies. Pollsters and political analysts have been predicting the 'swing to moderation' for so long, that they might well have simply created Social Democracy themselves, if Dr Owen and Mr Rodgers had hesitated much longer. Rarely in recent memory has a political grouping looked forward with such confidence to becoming the decisive element in a hung parliament on the basis of so sketchy and gestural a programme. The argument is that there is a vacuum in the centre which has to be filled. The CSD has so far responded to this challenge by being as vacuous as they could possibly be.

Journals like the *Economist,* which abhors a vacuum, have rushed in to provide the CSD with a programme which they so conspicuously lacked.[1] The economic part of the programme included, inter alia, a commitment to 'the pursuit of equality' (a 'fundamental ambition of social democracy') and a wealth tax. It was clearly too extreme for Dr Owen, whose own recent writings have avoided the theme of equality like the plague. The polls had to construct a hypothetical set of policies to provide their interviewees with some credible basis for responding to the question, 'Would you vote for a Social Democratic party – and, if so, why?' The results have simply compounded the confusion. One *Sunday Times* poll suggested that the Social Democrats would attract support for (among others) the following reasons: they supported (a) more public spending on welfare, and (b) wider worker participation in industry. Neither immediately distinguishes them from their Labour and Liberal rivals. Is Social Democracy, then, just a nine days' wonder, which is not worth discussing seriously? Not necessarily. Though this doesn't mean, either, that we should take it at its own, highly-inflated self-evaluation.

For one thing, it now represents a significant regrouping of parliamentary forces. Postwar parliamentary politics have been marked by many contradictory cross-currents. But the big parliamentary formations and the two-party system have, despite several flutters, remained remarkably stable and durable. There have been few significant regroupings. Open splits and group defections from the Labour Party are even rarer, despite prolonged internecine warfare. It is fifty years since the last one. The left has more often looked like splitting off than the right, which, until recently, has maintained its dominance. Moreover, the departure of the doctrinaire right (for the CSD is nothing if not militant in its 'moderation') marks the isolating out of certain political elements which, up to now, have coexisted with other currents in the unholy mix of 'Labour Socialism'. For years Mr Crosland was the spiritual leader of the group which has now formed the CSD. But Croslandism retained links with more traditional Labour themes (e.g. the strong commitment to equality of opportunity), even though he regarded them as old-fashioned. Mr Hattersley is the last representative of this current, the rest have given up on the labour movement. This represents the breaking of certain historic ties. Their appearance as an independent force thus signals a crisis and break in the system of political representation. And though such breaks do not always mark significant movements (the 'Lib–Lab' pact was more or less pure parliamentary opportunism, marking only the deep degeneration of the Callaghan government in the squalid evening of its rule), they sometimes do – as the breakup of Liberalism at the turn of the century undoubtedly did. It is hard to know, sometimes, just which conjuncture one is in. But, as Gramsci once reminded us, 'crises of representation', when 'social classes become detached from their traditional parties', and organizational forms and leaderships 'who constitute, represent and lead them are no longer recognized . . . as their expression' can form part of a more general crisis of ruling-class hegemony. The question, then, is whether Social Democracy is simply a new allocation of seating arrangements in the House of Commons, or part of a deeper process of the realignment of political forces. This possibility should not be dismissed as easily as it has been by the left in recent months.

Gramsci offered two reasons why such crises of authority might arise; the most relevant being that 'the ruling class has failed in some major political undertaking for which it has requested or forcibly extracted the consent of the broad masses'. In those terms, the 'objective conditions' look remarkably favourable. For such a historic failure – to wit, the task of stemming the precipitate decline of British capitalism – is precisely what is now before us. *Both* the major variants within the governing political repertoire are in various stages of collapse. The social-democratic version, Mark I – the management of capitalist crisis by neo-Keynesian strategies, corporatist politics and the disciplining of working-class demands through incomes policy – is deeply discredited. Its viability seeped away through two long, disheartening Labour regimes. And now the 'radical alternative' – the restoration of capitalist imperatives through the application of unmodified market principles – seems to be also coming apart at the seams. The monetarist, free-enterprise credentials, economic strategies and capitalist revivalism of the Thatcher government are in deep disarray. The Great Reversal, on which everything was staked, has so far failed to appear. The government is losing its struggle with public spending and money supply at approximately the same rate as it is losing its most powerful allies. The CBI is as close to open revolt as so weak-kneed and suppliant a body can ever come. The Treasury Select Committee, led by one of the most powerful independents in the Tory Party, Mr Du Cann (maker and destroyer of leaders before now) has delivered the new doctrines a near-mortal blow. The apostle of anti-statism, Sir Keith Joseph has given away more public money to prop up failing or near-bankrupt state industries than the last three or four chancellors put together. Faced with the long awaited showdown with the unions, the government looked into the face of the NUM, and withdrew. Mrs Thatcher's bellicose adventurism on the world scene – exceedingly dangerous as it is in its own terms – cannot be relied on to divert attention forever from the harsh economic realities at home.

'Thatcherism' has certainly already succeeded in shifting the balance of social forces in the country decisively to the right. But it has so far failed in the second task of the great populist adventure – to flush out the social-democratic vestiges within the power bloc and then reconstruct it, so as thereby to restructure society and the economy. 'Thatcherism' may have *already* fulfilled its 'historic mission'. But neither of the major electoral machines now offers itself as a credible occupant of power at another turn of the electoral wheel. Not only is Thatcher clearly in difficulties but the Tory Party is very divided. Labour is no longer what it was: but what it is, and even more, what it will become as a result of the internal crisis which Thatcherism has provoked within its ranks, is not yet clear. Its political character is highly indeterminate. The signs are therefore well set for the 'recovery' of more centrist ground. If the Social Democrats were prepared, selectively, to reflate; to restore some version of incomes policy; and to mastermind a modest revival by ditching the struggle against inflation and ruthlessly backing private industry against the state sector, they still might not attract popular support; and there is no evidence that they would succeed in the 'historic task' any better than their rivals. But they could look like another – the last? – viable political alternative. And they could secure powerful support 'from above', amongst all those forces currently detaching themselves from the Thatcher path to the brink. They are British capitalism's last political ditch.

This makes Social Democracy a powerful pole of attraction of a cross-party coalitionist type – the 'exceptional' alternative towards which, since the Lloyd George coalition, the British political system has tended to veer in moments of severe crisis (remember Macdonald, and Mr Heath's 'Grand National Coalition'?). This does not guarantee it popular support. But here there may be other trends which strengthen its case. There is what political scientists have been calling the 'growing electoral volatility' of the British voters. Between 1945 and 1970, each of the two major parties polled over 40 per cent of the votes at general elections. Their electoral base seemed reasonably secure. But in the 1970s their share of the vote has fallen significantly. Party identification has weakened, votes have become more fluid. No administration has gone its full term and then succeeded in being re-elected. The old rotation of parties in power has continued: but on an increasingly weak base. This now finds supporting evidence in the findings of the polls that a hypothetical Social Democratic–Liberal alliance would attract a significant proportion of 'floating' and fed-up voters in about equal numbers from both Labour and the Conservatives. The scenario then goes that they would form the decisive bloc in a divided parliament. Electoral reform would become the principal political bargaining point. Proportional representation would then destroy the hegemony of the two-party system forever, and secure a permanent majority for 'the centre'.

The trends are certainly clear, even if the scenario is less convincing. Mrs Thatcher may make royal progresses; but the two-party political system is in deep disrepute. Her popularity may well reflect the fact that she appears to transcend it, with her appeal to nation and people above 'party', and is prepared to destroy it in order to reconstruct it. But people do sense that we are at or near the limit of the present political arrangements and dispositions. Yet the meaning of this phenomenon is hard to interpret. The political scientists and polling fraternity explain it in one way. Here, at last, appears the 'true' voter: less traditional in political alignments, unattached to dogma and doctrine, rationally calculating political choices on a purely pragmatic, non-ideological, non-class basis: 'Economic Man' in the polling booth – the great pluralist dream. It confirms the wished-for breakup of the class structure of British political culture. And it is said to 'prove' that the true heart of the political system and of the 'British voter' lies in the centre. Rationality and moderation have fallen into each other's arms.

This is more self-fulfilling prophecy than hard political analysis. The interpretation of a natural gravitation of British politics to 'the centre', eschewing all extremes, would make more sense if the parties had represented over the decades the spectacle of alternating extremes. But, until recently, judged in terms of real strategies rather than ideological polemics and stage-managed caricatures, both parties have long struggled precisely to occupy this mythical 'middle ground', provided by a capital-led mixed economy, incomes policy, neo-Keynesianism and corporatism. The social-democratic consensus has been the base-line from which both sides have attempted to govern, and to which, in the end, even adventurists like Mr Heath (in his 'Selsdon Man' period) were ultimately driven back. It is the failure, precisely, of the centre, old-style, and the steady erosion of its repertoire of crisis-management, which has provoked successive movements in recent years towards more extreme alternatives. It is the collapse and bankruptcy of 'the centre' which generated increasing pressure towards these extremes. And if the revival of the left within the Labour Party is one way of inheriting this collapse, it has been much more evident on and towards the right. First, the populist undercurrents of 'Powellism'; then Mr Heath's boom-or-bust excursion, before the miners and the U-turn; then the formation of the Keith Joseph 'Adam Smith' kitchen cabinet; finally – as it became clear that the doctrines of Hayek and Friedman would need to connect with the reactionary instincts of the Tory backwoods – the formation, radical offensive and electoral success of the 'Thatcher party'. This progressive abandonment of 'the centre' has taken place for the best of all possible reasons: it failed. Things got worse, not better, under its increasingly

weak and nerveless leadership. This suggests that the increasing volatility of the electorate is best explained, not in terms of the natural and
inevitable gravitation of British politics to the 'middle ground', but
because of the manifest inability of the two variants of consensus politics
to stem the tide of British economic disintegration and progressive deindustrialization. 'Because the ruling class has failed in some major political undertaking for which it has requested, or forcibly extracted, the
consent of the broad masses ...'

What's more, the evidence from the movement of public opinion
suggests, not the permanence and stability of 'centrist' ideas, but a
steady gravitation towards the extreme right. An unpublished paper on
movements in public opinion by Tony Fitzgerald has shown that, among
voters strongly identifying with Labour, support for more nationalization, more spending on social services, retaining Labour's links with
the trade unions and sympathy with strikers all fell between the 1960s
and 1970s. Support among the same sections for the sale of council
houses, keeping the grammar schools, cutting government spending,
cutting profits tax, and strengthening law and order and immigration
controls have all swung significantly in Mrs Thatcher's direction. Manual
workers who are also Labour supporters and trade unionists showed
markedly higher shifts of opinion – again in this direction – than other
groups and long before the very significant swing to the right in 1979
which brought the most radical right government of the postwar period
to office. This is particularly strong in the area of the Thatcherite populist issues – anti-unions, anti-statism, anti-welfare. When these are
placed alongside the cluster of issues which Crewe and others have
called 'populist authoritarian' – the so-called 'moral' issues of race, law
and order, private initiative and self-reliance, where even Labour
supporters, strongly pro-Labour on other issues, suddenly become
explicitly 'Thatcherite' – the evidence of a natural gravitation to centrist
politics is thin. The underlying movement is undoubtedly rightwards.
Lack of faith in the two major parties may, therefore, draw people in
desperation towards a middle-ground alternative. But not because this is
where the natural fulcrum of the British voter permanently and
inevitably comes to rest. Social Democracy must occupy 'the centre'
because it is *there*. Besides, that is where *they are*. But their strongest
card will not be the promise to 'restore the centre', but the vaguer threat
to 'break the political mould'. In so doing, they inherit, not the mantle of
Attlee, but the legacy of Mrs Thatcher – for, though they may deflect it
in a different direction, that is what she promised too. Whether it is
possible to 'break the mould' and 'return to the centre' at the same time
is the particular card trick or sleight-of-hand on which the fortunes of Dr
Owen, Mr Rodgers, Mrs Williams and Mr Jenkins (a 'breaker of
moulds'?) now depend.

What, then, is its real political character and content? The break with 'Labour Socialism', however muted in some instances, is real and deep. It is a final break with the historic Labour–trade union connection. This is mounted as firmly on the back of the 'trade-unions-are-too-powerful' crusade as anything in Mrs Thatcher's vocabulary, though it is less virulently put. It is also a break with even a residual connection to working-class politics – even the rudimentary form in which this is still acknowledged by the traditional Labour right – 'Labour as the party of the working class in government'. At this level, Social Democracy is thoroughly managerialist in its political style. It will have no organized political base – only the 'detached voter' combined with a power-base in parliamentary rule. It is 'for' democracy – in so far as this highlights the undemocratic nature of British trade unionism; and especially in so far as it means (or meant) 'one-man-one-vote' for the Labour leadership, and the total independence of the parliamentary party from democratic accountability. This is nothing positively new, since for both the press and for Mrs Thatcher, 'democracy' only works when it allows the 'silent majority' to out-vote the left. In earlier days, the Social Democrats were the group within the Gaitskell orbit most prepared to put its democratic conscience into permanent cold storage, so long as the trade union block vote delivered the result to the right. It is deeply and passionately hostile to every manifestation of the left. The media have signally failed to bring out that the single, most important factor which precipitated the final break was the very thought that non-Labour trade unionists might somehow be able to exert an indirect influence over the leadership election – and I don't think it was the Federation of Conservative Trade Unionists they had most in mind!

On the economic front, it is the party of 'incomes policy' in the classic sense: i.e., as an instrument with which to discipline the demands of labour and restore them to their rightful position – led by the overriding imperatives of capitalist profitability and competitiveness. Neo-Keynesian in their sympathy for reflation, the Social Democrats are nevertheless as committed as Mrs Thatcher and Sir Keith are to the leadership of big industrial capital and the play of market forces. That is what they mean by a 'mixed economy'. They emerge as the only, true EEC 'party' – not even in the robust sense of Mr Heath, blowing the cold wind of European competition through the cobwebbed boardrooms of British industry: more as an article of faith. The unity through competition of free-market capitalisms is what they mean by 'internationalism'. 'A socialist who works constructively within the framework of a mixed economy, is the image to which Dr Owen recently aspired. His reference points – Sweden, Austria, West Germany and Holland. His memorable dates – the assimilation of the German SPD to reformism at the Bad

Godesberg meeting in 1959, and the overturning of the 1960 Labour Conference decision for unilateralism. Which 'moulds' are likely to be broken by these ancient instruments is something of a mystery.

Despite its cavilling at the cost of Trident, Social Democracy is fervent in its support for NATO and the Western shield. Indeed, in being less committed to the British independent deterrent, it is likely to be more suppliant to Washington's grand Alliance strategy than even its Labour predecessors. The Social Democrats, in the week of the Thatcher–Reagan resumption of the role of world policemen, and amidst the talk of NATO Retaliatory Forces and offensive Cold War postures, did not allow themselves to blink an eye at what precisely this loyal subordination to NATO strategy promises to become under the Reagan–Haig–Thatcher hegemony. Instead, they chose to open their parliamentary career by taking Labour to the cleaners about its wobbling indecisiveness over unilateralism.

This may look, when pieced together, like a very ancient and familiar concoction. The novelty appears to lie in the terminology with which their politics of the centre is verbally glossed. Despite their commitment to 'the new', the Social Democrats have failed to identify a single new political constituency around a single new issue. Feminism is a good case in point, where a strong, vigorous and radical movement has developed, to which the traditional political cultures of both the established left and the right are deeply inhospitable. If *any* organized force were in a position to disconnect the feminist movement and women from the left, and to articulate a limited version of feminist demands to a 'new' kind of political programme, Social Democracy ought to be. One or two public figures have indeed given this as their principal reason for evacuating the left for centre ground with embarrassing speed. But it must be said that this is more in the eye of the beholders than it is anywhere evident in the political complexion of the new centre. Apart from offering the person of Mrs Williams to fortune, Social Democracy has not made a single gesture towards attracting this new social force. It gives every appearance of not knowing it exists and of not knowing how or where to identify and address it, if it did. Indeed, despite the promise of nationwide campaigns and local groups, Social Democracy is at present totally devoid of any single vestige of popular politics or popular mobilization. It is exclusively and doctrinally attached to the prospects of 'politics from above'.

The only single gesture in this direction is in the fulsome talk about 'participatory democracy'. This is Social Democracy's way of attempting to colonize the growth of anti-corporatism and anti-statism which have become the principal forms of popular alienation from Labour. Here, like Thatcherism before it, Social Democracy is indeed working on a real contradiction. Labour-in-power became, not the means for generating a decisive shift of wealth and power towards the popular classes, but a mode of representing the popular classes in government – which, in conditions of recession, rapidly became a means of disciplining popular demands. The corporatist triangle is now, and rightly, seen as a directive style of political management – directed against the people, while at the same time incorporating them through their representatives. This has consolidated the Big State *over* the people – an identity which Mrs Thatcher was quick to exploit. This is a contradiction within the very heart of Labourism, with its deep parliamentary constitutionalism, its conception of the state as a neutral instrument of reform, its inexplicable belief that Labour governments can *both* 'represent working-class interests' *and* manage capitalism without something giving, and, above all, its fear and suspicion of popular democratic politics in any form. Mrs Thatcher exploited this identity between Labour and the state to considerable advantage. By 1979, Labour seemed much the same as Big Brother, much involved in pushing people around to no visible effect; while Mrs Thatcher was the populist champion of 'the people' *against* the power bloc: a pretty remarkable reversal.

Social Democracy is gunning for the same space. But whereas Thatcherism sought to master the antagonism between 'people' and 'power bloc', transforming it, at a critical point, into a populist movement for national unity around the new free-market programme – bearing Mrs Thatcher, at the same time, into the power bloc – Social Democracy hopes to exacerbate the contradiction and transform it through the programme of 'participatory democracy', and 'decentralization'. Dr Owen and Co. are doctrinaire 'decentralizers'. This new doctrine circles around the same themes: the 'bureaucratic centralizers, the corporatists who now dominate British socialism, the mood of authoritarianism ... the state ... seen as the main instrument of reform'.[2] It operates on the same dichotomies: liberty versus equality. Like Mrs Thatcher, and against the long socialist tradition, it privileges liberty over equality. In this sense, it belongs firmly within a much longer process – that of bending and articulating liberalism (and liberal political economy) to the conservative rather than the radical pole. Authoritarianism and the state as an instrument of reform, Dr Owen argues, has not been 'counterbalanced' by a 'libertarian streak'. But whereas Thatcherism, detaching 'liberty' and 'equality', connects it with *authority* ('free market' – liberty: strong state – authority); Social Democracy deflects it towards a third pole, in its struggle to win space from the left. Not authority but – fraternity: 'the sense of fellowship, cooperation, neighbourliness, community and citizenship'. The authentic centrist, cross-class, coalitionist codewords. Participation gives people a feeling of belonging. Decentralization gives them the illusion of real popular power. 'Small is beautiful' is a popular slogan in the era of state capitalism. There is no question but that, somewhere in this space, socialism has long since ceased to operate – to its profound cost. It has deeply lost its popular, anti-power bloc, democratic vision. There is space, after all, here – as the enemies of socialism in both the right and the centre know well.

But 'participation' without democracy, without democratic mobilization, is a fake solution. 'Decentralization' which creates no authentic, alternative sources of real power, which mobilizes no one, and which entails no breakup of the existing power centres and no real shift in the balance of power, is an illusion. It is a *transformist* solution. It conflates the unthinkable with the improbable – all the while giving the strong illusion of 'moving forwards'. Transformism is the authentic programme of the moderate left in a period of progressive political polarization along class lines. Its function is to dismantle the beginnings of popular democratic struggle, to neutralize a popular rupture, and to absorb these elements passively, into a compromise programme. Its true novelty is that it conflates the historic programmes of the classic, fundamental parties of the left and the right. It is the restoration of the old through the appearance of constructing something new: 'revolution' without a revolution. Passive revolution 'from above' (i.e. parliament). Gramsci noted two aspects of the programme of 'transformism' which are apposite to our case. The moment when 'individual political figures formed by the democratic opposition parties are incorporated individually into the conservative–moderate political class': and the moment when 'entire groups of leftists pass over into the moderate camp'. We are entering the second stage.

Since the breakup of the great Liberal formation in the early years of this century, the British political system has shown an increasing tendency, in periods of crisis, to turn to Caesarist solutions. 'Caesarism' is a type of *compromise* political solution, generated from above, in conditions where the fundamental forces in conflict so nearly balance one another that neither seems able to defeat the other, or to rule and establish a durable hegemony. Gramsci reminds us that 'Caesarist solutions' can exist without 'any great "heroic" and representative personality' – though in the earlier period there were indeed contenders for this role 'above party and class'. But, he adds, 'The parliamentary system has also provided a mechanism for such compromise solutions. The "Labour" governments of Macdonald were to a certain degree solutions of this kind ... Every coalition government is a first stage of Caesarism ...' The Social Democrats are our 'little Caesars'.

In a period when the discipline of unemployment is sending a shiver of realism through the labour movement, it may seem overoptimistic to argue that we now confront a situation of stalemate between the fundamental classes. Yet this does once more seem to be the case. Thatcherism lacks the economic space or the political clout to impose a terminal defeat on the labour movement. The working class and its allies are so deep in corporate defensive strength that they continue to provide the limit to Thatcherism despite their current state of disorganization. Irresistible force meets the immovable object. On the other hand, the labour movement lacks the organization, strategy, programme or political will to rule. So far it has failed to act as the magnet for new social forces, thereby itself embracing new fronts of struggle and aspiration. It still shows no major sign of reversing its own long decline. Such statements are readymade for the appearance of grand compromise.

Whether this is a solution which can more than temporarily stem the tide, remains to be seen. Sometimes 'Caesarism' is only a temporary staving off of deeper currents. Sometimes it can lead, through successive variations, to the formation of a new type of state. More often, it is 'an evolution of the same type along unbroken lines'. This is certainly not to say that it cannot temporarily succeed; or that, having succeeded in winning electoral support, it will not (as Thatcherism has done before it) have *real effects* in preventing that reshaping of the left and of socialism which alone can provide a real alternative – permitting, instead, Labour in a parallel way, only to recompose itself along familiar lines. A Labour government, succeeding to its third rotation in power, under such conditions, would certainly neutralize socialism for a very long time to come. That, after all, may be what Social Democracy is *really* about.

1981

Notes

1. 'A Policy for Pinks', *Economist*, 14 February 1981.
2. David Owen, 'Power to the People', *Sunday Times*, 25 January 1981.

4

The Empire Strikes Back

Empires come and go. But the imagery of the British Empire seems destined to go on forever. The imperial flag has been hauled down in a hundred different corners of the globe. But it is still flying in the collective unconscious.

As the country drifts deeper into recession, we seem to possess no other viable vocabulary in which to cast our sense of who the British people are and where they are going, except one drawn from the inventory of a lost imperial greatness. And now the country is going to war. Going to war for a scatter of islands eight thousand miles away, so integral a part of the British *Imperium*, so fixed in our hearts, that we have not managed to build a decent road across the place or to provide it with a continuous supply of power.

But this all-too-familiar story – the real history – from our imperial annals has been displaced by a more potent myth. *Civis Britannicus Sum.* We have set sail in defence of a high principle – and now, as if by magic, the powers we thought had departed from us have returned. In a dangerous, difficult and complex world, it is still possible to let a few of the old truths shine forth. 'Our boys' are 'out there' again; and despite 'the tragic loss of life'. Britain can show the 'Johnny-Argies' a thing or two, yet. No tin-pot, banana-republic, jumped-up dictator can tweak this lion's tail. Pull it – and the Empire still strikes back!

Rumour and speculation to the contrary, Mrs Thatcher did not invent the Falklands crisis. But she certainly now regrets that it was General Galtieri, not she, who thought of it first; for it is doing her government and its historic mission a power of good. What else is Mr Cecil Parkinson – Tory Party chairman, but with no high ministerial responsibilities and not, so far as is known, a notable naval strategist – doing in the War Cabinet, if he's not there for the purpose of exploiting the crisis to the political hilt in the best and continuing interests of the Conservative Party?

It has already delivered tangible rewards. Three million people and more are unemployed; the whole social infrastructure is being savaged by cuts; the economy continues to bump along the seabed. Our Hunter Killer subs seem able to surface, but the economy stubbornly refuses to do so. Yet, even before the Falklands crisis, these facts had failed to convert themselves into a popular revulsion against the government – due to the absence of a credible alternative. (Oh, economic determinism – three million unemployed equals a 100 per cent swing to Labour – where art thou now?)

The programme of the radical right is still very much in business, with no U-turn in sight. It is, clearly, still the dominant political force. And now, powered by an imperial adventure that would have seemed out of date in 1882, the government is riding high in the opinion polls, some fifteen or twenty points ahead of its nearest rivals – at the mid-term, when most other postwar governments have been clutching at straws.

It has come, unscathed, through the local elections. Were Mr Parkinson to stoop his unyielding back so low as to give the Prime Minister the opportunist advice to call a snap election tomorrow, the latest poll suggests that 52 per cent of manual workers, a lead of 9 per cent among trade unionists, as well as more men than women, would be prepared to vote Conservative: a historic reversal, were it to be realized.

The opposition has been effectively disorganized. Labour is split. The leadership and the parliamentary majority, hoisted aloft by the windy gases exhaled in frontbench speeches – sound and fury, signifying a total loss of grip on the political reality – is firmly attached to the tail of a patriotic war. As if Labour's cause has anything to gain from dabbling in patriotic jingoism except more Tory votes.

The left, opposed to the war in a principled stand, is nevertheless isolated, silenced by the usual media blackout. And – speaking of the media – SDP support is crumbling, as the South Atlantic steals the headlines: except, of course, for Dr Owen, man of the future, reliving each intense moment from past heroic engagements when he was at the Falklands helm, as if from the bridge or operations room of some imaginary aircraft carrier. Worst of all, is the spectacle of a Conservative government leading the nation towards the sunrise, into what is indisputably a popular war. The naval imperialism – 'mistress of the waves' – on which past British greatness was built paid a few off better than it did the majority. But it has been a popular cause before and – with so much else that is nasty, brutish and unpromising to think about – has become so again.

'Public opinion is fickle. Wait until the casualty lists start rolling in.' They will have to be British names, for Argentinian dead don't rank. For the moment, the most solid hope of halting the fighting is the sombre calculation of how the country would take the despatch of some ship of the size of the *HMS Invincible* to the icy depths of the South Atlantic, courtesy of a French, South African, Israeli or international arms trade Exocet missile. Empire has struck.

Its antiquated character remains one of the most striking features of the Falklands crisis. The early inaction of the left was no doubt attributable to sheer disbelief at this return of the repressed in the middle of the nuclear missile age. The task force is a great armada – though the last one was blown out of the water, breaking up in the outer Hebrides. The fleet can no longer fire a broadside or get an Exocet missile off its trail or keep the skies free of 'Argies'.

Yet the language of the Battle of Jutland and the Battle of Britain survives. Those great vessels, named after historic cities, with their expensive equipment and their precious human cargo, would be so many sitting ducks – of the bathroom variety – if only the 'Argies' had learned the lesson of the stockpile. Others will. That the common humanity and emotion of families waving their relatives off at the quayside should be recruited into this quest for past glories is an obscenity – a piece of political recidivism. But it would be wrong to assume that the charge of anachronism would make Mrs Thatcher stumble or hesitate for a moment.

After all, the return to the traditionalist reference points of the past has been one of the main lynch-pins of Thatcherism's ideological project. It is at the heart of its populism. 'Mrs Thatcher called yesterday for a return to traditional values' the *Guardian* reported in 1978. She has been advancing steadily towards the past ever since. 'Together,' she assured her audience about her visit to President Reagan in 1981, 'we have discovered old verities'. Again and again, the simple, tried and trusted virtues and ideals which stood our fathers and mothers in such good stead have been identified with the definition of what is 'great' about 'Great Britain'.

'I think it's astonishing how true many of the deep, fundamental values have remained, in spite of everything. Things may have changed on the surface, but there is still tremendous admiration for true values,' she assured the readers of *Woman's Realm* in 1980. The return of Britain to greatness has been identified with the fixed reference points of good old British commonsense. In search of the populist connection,

Mrs Thatcher and her allies in the press and elsewhere have unashamedly gone for the great simplifications.

The economy can be managed on the same principles as the family budget: you can't spend what you haven't got. Mrs T is simply our most-beloved Good Housekeeper. Children should be brought up as our parents brought us up. Mothers should stay at home. Tin-pot dictators must be stood up to. These are the grand truths which history and experience teach: what she called, to the Conservative Women's Conference on the eve of her election victory, the 'tried and trusted values of commonsense'. Better than 'trendy theories' – and all that thinking.

Her approach is instinctual. 'If you can't trust the deeper instincts of our people, we shouldn't be in politics at all.' And essentialist: these are the essential human qualities of the British people, inscribed in their destiny. The assumption of the radical right to power has been safely located within Tory traditions, by a highly selective form of historical reconstruction. 'I know you will understand the humility I feel at following in the footsteps of great men like our leader in that year, Winston Churchill, a man called by destiny to raise the name of Britain to supreme heights in the history of the free world.'

What event, what image, is more calculated to draw these different strands together and condense them into a compelling symbol in popular consciousness than one more great imperial adventure on the high seas – especially when gut patriotism is laced with gut moralism. 'Nothing so thrills the British people as going to war for a just cause.'

The Falklands crisis may have been unpredicted, but the way it has been constructed into a populist cause is not. It is the apogee of the whole arc of Thatcherite populism. By 'populism' I mean something more than the ability to secure electoral support for a political programme, a quality all politicians in formal democracies must possess. I mean the project, central to the politics of Thatcherism, to ground neo-liberal policies directly in an appeal to 'the people'; to root them in the essentialist categories of commonsense experience and practical moralism – and thus to construct, not simply awaken, classes, groups and interests into a particular definition of 'the people'.

At different stages of the populist project, different themes have been drawn into service in this attempt to capture commonsense for traditionalism and the right: race ('people of an alien culture'), nationality (the new Act, under which, incidentally, the Falklanders ceased to be citizens of any special kind), foreign policy (the Iron Lady episode) and law and order have helped to give 'what the nation is' and 'who the people are' its particular traditionalist inflection.

This is a high-risk strategy for the right. It entails mobilizing the people in a populist arousal, sufficient to cut across and displace other, more compelling definitions, interests and contradictions and to supplant alternative images and meanings. 'The people' must be mobilized if they are to join the party in the crusade to drive from the temples of the state all the creeping collectivists, trendy Keynesians, moral permissives and soft appeasers who have occupied it in the era of the social-democratic consensus. Yet in order to prevent a populist mobilization from developing into a genuinely popular campaign, the arousal of populist sentiment must be cut off at just the correct moment, and subsumed or transformed into the identification with authority, the values of traditionalism and the smack of firm leadership. It is an authoritarian populism.

It is also a delicate and contradictory ideological exercise. It has been required, for example, to square the circle consisting of the free market, competitive individualist tenets of neo-liberalism, as well as the organic metaphors of flag, patriotism and nation. This work of populist transformation and synthesis can be seen in the very person of the great populist herself: the steely manner; the lugubrious approach; the accent, revealing the expropriation of provincial Grantham into suburban Finchley; the scrupulously tailored image – just now, draped in black, as if half anticipating sorrowful news from abroad about 'our boys' doing so well 'out there' against 'them'; the smack of firm leadership; the oceanic reserves of class patronage and – from the heights of this assumption of authority – the popular touch.

It is the success with which all the chords of populist sentiment, feeling and memory have been struck at once, which testifies to the sureness of touch with which the Falklands crisis has been handled ideologically. The most powerful popular memory of all – the war, when we came to the rescue of oppressed people 'under the heel of the dictator'; 1940, when 'we stood alone' against enormous odds; and '1945' – Churchill's triumph, not the founding of the welfare state – has been totally colonized by the right.

We have been invited to relive our last great moments of national greatness through the Falklands war. In the process, the legitimacy, the popularity and the justice of the one is transferred to the other. In this way, and to the astonishment of the left, Thatcherism has literally stolen the slogans of national self-determination and anti-fascism out of mouths. The sovereignty of people, the right of self-determination, the wickedness of dictators, the evil of military juntas, the torch of liberty, the rule of international law and the anti-fascist crusade: in a hideous but convenient ventriloquism, they have been run up the flagpole of the right.

As the 'war cabinet' drapes itself in the ensign of the Royal Navy, and the *Mail* remembers its past, who cares that the long-standing, well-documented obscenities of the Argentine regime against its people did not disturb Mrs Thatcher's sleep until the day before yesterday? Who minds that Argentina has so speedily become the only offending fascist military junta in Latin America, and that neighbouring Chile, where the roll-call of 'the disappeared' is almost as long, is a friend of democracy?

Until a few weeks ago, the Argentinian generals were slipping in and out of quiet briefing rooms in Western military establishments and training schools around the globe. Until yesterday, Mrs Thatcher's only concern about the international arms trade was how Britain could – to coin a phrase – 'make a killing' in that lucrative market.

Tomorrow, once the junta has been taught a lesson, and the national spirit revived by a little blood-letting, things will no doubt slowly return to 'business as usual'; a much-relieved General Haig will send his advisers back to Buenos Aeyer-es, where they naturally belong. When flags unfurl, there is no time – fortunately – for awkward contradictions. The British can take heart. The navy, with a little effort, sails. Flags fly. Things are simple, after all.

We are up against the wall of a rampant and virulent gut patriotism. Once unleashed, it is an apparently unstoppable, populist mobilizer – in part, because it feeds off the disappointed hopes of the present and the deep and unrequited traces of the past, imperial splendour penetrated into the bone and marrow of the national culture. Its traces are to be found in many places and at many levels. An imperial metropolis cannot pretend its history has not occurred. Those traces, though buried and repressed, infect and stain many strands of thinking and action, often from well below the threshold of conscious awareness. The terrifying images of the past weigh, 'like a nightmare, on the brains of the living'.

The traces of ancient, stone-age ideas cannot be expunged. But neither is their influence and infection permanent and immutable. The culture of an old empire is an imperialist culture; but that is not all it is, and these are not necessarily the only ideas in which to invent a future for British people. Imperialism lives on – but it is not printed in an English gene. In the struggle for ideas, the battle for hearts and minds which the right has been conducting with such considerable effect, bad ideas can only be displaced by better, more appropriate ones.

Ancient thoughts will only cease to give us a compelling motive for action if more modern thoughts can grip the popular imagination, bite into the real experience of the people, and make a different kind of sense. To do this would require a recognition of the critical importance of the ideological terrain of struggle – and the construction of the instruments by which such struggles are conducted. Yet the Labour Party, the labour movement and the left have no national paper: all we can do is read the *Guardian* and pray! No powerful journal of opinion, no political education, no organic intellectual base from which to engage popular consciousness, no alternative reading of popular history to offer, no grip on the symbolism of popular democratic struggle.

The left thinks it is 'materialist' to believe that because ideas do not generate themselves out of thin air, they do not matter. The right of the labour movement, to be honest, has no ideas of any compelling quality, except the instinct for short-term political survival. It would not know an ideological struggle if it stumbled across one in the dark. The only 'struggle' it engages in with any trace of conviction is the one against the left.

More scandalous than the sight of Mrs Thatcher's best hopes going out with the navy has been the demeaning spectacle of the Labour frontbench leadership rowing its dinghy as rapidly as it can in hot pursuit. Only, of course – here, the voice of moderation – 'not so far! Slow down! Not so fast!'

1982

5

Cold Comfort Farm

In the immediate aftermath of the rioting in Tottenham, you could command any journalist's attention for hours if you could address such critical matters as – the exact location of the walkways on the Broadwater Farm Estate; or who it was who actually first spread the word that Mrs Jarrett was dead; or exactly what is the street price of the cocaine which the police were after when they put the 'squeeze' on the area some weeks ago. But for the wider social and political context there was no interest whatsoever.

It was several days after the dust settled, that *some* of these broader questions were posed. By then, however, the dominant definition of 'the riots' was firmly set in place. So far as the government is concerned, the matter was settled to its profit as soon as the problem was framed as a question of 'law and order'. As with the miners' strike: as soon as the 'law-and-order' perspective prevails, all wider questions pale into insignificance. Anyone who raises them is immediately tarred with the brush of being a 'soft do-gooder' or – worse – a secret fellow-traveller with violence. Everything is concentrated on the black-and-white (sic.) question of 'who broke the law?'

Behind that banner the legions of the righteous and the self-righteous gather. Under that rubric, the escalation takes place; the force can be legitimately wheeled out. Metropolitan commissioners and chief constables can frighten themselves and the public by giving their private fantasies an airing on television. The water cannon and the plastic bullet can quietly take their place in the repertoire of normal policing. Intelligent human beings, like Sir Kenneth Newman, can actually be heard on the radio and seen on television, persuading themselves that this is an adequate answer to the problem of social unrest in Britain's cities.

For a few, brief hours, the police may have been held to a standstill in Tottenham. But in the country at large, where these matters are ultimately settled one way or another, the government, the right and the cause of racism won hands down – another famous victory.

The media, wittingly or unwittingly, played a small but crucial role in securing that victory. For days following Brixton and Tottenham, I was contacted by media persons saying, 'Of course, there's unemployment and all that, but we've heard all that before. There must be some *other* reasons.' There is nothing to beat the relentless ignorance of the media in search of novelty. Even serious journalists seem prey to the illusion that, because a story on the underlying social and economic causes of tension in the inner cities has once or twice appeared in the pages of the paper they work for, therefore *something has been done about it.*

It then appears to be a platitude to say that, since in fact nothing whatsoever has happened about it – indeed, things have gotten worse, not better, since they last turned their reluctant journalistic eye in its direction – the likelihood of an explosion has moved nearer, rather than become more remote.

I repeat the summary judgement I offered above. The right, broadly speaking, *won* at Tottenham, whatever symbolic victories people think were achieved on the night. By that I mean, quite specifically: the government presided over by Mrs Thatcher and her 'team' of sound folk; the forces within the police (not *all* of the police, incidentally), unleashed by the whole policy and tenor of that government, powered by a simple, blind set of racist simplifications, who have been waiting, ever since the Scarman report, to 'have another go'; the quiet – and the not so quiet – respectable, Tory backbenchers who have taken every single opportunity in the last few years to steer their constituency parties into a more openly anti-black and repatriationist stand; the core of hard-faced street racists, who have been worming and boring their way into the cracks and rifts of a rapidly disintegrating social fabric; and the latent reservoir of 'little Englandism' which Thatcherism has been stirring and inciting up to, during and since the Falklands episode.

This complex 'bloc', or formation, *is* the social core of racism in the country. Far from being stifled underground until recent weeks, it has been enjoying a steady and unremitting rise in popularity and growth in scale throughout Mrs Thatcher's reign. It is, whether she and her colleagues are willing to recognize it or not, the unacceptable face of Thatcherism and as much part and parcel of the whole ethos and climate of its ascendancy in the country as boiled beef and carrots, or whatever it is they eat these days for Sunday dinner in upper Finchley. In the only important sense that matters – the political sense – Thatcherism produced the riots; as certainly as it produced the rioting skinheads on the football terraces a few months ago, itching to 'get at the Eyties' just as the fleet was 'itching to get at the Argies' – both swathed to the eyeballs in Union Jacks.

I put it in that stark and simple form because, even amongst black commentators, the tendency has been to point the finger at the police rather than at their political masters and mistresses. Don't misunderstand me. Racist policing there certainly is. In the inner cities, despite Scarman and neighbourhood policing, it has gradually become the norm. Any black man or woman, in such areas, seen – for whatever reason – in the company of the police, is instantly understood as 'being questioned', and as likely to be hassled at some point, not to mention casually abused, before being released.

It hardly matters whether he or she is, indeed, one of the many people stopped and questioned on the sole grounds that, since they are black; they must be suspect of *something*. They may simply have been asking the time of day – or, even more unthinkably, reporting a crime or vainly attempting to persuade the police to do something about it. No matter. Any such incident is immediately interpreted by the black community as 'trouble', because 'trouble' of that sort is now the norm – the regular, routine, everyday, everynight, experience of policing in black neighbourhoods.

The plain truth is that, in the black communities, policing is now 'out of order'. The fact that an example of casual neglect in one part of London triggered off a riot does not seem in any way to have made the police – even in a self-interested way – cautious about their behaviour in other parts of the city the following week. The police ethos in these areas has become impenetrable, impervious to outside influence. They appear to have forgotten any other means of entering a black person's home than breaking down the door.

Insulated against reality by the whole 'law-and-order' climate, their powers considerably enhanced, their every move justified by a subservient Home Office, the tempo and strategic goals of their policing set by the range-riding hawks among the chief constables, they have simply gone over the top – gung ho. Their every move is bathed in the soapy bubbles of the prime minister's sycophantic adulation. They have become, as many of us predicted ten years ago, Mrs Thatcher's 'boys' – the front line in the crisis of Britain's cities.

Any journalist still in search of a 'riot story' could be profitably employed piecing together the so-called pattern of what exactly it is, in the last weeks, which made another casual act of racist policing trigger the inflammable materials accumulating in our inner cities.

So there is no question of the centrality to the whole story of the terrifying and still unconcluded story of racist policing. Nevertheless, in my view, the blame for the disturbances which have ripped through the inner cities in the last few months cannot be solely and entirely placed at the door of the police.

The fact is that Britain has a long and distinguished history of urban and rural riot. And that history has an unmistakable pattern to it. It occurs amongst that section of a population excluded from the social, political, economic and cultural life of society. It results from a long and gruelling period of deepening poverty and neglect, so that people begin to feel as if they are permanently out of sight of the society at large: living behind God's back.

As the screws tighten, the fragile bonds which tenuously link such communities to the dominant society loosen. Those who have no stake in society, owe it nothing. They have nothing but their poverty, their exclusion, to lose. At that point, 'the riots' have already begun, though no one has yet thrown a single brick. But everything that creates riots and disturbance, the spontaneous explosion of rage, anger and frustration that flows over like lava when things start, is already in place. No one – not the best historian, social analyst or police commissioner – can predict exactly what precise event will trigger that explosion. But the fact that, one day or night, something – great or trivial – will set the process in motion is as inescapable as night follows day.

That is the position into which the dispossessed, accumulating in the crevices of chancellor Nigel Lawson's 'recovery', have been remorselessly driven over the past few years. They have always been poor and disadvantaged. But now, in Mrs Thatcher's Britain, it is 'right and proper' that they should be poor, because, otherwise, how are they to toughen their moral fibres, acquire self-sufficiency, stop leaning on the welfare state, get on their bikes and off Tebbit's unemployment list, 'put Britain back to work' or 'start up a small business'?

Thousands of such people up and down the country have not and will not see a job of any kind in the next five years. What, pray, is the stake they are supposed to have in the country which would make them regard its laws and mores as 'binding' on them, as 'unbreakable'? Many of them are young, and since hard work has long been the discipline of the labouring classes, it is not difficult to imagine why their commitment to 'working Britain' is so tenuous. When Britain does something for them, they *might* be persuaded to do something for Britain. Until then ...

And, down at the bottom of this pile, are the blacks. The dispossessed, the excluded, Mrs Thatcher's 'alien wedge'. Here is a recipe for Norman Tebbit showing how to get the alien wedge moving. Cut off the lifeline of government spending to the inner cities and destroy the fragile community groups and activities which provided these areas with the faint possibility of self-activity. Punish the local authorities who could be pressured into doing something and starve the networks of material support by ratecapping. Then, widen the powers of the police, virtually setting them up as an alternative source of moral and social authority in these areas, and start to penetrate into the community, into people's homes, in relentless pursuit of 'the criminals' ...

The fact of the matter is that it is no longer possible to fight racism as if it had its own, autonomous social dynamic, located between white people or the police on one side, and blacks on the other. The problem of racism arises from every single political development which has taken place in Britain since the new right emerged.

Blacks have themselves, at times, tried to isolate the issue of race from the wider questions of social politics in Britain – as if black people have nothing to do with rates and ratecapping and monetarism and the Falklands factor until they affect the black communities directly. This separation, if it ever existed, has long since departed. In *Policing the Crisis*, a book some of us wrote in the mid-1970s when Thatcherism was still only a tiny gleam in Sir Keith Joseph's eye, we argued that race was deeply and intimately intertwined with every single facet of the gathering social crisis of Britain; and that it was no longer possible for blacks to have a political strategy towards that part of the dynamic which affected them without having a politics for the society as a whole. That argument has immeasurably strengthened over the years. The disturbances of 1985 have placed it squarely at everyone's front door.

It remains extremely difficult to forecast the exact forms in which the black political response will be made. But it seems to me undeniable that the crisis of Tottenham is now also a crisis of and for black politics. Keeping faith with the people who, in the teeth of relentless oppression, spontaneously resist, is all right on the night. But it is not enough when the next day dawns, since all it means is that, sooner or later, the front-line troops, with their superior weapons and sophisticated responses, will corner some of our young people on a dark night along one of these walkways and take their revenge for Tottenham.

There has never, in my view, been so urgent a need for the most radical and searching black political response as there is now, as the kick-back on the Broadwater Farm Estate begins and the 'law-and-order' juggernaut rolls back into place.

1985

6

No Light at the
End of the Tunnel

The election wheels have begun to turn. The government has once again taken the high ground in the public opinion polls. The Chancellor's giveaway bonanza has taken place. The press has greeted this as the long-awaited U-turn, but those with their political heads screwed on know that it is only a Z-turn: an increase in public spending now, then the election, then back to the old-style monetarism. On this tacit understanding, the hardliners have swallowed hard. It is good for 'presentation', good for pulling the rug from under the feet of Labour and the government's critics.

It is time to make an assessment. Where is Thatcherism now? How does it stand as a political force? How much have its recent troubles placed the whole political project in jeopardy?

Thatcherism is certainly in difficulties. It is a much less stable political formation than at any time since the period immediately before the Falklands war, when its popularity was at a very low ebb. Some of the reasons for this are immediate, others stem from deeper trends and tendencies. It is clear, now, that Thatcherism has not succeeded in stemming or reversing Britain's long-term economic decline. The manufacturing base remains in a collapsed state. The attempts at restructuring, while creating wholesale regional dislocation and generating a few 'sunrise' industries (mostly funded by imported capital), are extremely fitful. The cabinet continues to put a bold face on it – recovery is, as ever, just around the corner. Most people know they are whistling in the wind. The turnaround is not happening.

Politically, the impact of this is not so easy to assess. Thatcherism always told us that the road to recovery would be long and stony. It made no easy promises. Rather, appealing to well-founded British masochism (every summer of affluence, pleasure and permissiveness must be paid for by twenty winters of discontent), it promised, in the short term, only economic 'blood, sweat, toil and tears'. However, the message that even the long haul is not paying off has begun to penetrate popular consciousness and taken the edge off Thatcherism's drive. Of course, part of the message – that this is due not to Thatcherite policies but to long-term, structural weaknesses in the British economy and world trends – has also taken root. And since there is a small, rational core to this proposition, it does not translate itself directly into a swing to Labour.

Secondly, in spite of the extensive manipulation of the figures (one of the government's undeniable successes) there is very little sign of a turn-around on unemployment. School-leavers can be shunted sideways by Lord Young into schemes with little prospect of full-time employment at their end; their entry to the dole can be delayed; a proportion of the marginal and long-term unemployed can be squeezed off the register. But the underlying trends stubbornly remain unacceptably high. This is a real setback, politically.

In the early days, Thatcherism succeeded in putting the fight against inflation higher than unemployment in the national agenda. Inflation has come down. And it remains in the background, as a sort of warning light. People are aware that certain kinds of reflation lead to inflation rates which erode their standards of living. However, in popular consciousness, unemployment is now a make-or-break issue. It symbolizes the human and social havoc which has become monetarism's trademark.

Thirdly, in the areas of public spending and the cuts, we have witnessed perhaps the most dramatic turnabout of all. A majority still favours public spending even at the expense of lower taxes. Some recent figures published in *British Social Attitudes* suggest that this is a long-term not an immediate trend. It has been in progress since at least 1984 and affects Conservative supporters almost as much as Labour and Alliance voters. 'Only 8 per cent of Conservative supporters opted for lower taxation if it meant less being spent on health, education and social security benefits. Overall, only 6 per cent favoured such cuts.'[1]

This is a major reversal – and the Chancellor's Z-turn on public spending clearly acknowledges it. It is important, however, to note the sectors where this turn has occurred – health, education, and social security. The NHS has been, from the very beginning of Thatcherism's assault on the welfare state, Mrs Thatcher's 'Maginot line' – the point where the cutting had to stop. Remember how early it was that Mrs Thatcher had to assure the country that, contrary to all appearances, the NHS was 'safe in my hands' (sick)?

Of course, the cuts and privatization of services, where possible, continue apace. The new, private London Hospital shines forth like a glowworm on the south bank of the Thames. Round the corner, operating theatres at Guy's Hospital are being closed. The deception that, because investment in the health service increases, it is keeping pace with either costs or needs, continues to be advanced. Nevertheless, the principle of universal health provision – one of the cornerstones of the welfare state whose basic structure Thatcherism set out to dismantle – remains intact.

Education now turns out to be another area of major miscalculation. Sir Keith Joseph seemed determined that he would pass into a well-deserved oblivion, fighting to the last drop of ideological blood to reverse postwar trends in education. His aim was to decimate higher education, harass the schools, reverse the 'permissive' revolution in the classroom and exploit the anxieties and worries of parents as a weapon to break the teaching unions and face down the teachers, as Mrs Thatcher had faced down the miners. What he forgot is that the majority of parents who were expected to provide the cutting-edge of this populist strategy have nowhere else to send their children except into the hard-pressed, crumbling, under-resourced schools in the public sector. In the end, their alliance with the teachers – a fragile one, which the teachers did not effectively consolidate on a long-term basis and which they would be ill-advised to regard as automatic – nevertheless held for just long enough to float Mr Baker, one of the new 'third force' Thatcherites (monetarism with a human face), to power.

In spite of all that, the situation with respect to local authority spending is not quite so clear-cut. The erosion of the social fabric of the urban environment is now so widely acknowledged that local authorities are to get an additional £3.8 thousand million this year. Nevertheless, it would be wrong to assume that the drive against local authorities and local democracy (and, incidentally, Labour's strongholds in the large urban constituencies) is over. Mr Ridley, a flint-faced Thatcherite of the first phase if ever there was one, continues to exploit the rich vein of town hall unpopularity.

The rates campaign – 'spending *your* money' – continues, ideologically, to mobilize the 'ratepayer' in us all. The attempt to bring to a halt the rising needs and expectations of the inner urban constituencies (the welfare-dependent poor, especially women, blacks, the unemployed and the marginally employed, single-parent families, and the low-paid unskilled) and redistribute power and wealth to the suburbs and the shires is part of a long-term reversal of the dispositions of welfare social democracy to which Thatcherism remains committed.

To complete this assessment, on the negative side, so to speak, of Thatcherism's current troubles, we must add the more immediate succession of errors, mistakes and other little local difficulties in which the prime minister has been ensnared in recent months (backing off on the sale of British Leyland, the Libya bombing, Westland, the loss of two ministers, etc.). These have shaken public confidence in her 'mastery' of the political scene and weakened her political credibility.

In considering Thatcherism's troubles so far, we have been looking at important areas of policy where either it has failed to deliver or has been obliged to change emphasis or even shift direction. But now we have to dig a little deeper. Thatcherism was never, after all, only a set of policies. It was always a whole political project, and a radically novel political formation. How do we assess Thatcherism at this level, now?

In terms of this broader question, the most significant feature to my mind is the growing unpopularity of the whole authoritarian form of politics. This constitutes an important turning-point because, in the early days, strong leadership and conviction politics operated in Thatcherism's favour. Here was an end to the shilly-shallying of the old consensus politics: a regime with a bold political purpose, driven by a clear and alternative set of ideological goals towards a clearly perceived – and radically different – end. This spoke to something deep in the political psyche – a sense that only a radical rupture with the past and an authoritation leadership in a new direction was equal to the profound sense of unstoppable national decline.

'Authoritarianism' no longer holds this position in the popular imaginary. The image of 'conviction' has been replaced by that of 'intransigence'. The government is seen as increasingly isolated, insensitive to the changing winds of public opinion, cavalier in relation to the trail of dislocation which follows in its wake and determined to 'press on regardless', so long as the parliamentary majorities hold up. An 'elective dictatorship' with a vengeance.

It is difficult to date precisely when this 'turn' occurred. Some pinpoint the brutal assault on the unions at GCHQ (which, after all, is staffed by thoroughly loyal, endlessly vetted, 'sound' intelligence officers). Some cite the abolition of the GLC and the other large metropolitan authorities. Within its own lights, Thatcherism was perfectly correct to perceive that it was necessary to blow away the GLC as soon as it was convenient to do so. It always understood – as Mr Kinnock and the Labour leadership never have – the innovative character of the 'new politics' of municipal socialism and its positive 'demonstration effect' on the morale of the left.

Nevertheless, abolition was a deeply unpopular move – unpopular with the majority of Londoners, with young people and the new social movements whom the new cultural politics had begun to address, with old-style Tories and their commitment to the balance between central and local government as a keystone of the unwritten constitution. It was even, for once, unpopular with the Alliance, which left the government, on this issue at least, totally isolated. In short, the abolition of the GLC looked what, indeed, it was: a naked exercise in political assassination.

We have been talking about the growing unpopularity of a political style. But this is no mere matter of style. Or rather, style is a more important issue than the left believes. Thatcherism's 'authoritarian style' does not simply refer to the bossy, governess style of the prime minister, or the self-righteous way in which she lectures everyone in sight with her Finchley-spun homilies. It relates to the whole form of politics which has come to be part and parcel of Thatcherism's political project: the politics which we have learned to describe as 'authoritarian populism'.

Authoritarian populism is a way of characterizing the new form of hegemonic politics which emerged on the British scene with the formation of the 'new right' in the mid-1970s. It described a shift in the balance of social and political forces and in the forms of political authority and social regulation institutionalized in society through the state. It involved an attempt to shift the centre of gravity in society and the state closer to the 'authoritarian' pole of regulation. It attempted to impose a new regime of social discipline and leadership 'from above' in a society increasingly experienced as rudderless and out of control. However, the 'populist' part of the strategy required that this move to new forms of social authority and regulation 'above' should be rooted in popular fears and anxieties 'below'. Central to this movement – of which the drift into a law-and-order type of society was one clear index – was that the shift to greater social discipline should be made while retaining intact the formal paraphernalia of the liberal-democratic state.

The growing unpopularity of the more superficial forms of an authoritarian style of government, then, probably has at least two deeper meanings. The first is to remind us how deeply rooted democracy, in a broad sense, still is in British political culture and the limit this sets to any political force which attempts to push the long, historic, democratic gains of the British people back too far. The second is the evidence it offers of the problems which are beginning to beset 'authoritarian populism' itself. This is of the utmost importance, if it is true, and merits further exploration.

The engine of this 'authoritarianism' has been, in narrow terms, the cabinet (or the Thatcherite caucus within the leadership). But in broader terms, it is really a question of the state and the role which it now plays in Thatcherism's projects. The left sometimes finds the role of the state in the current period of Thatcherism hard to understand since it continues to represent itself, ideologically, as unremittingly 'anti-statist'. In part, this is because the left continues to believe that ideology is unified, uncontradictory and coherent – its coherence guaranteed by the unified class interests it is supposed to reflect. We also imagine that the subjects of ideology – 'the people' – are similarly unified. Either Thatcherite forever, and to the core: or already paid-up members of the collective revolutionary subject.

In fact, Thatcherism has effectively exploited the necessarily contradictory structure of popular ideology, playing the discourse of liberal economy and the free market off against the discourse of the organic nation and the disciplined society. In the 'logic' of Thatcherism, the free market and the open economy was always the route to the strongly integrated, thoroughly 'British' society. This is not as much of a paradox as it appears at first sight. Ideologically, Thatcherism has always set the national-moral question *above* the economic one (not below it, as the left, who do not consider moral-ideological questions to be serious, imagines). 'Serious as the economic challenge is, the political and moral challenge is just as grave, and perhaps more so, because economic problems never start with economics,' Mrs Thatcher reminded us at the Conservative conference in 1975. 'They have much deeper roots in human nature, and roots in politics, and they do not finish at economics ... These are the two great challenges of our time – the moral and political challenge, and the economic challenge. They have to be faced together and we have to master them both.' The moral language and agenda of Thatcherism was never simply an ideological convenience. It was always the 'leading edge' of its populism.[2]

Of course, Thatcherism has always had, ideologically, to negotiate the contradiction between the freewheeling 'enterprise culture' and a 'return to Victorian values'. There is a historical precedent for this apparently unstable combination. In the Victorian society to which she appears to be so attached, there was a similar split between the two spheres: between the vigorous cut-and-thrust of entrepreneurial capitalism, which, of course, was reserved for bourgeois men; and its separate, but complementary, sphere – domesticity and patriarchal respectability, the private sphere or 'little kingdom' of family, hearth and home, to which the men retired from their hard graft, wheeling and dealing in the public world and over which, of course, the Victorian wife, mother and 'helpmeet' reigned supreme.[3] To some extent, the whole ideological thrust of Thatcherism has continued to play on and reproduce this gender-inscribed complementarity. The language of the market as opportunity, computer technology as power, of financial 'big bangs' and competitive frontiers to conquer, is a discourse clearly addressed to Thatcherite men (or the Thatcherite 'man' in all of us). The language of moral discipline, law and order, sexual conventionalism, family values, and 'one (white) nation' is clearly a language for the female guardians of the national hearth (the little Thatcherite 'woman' in us all).

These, then, are Thatcherism's 'two faces'. Thatcherism continues to play off both ends of this repertoire. Rational logic may not find it easy to explain how these two, apparently contradictory discourses can coexist within the same position. Ideology, however, works according to 'logics' of its own – ones which are capable of sustaining apparently mutually exclusive propositions, in a discursive structure closer to the logic of the dream-work than that of analytic rationalism.

The same is true of Thatcherism's contradictory attitude to the state. The project was to 'win' the state, in order to restructure it – in order to 'roll it back'! It continues to be both inside *and* against the state although occasionally, of course, the negotiation cannot be managed, and credibility sags. That is the true meaning of the 'Westland affair' – where the party of 'Great Britain' was caught, redhanded, inviting the Americans to avail themselves of the open economy and help themselves to yet another bit of British industry.

Nevertheless, despite its merciless use of the state as the agent of social regulation, Thatcherism's 'anti-statism' is no mere ideological fig-leaf. In relation to the economy, particularly the state sector and a welfare state swollen by so-called 'unrealistic' popular aspirations, 'anti-statism' signified something real and profound – the project to reverse the postwar, Keynesian, welfare-corporatist consensus: the undiminished thrust towards privatization and deregulation are there to prove it. But on *social* questions, Thatcherism in power has been the most 'interventionist' government of the whole postwar period. This is not a paradox. It is possible to *use* the state, strategically, to *divest* the state. At the beginning of the last century, Bentham and his disciples pioneered just such a reforming, state-inspired type of 'laissez faire'. In some ways, the Thatcherites are the 'new utilitarians'. States do not dismantle themselves. In any case, advanced industrial capitalist societies like ours cannot reproduce themselves socially and culturally without a strategic role being played by the state. The idea that 'neo-liberalism' meant the abolition, rather than the *recomposition*, of the state was always inaccurate.

The growing unpopularity of the authoritarian style of Thatcherite politics finds its reverse side in the open manipulation of public opinion. Where a populist consensus cannot be won, it must be seduced into place. The massaging of the unemployment figures by Lord Young's department is remorseless. When ministers deceive the House of

Commons, it is their civil servants who are hauled before the courts. The unquotable Bernard Ingham is the master of misrepresentation – government reduced to an exercise in public misinformation. Mr Tebbit is in charge of intimidating the media into line. Whatever is the truth of the Westland affair, nobody believes Mrs Thatcher has been speaking it. Civil servants are reluctant to talk to select committees because they do not always relish being forced to take the flak for their political masters, and they may just blow the gaff. Not to put too fine a point on it, lying and double-dealing have become part and parcel of the politics of Thatcherism, just as they have long been the hallmark of Reaganism.

Does all this mean, then, that Thatcherism has finally been blown off course? Before we jump to this conclusion, we must consider what is still ongoing, still 'in place' in the Thatcherite project, despite its many little local difficulties. What, indeed, are Thatcherism's long-term prospects? Here, it will not do to remain solely on the ground of the immediate, electoral, tactical and conjunctural questions. We must try to understand how these conjunctural twists and turns relate to, in fact are rooted in, deeper trends and tendencies in the society.

Against Thatcherism's failure to turn round the economy, we have to set its success in reconstructing Britain as an 'open economy'. The move to flexible exchange rates, the free flows of capital, the leading place Britain now occupies in the internationalization of capital, tell an important story. Many of us still imagine that Thatcherism is aiming to restore Britain as a first-rank manufacturing capitalist power. We are waiting for the chimneys to sprout, the factory gates to open once more in the declining regions. The only problem is its inability to deliver.

The 'open economy' reminds us that Thatcherism is pursuing an alternative image of 'prosperity': Britain as an open playground or permanent 'green site' for international capital. This multinationalization and internationalization of capital, to which Thatcherism has hitched its star, for good or ill, is the most significant process going on globally just now. It is based on the opening up of the new financial markets and harnessed to the new information technologies. It is this which is lending the world capitalist system so much of its dynamic thrust, despite all its problems (like high, competitive interest rates and growing indebtedness).

This has some consequences, socially and politically. In order to clear the decks for this development, far from advancing the interests of the capitalist class as a whole, Thatcherism is driven to displace some of the older echelons in order to bring itself into line with the new social forces aligning themselves with these new developments. The political 'unity' of capital is neither given nor guaranteed. It has, continually and with difficulty, to be politically produced. That is the basis of Thatcherism's 'relative autonomy' of class interests, narrowly conceived.

Hence the phenomenon of Thatcherism often moving hard against certain old, vested social interests, which it is obliged to dismantle if it is to harness to itself some of the new social forces. The big battalions of the CBI are reluctant allies. They are still attached to the project because of its political thrust in restoring the 'right to manage' and the primacy of profitability and efficiency. But they continue to hope for a little controlled reflation. They prosper in an 'enterprise culture'. But they have noticeably not availed themselves of the opportunity to rush into court provided by the anti-trade union legislation. The same is true of the 'older professions' – the solicitors, the estate agents, the old stock-brokers of the City, even the BMA; all are ruffled by a riot of deregulation.

These things open a path for what Thatcherism regards as the new, vital forces of capitalism: the small businessmen, the do-it-yourself conveyancers, the department stores willing to undersell the NHS to provide optical wares, on the one hand; on the other hand, the new, young managers and city-men, the paid-up subscribers of the yuppie international. Who cares if the 'Big Bang' dislodges the grey-suited brigade of the City, if it licenses the new answerphone young men of Merrill Lynch?

Alongside that, and closely linked with it, we must acknowledge the relative effectiveness and continuing energy of the thrust towards privatization and deregulation. The continuing élan of this part of the project cannot be attributed to any one cause. It generates shortfall money which can be turned back in the form of tax cuts just before the next election. It returns crucial sectors of the economy to the private sector, divesting the state.

It appears to widen share-ownership, securing the commitment to what Thatcherism now calls 'popular capitalism'. ('It is estimated that the sell-off of British Gas will bring the number of individual share-holders in privatized companies to at least 6–10 million or an average of 10,000 to 15,000 voters in every constituency in the country with a financial stake in a Tory victory', as Adam Raphael recently calculated in the *Observer.*) Privatization continues to valorize the free market as the only source of energy, drive, goodies. It outpaces and makes obsolescent outmoded notions of the 'public good' and 'social need'.

Another important area concerns Thatcherism's attempt to root its political strategy in the growing fragmentation and the individualization which increasingly characterizes British society under the double impact of recession and restructuring. One tiny clue to this may be found in Thatcherism's use of differential incentives and selectivity to segment the older political constituencies and to disorganize the opposition. This relates to Thatcherism's growing fluency in building directly on the crucial dividing line which now separates those in from those out of work, the 'loadsamoney' minority from the growing ranks of the poor.

One can find evidence of this at both the tactical and strategic level. Incentives for head and senior teachers have succeeded in 'buying off' the upper echelons from the mass of teachers. 'Selectivity in welfare' arguments are making deep inroads into the principle of universalism. Selective tax cuts cream off, in rotation, one minority after another. This may not look like a successful exercise in hegemony, but it is evidence of something else which may be almost as important: Thatcherism's capacity to constantly compose and recompose – to permanently rotate – the required social 'minorities'.

However, this is certainly not simply a matter of tactics. The strategy is rooted in deeper social and material realities. Fragmentation and segmentation are now deep features of the British society. The breaking down of traditional skills, the introduction of more part-time and flexible working, the decentralization in the sphere of employment, the new 'home working', the penetration of new technologies, all drive individualization ahead, break down social milieus and fragment the communities of skill and work typical of the older forms of industrialization and the social identities and political solidarities typical of that phase.

This is what Peter Glotz has recently called 'the dark side of individualization'. An immense process of liberation has fragmented social milieus, put class solidarity in question, and forced politicians to toil at merging discrete groups into temporary "majorities".'[4]

This begins to explain a paradox, which otherwise is unintelligible and the left finds hard to understand. The fact that, despite the depth of the recession and unemployment, a significant number of people have been doing very well out of the recession. 'Despite the abysmal performance of manufacturing industry in the UK,' Grahl and Rowthorn argued in the November 1986 issue of *Marxism Today,* 'real wages for those fortunate enough to keep their jobs have risen faster in the UK since 1979 than in *any other major Western country*' (my italics). This is 'prosperity for some, purchased at the price of poverty for others'.

We are only just now beginning to glimpse the outlines of what 'Thatcherite Britain' might be like as a stable formation. Therborn has described it as 'Brazilianization': mass unemployment as a permanent feature; at the bottom, the permanently unemployed and the marginals, dependent on falling welfare entitlements; in the middle, the regularly employed, increasingly divided by enterprise, sector and hierarchy; at the top, the increasing wealth and incomes of capitalists and top managers.[5]

Glotz spoke of the 'two-thirds society'. The social decline of the weakest third becomes a permanent feature – 'the unemployed, the odd-jobbers, the elderly of the lower classes, the migrant workers, the physically and mentally handicapped, the teenagers who cannot find their way into the job-market.' The rest are divided from the marginals by full-time work, the competitive society and economy with its privatized rewards.[6] Ralph Dahrendorf has recently argued (in the Haldane Lectures) that, in such societies, the question of social discipline or the politics of law and order (which, in British society, is also a politics of race) becomes the characteristic form of political conflict.

Finally, we come to the crucial terrain of the ideological offensive. Here we have to address the recharged nature of what we might call Thatcherism's 'moral agenda'. The baton in relation to the moral agenda has passed from the front bench to the moral entrepreneurs and range-riders of the far right. Mr Bruinvels and his cohort, inside the House, coupled to Mrs Gillick and her cohort outside represent a powerful, new, grassroots 'moral majority' pressing the all too willing but rather more circumspect sympathizers inside Mrs Thatcher's inner circle.

These discourses about crime, law and order, abortion and sexuality, the position of women, sex education, homosexuality and social and moral respectability have always been key bastions of Thatcherite ideology. They have been 'manned' (sic.) with renewed energy and vigour in recent months. We have had Mr Tebbit's sweeping attack on the 'permissive society' and – taking their cue from that – the massive 'moral panics' about homosexuality (fuelled by the AIDS scare) and drugs; then the mobilization around school libraries and sex education; and, always, as a continuous subterranean theme, the restoration of the family, the bulwark of respectable society and conventional sexualities with its fulcrum in the traditional roles for women.

Parallel with this, in another part of the moral agenda, we have had the crude revival of cultural racism, which is now so powerfully organized around beleaguered conceptions of 'Englishness', evidenced in the thinly disguised scenes of barbarism over Asian visitors and visas. Thatcherism's 'tight little island' – culturally, sexually – is back in business with a vengeance.

This, too, may seem surprising, for it is highly contradictory terrain. There is no clear evidence that ordinary Conservative folk – let alone the Conservative Party chairman – are actually giving up the so-called permissive society. It seems, from the scanty evidence we have, that this is even less the case with the younger generation. How, then, can we explain the discrepancy between what Thatcherite children are actually doing with and to one another, and what Thatcherite parents are represented as wanting or not wanting their children to be taught in schools?

This is a continuing contradiction inside the Thatcherite sexual psyche.

However, Thatcherism does not need to organize the heart or the body if it can organize the ideological terrain. The moral discourses of Thatcherism remain important, whatever the discrepancy between them and actual social behaviour, because into them a whole range of other languages have been condensed. They are the site for the mobilization of social identities and, by appropriating them, Thatcherism has put down deep roots in the traditional, conventional social culture of English society.

Its capacity to do so, and thus to capture and bend to its political project some of the profound cultural formations of English society, represents the truly hegemonic character of its historical project. Nevertheless, this does not mean that it can continue to hegemonize the moral discourse of the society unchallenged. As contemporary cultural attitudes among young people increasingly move, in the aftermath of feminism, sexual politics and the cultural coming-of-age of young urban blacks, in one direction, and the public morality of Thatcherism moves the opposite way, this is increasingly likely to become a key arena of social contestation.

Thatcherism, then, has been obliged to change and adapt to a changing and difficult terrain. It has encountered some areas of genuine resistance and difficulty. It has had, to some extent, to recompose itself. But its long-term, fundamental political project is still, substantially, in place. Thatcherism has never been 'hegemonic' if by that we mean that it succeeded in unifying a major social bloc and 'winning the consent' of the great majority of the subordinate classes of society and other key social forces to a major task of social reconstruction. Especially if we conceive 'hegemony' as a permanent, steady state of affairs.

What we have always argued is that it had a 'hegemonic project'. It was designed to renovate society as a whole. And, in doing so, it understood that it must organize on a variety of social and cultural sites at once, both in society and in the state, on moral and cultural, as well as economic and political terrain, using them all to initiate the deep reformation of society. It has not achieved the goal of securing a period of social and moral ascendancy over British society, whose problems remain as yet too deep and intractable for such an enterprise. But it remains, by dint of a more 'directive' form of authoritarian populist politics, the leading force in British political life.

This is not the place to make a parallel assessment of Labour's alternative, but it must be said that, in comparison, the gains which the non-Thatcherite forces have made out of Thatcherism's troubles are extremely shallow. The presentation of Labour's case has improved. The Kinnock leadership has taken a firm, managerial grip on the party machine. The realigned left has failed to establish an alternative agenda or to provide a powerful political alternative to the fundamentalist left or the centre-right.

But politically, the so-called recovery has no depth to it. It still lacks an alternative popular politics or a convincing alternative economic strategy or a cultural politics capable of mobilizing alternative social identities. It has become, technically, more adept at telling the electorate what is 'wrong' with Thatcherism. But it is not yet capable of convincing significant numbers of the unconverted or the disillusioned about what, in the last decade of the twentieth century, might be 'right' about social-ism. In part this is because, though it has some plausible answers to the tactical and more superficial questions where Thatcherism has run into difficulties, it has no long-term, strategic stake in the deeper, and rapidly shifting, contours of British economic, cultural and social life into which, in its own contradictory way, Thatcherism has inserted itself.

From a more short-term perspective, it will not do to argue that it is the electoral split between Labour and the Alliance which is allowing Thatcherism to survive on a minority basis. It is now clear that, in the event of a close election, the Alliance would deliver as many votes to Thatcherism as it would against it. So far as public opinion in relation to immediate electoral prospects is concerned, on the question of Thatch-erism (not Mrs Thatcher), the country seems split down the middle. Those who are not 'for' it are not very convincingly 'for' anything else. It is a sobering thought that, despite Thatcherism's many difficulties and the wave of revulsion against its narrow utilitarianism, the safest bet one could currently place is still on a third innings for Thatcherism, on a reduced but operational majority. The end of the nightmare is still nowhere in sight.

1986

Notes

1. Jowell, Witherspoon and Brook, eds, *British Social Attitudes*, London 1986, p. 81.
2. For an impressive account of that language, see Alan O'Shea, 'Trusting the People' in *Formations of Nation and People*, London 1984.
3. See the account in L. Davidoff and C. Hall, *Family Fortunes*, London 1987.
4. Peter Glotz, 'Forward to Europe', *Socialist Affairs*, 1, 1985.
5. G. Therborn, 'West on the Dole', *Marxism Today*, June 1985.
6. P. Glotz, 'Forward to Europe'.

PART TWO

———◆———

Questions of Theory

PART TWO

Questions of Theory

7

State and Society, 1880–1930

with Bill Schwarz

The broad lines of our interpretation of the recomposition of British society, politics and the state from the 1880s to the 1920s can be summarized by the following points. First, from the 1880s there occurred a profound crisis of the British state which became acute from 1910 to 1926. The general crisis of the state marked a sharp historical *discontinuity* from the period which preceded it. One important way in which we characterize this crisis is as a 'crisis of liberalism'.

Second, out of this crisis, or succession of crises, there developed a transition to new 'collectivist' forms of state organization and social regulation which were qualitatively distinct from the laissez faire individualism of the mid-Victorian period. This new form of the state can be described as the interventionist state.

Third, although we insist that a transition from individualism to collectivism (or laissez faire to monopoly capitalism) was accomplished in Britain by the end of the 1920s, we reject the idea of any adequate general theory of the state from which British particulars can be deduced. Rather we wish to stress the necessarily contingent dimensions of the political forces which constituted both the 'crisis' and the 'transition'. This means emphasizing the peculiarities of the British route and – in contrast to Germany and Italy – the differences which led, in the British case, not to a fascist but to a democratic-interventionist 'solution'.

Fourth, the form of the state and the main agencies for mass political representation which are now seen as characteristically 'modern' first appeared between the 1880s and the 1920s. In this sense the major political forces of our own period first arose in these years. In the analysis of the crisis of the state which now confronts us in the 1980s, the 1880s to the 1920s remain the 'crucible years'.

Fifth, and last, we argue that the political solutions and compromises of the 1920s and the decades which followed carried with them new antagonisms and contradictions; these have become especially apparent from the perspective of the crisis of the state of the 1970s and 1980s. Each of these points needs to be discussed in turn.

Crises

The apparently precise period we have adopted – 1880 to 1930 – is only an approximate indication of the historical boundaries of our subject. Within these decades the first, formative moment in the consolidation of monopoly capitalism was completed. This was a transition which stamps the historical development of Britain as surely, but perhaps not as visibly, as the period from the 1640s to the 1660s (the establishment of the revolutionary constitutional regime) or the period from the 1770s to the 1840s (the formation of industrial capitalism). Each of these periods was an epochal moment, a time of organic crisis when the society as a whole was structurally reformed. The significance of the 1880s–1920s, however, is that although its epochal character is not so well established or studied, it is, nevertheless, the period most immediately formative *for us.*

Epochal transitions, in the sense used above, are notoriously difficult to theorize and specify. The key lies in the concept of crisis. Crisis is a term which has been weakened through overuse, forming the very staple of journalistic punditry. But none the less it has pertinence, and is peculiarly applicable to the analysis of the British state since the 1880s. It is, however, necessary to distinguish a short-term crisis of the state – one which is relatively localized and confined to the formal institutional apparatuses of the state – from a crisis which breaks across the social formation as a whole and threatens the hegemony of the dominant order. From the 1880s there occurred a succession of crises of the state, each only incompletely and partially resolved before new antagonisms arose, which in their combination amounted to a crisis of the social order itself. Crises occur when the social formation can no longer be reproduced on the basis of the pre-existing system of social relations. To be more specific, in the closing decades of the nineteenth century the liberal state and its attendant modes for regulating civil society could no longer be reproduced by means of liberal policies, practices and objectives. That is why the crisis was general – and also why it was a crisis of liberalism.

The onset of this crisis in the 1880s marked a deep rupture and discontinuity in British social and political development. This needs to be emphasized, given the continuing predominance of evolutionist explanations both within contemporary political ideologies and within historiography. Theories which are predicated on a fundamental continuity between the mid-Victorian period and the early decades of the twentieth century – such as seeing the Labour Party as the natural successor to the Liberals, or the 'growth' of the welfare state – fail to grasp the immediate determinations which impelled a change of course and the desperate attempts to organize new solutions. After the cataclysmic impact of the war the state formation which emerged in the 1920s was quite new, both in its internal organization and in the set of social relations in which it existed. No return to older forms was possible.

One reason why some commentators are so keen to assert an essential continuity in these years may be to distance themselves from the excesses of the thesis developed by George Dangerfield in his book *The Strange Death of Liberal England*, published some fifty years ago but which (with Halévy's monumental account, to which Dangerfield owed a great deal) still largely defines the terms of current debate.[1] This is a racy book, written with stylistic verve, stronger on anecdotes than it is on historiographical research. His argument, which he pursues in uncompromising terms, is that in the years from 1910 to 1914 the multiple threat to the social order – manifest in the struggles of the syndicalists, the suffragettes and the opponents of Irish Home Rule – had, even before the outbreak of war, brought about the death of liberal England. In their different ways, he contends, these struggles expressed the fundamental 'spirit of the age' in tearing to the ground the institutions and assumptions of high Victorianism. Historians have attacked his method as hopelessly idealist and his conclusions as extreme. They demonstrate, for example, that the Liberal Party still remained a major electoral contender until the end of the 1920s, and liberal social theory and philosophy, far from dying out before 1914, was an active force long after the First World War. These qualifications and counter-examples, however, may not be as damaging to the validity of his historical insight as his critics imagine. The Dangerfield thesis, in its pure form, cannot stand. Yet there is none the less a profound historical imagination at work in Dangerfield's account, for all its overdramatization. He grasps the fact and the depth of the crisis and he sees its connection to liberalism. If only as a marker in a complicated debate, his analysis provides our account with its initial bearing.

It is, however, necessary to have some indication of the various meanings attached to the term liberalism. First, and most obviously, it refers to the rule of the Liberal Party. As a party of government and as a major political force in the country, the Liberals did not survive the coalitions of Asquith (1915–16) and Lloyd George (1916–22), even when the shell of the party endured. The party suffered two great splits in this period, first in 1886 over Home Rule and then in 1916 over the conduct of the war. The decline of the Liberal Party was long and complex, and it was by no means out of the running until the early 1930s. Yet a decline it indisputably was, and as such must mark an important element in the crisis of liberalism.

But liberalism always carried much deeper connotations than the designation of a single party. It defined the relationship between state and civil society. In this area the key concept of classical liberalism was 'individualism' (to which the new term 'collectivism' was explicitly a counter). The sovereign individual in civil society, with his right to property and to his liberties of action and movement, was the central ideological figure. Individual liberty was determined by the workings of the free market, sanctioned and protected by the rule of law. The role of the state was to oversee the free play of the market and thereby serve as the defender of individual liberties: it should assume the role of 'night-watchman', intervening in the market economy as little as possible. This, briefly described, formed the ideals of laissez faire government, even when modified in actual practice. The identifications forged in this system between the free individual in civil society, the free market, private property and the patriarchal domestic household formed one of the most powerful and durable popular conceptions of state and society. But, as many of the conventional histories demonstrate, the tempo of state intervention increased sharply in the 1880s and 1890s; the boundaries between state and civil society began to be redefined; and the nightwatchman role of the state began to be steadily eroded. In this sense, too, liberalism was in crisis in the last two decades of the nineteenth century.

A third, broader meaning attached to the idea of liberalism is the notion of a liberal social *system*, referring not only to the relationship between state and civil society (concisely if too simply described by the term laissez faire) but also to the constitutive features of civil society itself. This includes the formal, philosophical elaborations of liberalism, as well as the lived, civic ideologies and practices which drew on liberal philosophy and which, by the 1860s, constituted the common sense of the mid-Victorian age. Crucial in this context are the conceptions which were dominant in the period – of the individual, family, constitution, law and nation – which defined the very core of liberal thought. These formed not a codified 'philosophy' or body of political thought, but the common sense ideas, the taken-for-granted points of moral reference, the practical ideologies of the leading classes in English society. The crisis of liberalism in the closing decades of the century was, therefore, also a crisis of confidence and of continuity in these practical–ideological conceptions. Each of the leading ideas noted earlier is challenged and redefined in our period – and not only by new conceptions, but in practice and in social organization.

The fissures and breaks in the practical organization of common sense represented – as Gramsci has argued – no mere shift in the 'spirit of the age'. They have a direct bearing on the mechanisms of power in both civic life and in political institutions. They lead us directly to the questions concerning the maintenance of social authority or hegemony. The question of liberalism in mid-Victorian society was, in the end, always a question of how the delicate power balance was maintained and reinforced in a rapidly changing society. The crisis of liberalism was, therefore, ultimately connected with a crisis of hegemony in the whole social formation.

Thus the crisis of liberalism was not just a crisis of the state, narrowly conceived (concerning the fortunes of the Liberal Party), nor simply of the technical relationship between state and civil society (the demise of laissez faire as a practical objective) but rather of the very *ideas* of state and civil society, of public and private. It is legitimate, then, to refer also to a crisis in liberal philosophy, and to note that this had direct effects on the intellectual and moral leadership of the dominant classes.[2] From this point of view it is possible to return to the original Dangerfield thesis and to rework and reappropriate it as an insight into the crisis of *liberal hegemony*.

From this historical moment the very means and modes by which hegemony is exerted in the metropolitan nations undergo a significant alteration. There is a shift not just in the disposition of forces but in the terrain of struggle itself. The nature of 'the political' underwent a profound transformation. Indeed, Gramsci's own notion of hegemony was specified historically in relation to this period. In distinguishing between the working-class movement of 1848, which relied only on direct confrontation with the power centres of the state, and the strategic questions facing the socialist movement of his own time in the 1920s and 1930s, Gramsci noted:

In the period after 1870, with the colonial expansion of Europe ... the internal and international organisational relations of the State became more complex and massive, and the Forty-Eightist formula of the 'Permanent Revolution' is expanded and transcended in political science by the formula of 'civil hegemony'.... The massive structures of the modern democracies, both as State organisations and as complexes of associations in civil society, constitute for the art of politics as it were the 'trenches' and the permanent fortifications of the front in the war of position: they render merely 'partial' the element of movement which before used to be 'the whole' war....[3]

It is this deepening complexity of state power which led Gramsci to adopt the idea of a war of position, in which the overthrow of the state is conceptualized as a protracted struggle waged on all fronts, cultural as well as political, economic and military, engaging with the '*focos*' of power distributed through political *and* civil society. The significance of this, for our purpose, is the idea that Gramsci conveys of the reconstitution of the relations between state and civil society, the expansion of the very idea of 'politics' and the incorporation of the masses in the nation states of the late nineteenth century.

Political Representation

Fundamental to this process was the means by which formal representation of the popular masses was secured. The second Reform Act of 1867 clearly demonstrated that the liberal state was organized to counter mass democracy and universal suffrage. The masses were to be incorporated in the nation, but indirectly, on the basis of a limited suffrage. It was along this fault-line that the disintegration of liberal hegemony first occurred.[4] This signalled the end of the period of relative stability in the mid-Victorian political order.

From the 1880s, established constitutionalism could no longer ensure the representation of the nation. Indeed, what social and political elements composed 'the nation' became a pressing political question. The pressures for the democratization and universalization of the political nation (such that every adult member had formal and equal rights of citizenship) undermined the established unity, organized by and through the state, of the liberal alliance. In the early moments of this collapse, party organization loosened and political affiliation became increasingly volatile. Gramsci's account of what he called an 'organic' crisis is instructive:

> At a certain point in their historical lives, social classes become detached from their traditional parties. In other words, the traditional parties in that particular organisational form, with the particular men who constitute, represent and lead them, are no longer recognised by their class (or fraction of a class) as its expression. When such crises occur, the immediate situation becomes delicate and dangerous, because the field is open for violent solutions, for the activities of unknown forces, represented by charismatic 'men of destiny'.[5]

The reference here to the 'men of destiny' is one to which we must return. But the emergent political forces which, from the 1880s, weakened the traditional organizations which had hitherto represented and constituted social classes need first to be located.

Perhaps the most significant factor in the political realignments of the late nineteenth century is the least researched: the recomposition of the capitalist class. The expansion of capital accumulation and the increasing opportunities for the diversification of investment tended to undercut traditional divisions between those who secured their wealth from capitalist agriculture and those whose primary concerns lay in manufacturing. These social distinctions had been reproduced in the political alliances of the Conservative Party and the Liberal Party respectively, giving each its distinctive social character. But in the period up to the First World War these divisions rapidly diminished in significance. As the process of capital accumulation became more complex, so the various functions within the ownership and management of capital increased. One feature of this was the emergence of a new plutocracy – bankers, stockbrokers, investors and so on – who through their spectacular wealth commanded immense prestige in Edwardian society, and who gravitated to the Conservative Party, especially from the 1890s. Despite the continued presence of the political grandees, an effective social revolution took place within the Conservative Party, allowing into its inner councils those whose wealth and position was directly dependent on the day-to-day fluctuations of business.

Yet the immediate trigger for this transformation of alignment stemmed from the disarray of the Liberal Party, provoked by the antagonism between Joseph Chamberlain's radicalism and Gladstone's more cautious conception of liberalism. This came to a head in 1886 when Chamberlain formed an organized Liberal Unionist grouping in order to oppose Gladstone's Home Rule Bill. This represented not only a disaster for the Liberal Party, but a grave split inside the ruling bloc as a whole. It was a break which permanently shifted the political terrain. In the following thirty years the Unionist (Conservative) alliance was to emerge as the all but exclusive representative of the varied interests which made up capital 'in general'.

The issue which drove Chamberlain towards Conservatism was *imperial* – the rejection of Home Rule for Ireland. Throughout the period, Ireland was perceived first and foremost as an imperial issue, with an immediate, continuous and overbearing impact on domestic politics. The issue of Ireland condensed the anxieties about Britain's imperial position as no other could, for if the empire were to be dislocated at its very centre its prospects looked bleak. In the last quarter of the century the concept of empire assumed radically new connotations.

Behind this shift lay the recognition that the rise of industrialized competitors for the first time decisively threatened both Britain's trade and its informal spheres of colonial interest. From this point on, Britain could no longer run on the steam of its own economic power, founded on the principles of free trade. British manufacturers were perplexed by the sustained period of stagnation and paralysis in capital accumulation which characterized much of the last quarter of the last century and which later came to be known as the Great Depression. This decline in the rate of growth was striking compared both with the pace of Britain's earlier economic expansion and with the astonishing acceleration of industrial output of Germany, Russia, Japan and the USA. Britain passed in this period from being the strongest to becoming one of the weaker links in the chain of industrial nations. This did not, in most cases, compel businessmen to adopt radically new solutions; but it did exert a new set of political pressures on those who most directly represented capital in the state. Chamberlain's conversion to Empire and tariff reform was the most celebrated instance.

Just as from the 1880s the dominant class underwent an important phase in recomposition, so too the working class was 'remade'. The drive of capital to break down the skills of those workers strategically placed in the production process had crucial implications in the restructuring of the division of labour and in fracturing and disorganizing the cultural and political ties which had held skilled labourers to liberalism. But equally important the socialist revival (conventionally dated from the great dock strike of 1889), combining with forces pressing from below for a system of *mass* democracy, coincided with the political splits in the dominant bloc and gave a strategic leverage to those political movements emerging outside the state.

The dock strike was the first major sign of the organized workers' movement disengaging from the Liberal Party and seeking to win independent political representation. In the socialist movement from the late nineteenth century up to the First World War political opposition to the state cohered as it had not done since Chartism. In these years, as in no other period before or since, the different strands of the 'socialisms' appeared as organic expressions of proletarian experience, though this process was always manifestly uneven and heterogeneous. One common impetus which lay behind these experiences, however, derived from the incipient internal collapse of the administrative solutions which had been institutionalized as state policy in the 1830s. The most obvious example of this is the New Poor Law, which demonstrated with singular force the inability of such administrative reforms to resolve or even mitigate structural economic problems. In such a climate, socialist and collectivist alternatives took on a more acceptable and positive profile.

The pressures for the expansion of democratic participation were not confined to the male working-class movement. For the first time there arose a mass feminist movement, organized initially as a campaign to repeal the Contagious Diseases Acts. By the early 1880s the repeal movement had moved to the centre of the public stage and feminism had become established as a major political force. The dynamic of popular and public concern over sexual matters reached a peak in 1885, the year which Jeffrey Weeks has called 'an *annus mirabilis* of sexual politics'.[6] A fundamental objective of this and later campaigns was concentrated on the suffrage. The aim was to win a political voice and thus articulate such matters on the parliamentary stage. The rationale for this objective was drawn in part from liberal philosophy, but at the same time challenged a principled liberalism on its own terms. The long-term effect of these struggles was to impose a further degree of fragmentation on the political and social alliances organized around the Liberal Party. In the later years, at the height of suffragette activity, this was symbolized in the most dramatic terms, when male political leaders looked out from the Palace of Westminster to see their female relatives and social acquaintances breaking through the police cordons in order to reach the parliament building and demonstrate their passionate and public condemnation of that exclusively masculine bastion of political power.

However, liberal hegemony was broken not only by an array of alternative political forces, but also by an alternative and expanded conception of politics. Liberty to sell one's labour in the market, and even to choose a parliamentary representative, was challenged in the name of *social* rights. This was made explicit in the socialist groupings of the time – which were insistent in their claims that they could supersede liberalism – and even more so in the feminist movement. This is not to suggest that there occurred a spontaneous alliance between the socialist and feminist movements. Quite the reverse. The effect of the feminist campaign was to activate new sources of contention and antagonism, as well as new potentialities for alliances, *across* the popular movements of the day. Feminism challenged the apparent unity of the male labour movement, just as the impact of socialism disrupted the women's organizations. The intellectual resources of feminism may have drawn from the socialist tradition as well as from liberalism, but they were primarily constituted by women's distinctive histories and concerns. The struggle for the vote was only one very particular aspect of a much wider conception of women's emancipation.

The political forces which broke up the liberal system at the end of the century were thus not premised on shared objectives; neither was there a common idea of what would be the most satisfactory political solutions to the varying conceptions of 'the crisis'. Nevertheless, the new political forces which arose in the 1880s were all positioned in different ways *against* the state and existing institutions of power. In varying degrees they all addressed popular constituencies in a bid to recruit them in reconstructing the forms and boundaries of the state. This included not only the socialist and feminist movements but also elements which, under the aegis of jingoism or Orangeism, became seriously involved in building mass movements of the right. There is a sense in which Danger-field is correct in seeing these different movements, from diverse sources, all coming to a head on the eve of the war. Although the fissures and breaks in the liberal system originated from distinct antagonisms, in terms of their effects they began to converge. The combined effect was to precipitate and then deepen the crisis of liberalism. Liberal constitutionalism and mass democracy, far from being evolutionary successors to one another, could not coexist in one state without there first being a major upheaval. Victorian constitutionalism consequently broke apart. Inside Parliament new mechanisms for compromise evolved for managing the pressing issues of the day; outside the constitutional arena, political forces generated by new mass movements assumed a radically new profile. The liberal state could no longer serve as a means to represent the new social forces, nor reproduce itself as a point of political and social stability. The issue at stake was how a new type of state could be constructed, capable of sustaining these new forces.

For each specific crisis innumerable new solutions, at once political and ethical, were proposed. A hundred different positions, philosophies and formations vied with one another to win ascendancy in defining the new rules of the game. Some politicians still hoped to save liberal society, even if this required illiberal means. Others subscribed to versions of a new social order. However, the social system was not so finely and functionally balanced that all the elements which composed the crisis were at some point resolved. The relations between state and society were dramatically reconstituted. But in some senses certain features of the British crisis were permanent, and in any fundamental sense, remained – and remain – unresolved.

Collectivism

The picture gets more complex when we see that each moment of crisis is also a moment of reconstruction: crises are the means by which social relations are reconstituted. The destructive and the reconstructive moments are parts of a single process of social transformation. Thus the emphasis on crisis is at the same time an emphasis on the remaking of the social formation. This process of reconstruction – 'reconstruction in the very moment of destruction' as Gramsci once put it – at the end of the last century was one in which many new possible solutions appeared on the horizon, each carrying potentially new dangers and contradictions. A central feature of many of the emergent solutions was the idea of collectivism.

There is a substantial but varied body of journalistic, theoretical and historical work, spanning contemporary liberal theorists such as A.V. Dicey and Marxists such as Lenin, which locates the crucial transformation in the metropolitan nations of the period in the transition from laissez faire to collectivism. Collectivism is as ambiguous a term as individualism. It refers to the process by which state policy became organized around class or corporate rather than individual interests. Thus, within the collectivist perspective, the state was seen as representing particular collective interests, and thereby required to intervene positively in civil society on behalf of these, rather than holding the ring within which individual interests compete. Underlying these theories was the idea that the state was linked to the organic interests of class, community or nation. It followed that the state should forsake its night-watchman role and become more actively interventionist, regulating more directly the civic and private spheres of individual decision. This tendency, explicitly counterposed as it was to the liberal conception of the state, gathered pace in our period, supported by a diverse and heterogeneous set of social forces. Some welcomed the drift to collectivism. To others, who feared the erosion of individual liberties, it was the cause for deep despair.

That was at the level of political theory, public philosophy, social attitudes and legislation. At a higher theoretical level, and within the specifically Marxist framework deployed by Lenin, the new collectivist system represented not simply a new form of state but a new phase of capitalism – monopoly capitalism – in which the contradictions inherent in the capitalist mode of production reached a new level. This Lenin conceptualized as the highest and last stage of capitalism, in which the state assumed a central role as the direct organizer of capital.

Those committed to liberal individualism frequently indulged in unwarranted hyperbole in making their case, unearthing the makings of a revolution in political and civil society, pioneered not by wild extremists from the barricades but from within the very citadel of parliament itself. However the publicists indulging in these polemics were never simply scaremongering. The pressures for collectivism *were* strengthening, as was the tendency for more direct regulation of civil society.

How did the forms of state regulation emerging in the early part of the twentieth century differ from state regulation in the period of laissez faire? This touches on a major historical debate. We have so far accepted a rather simple equation between classical nineteenth-century liberalism and laissez faire. Yet the ideal of such limited state intervention never came anywhere near realization in practice. In social terms, 'the population' had been the constant object of state regulation and surveillance since the early decades of industrialization, especially in matters of health, sanitation and hygiene which could be incorporated within the very broad rubric of medical discourses. Even in terms of the market, those most often committed to the principles of laissez faire were frequently, as state officials and administrators, the most inveterate 'interveners'. Those involved with the legislation on poor relief provide a striking example. By the mid-century the impetus of reform, involving a steady 'growth in government intervention', was in full spate.

Two general points which help to distinguish liberal from collectivist regulation can be made. First, the liberal reformers of the 1830s and 1840s were concerned above all to dislodge and break up the social institutions and practices inherited from an older social system which they perceived as inhibiting the free currency of market relations. Their objectives were in a sense, then, negative: to intervene in order to secure the conditions for regulation by economic or market compulsion. Second, the market and the conditions of wage-labour are *always* politically constituted, even if the role of the state is only remedial and deterrent. In this sense the state always has a positive role to play, even if that role is 'only' to ensure that the law of the free market prevails. We can therefore modify our definition of the key contrasting term to collectivism. Laissez faire describes not an absence of controls, but a specific means by which market forces are politically regulated.

In the process of capital accumulation itself there exists a tendency for the progressive socialization of the means of production (larger and more closely integrated units of production) and also for greater collectivization of owners on the one hand and workers on the other. In the latter stages of capitalist development there arises the tendency towards the organization of cartels of capitalists, overriding the laws of the market through price-fixing and trade agreements, ultimately leading to monopoly enterprises. Similarly, there develops a greater concentration of workers at the workplace (and in the great industrial cities) who attempt to protect their collective interests by regulating the price of labour, principally through trade unions. These pressures, inseparable from the process of capital accumulation itself, have the effect of destroying the classical rule of the 'free' market in its pure form, and with it the basis of a systematic and thoroughgoing laissez faire. Yet the decomposition of market relations can be counteracted by the reconstitution of the market, in new forms, by the state. Indeed it must be re-constituted since it is an essential condition for the realization of value and the reproduction of capital. Thus direct state regulation of the market in one sector tends to occur *in order to preserve* the system of 'unfettered' relations in another. Far from the reproduction of market relations depending on the state absenting itself from the free play of the economy, it now comes to depend on a certain level of positive inter-vention by the state in the economy. This is one of the great contra-dictions on which intervention by the capitalist state is founded. The state tends to become an active and more direct agent in the process of 'decomposition and recomposition' of the social relations of production.

For example, at the turn of the century William Beveridge devised a scheme for state-sponsored national insurance (to aid those temporarily outside paid employment) and for labour exchanges. To be effective these plans required direct state intervention in the labour market. Indeed, they were premised on the belief that free-market relations were *no longer able* to direct a particular worker to the job to which he (the worker was generally thought of as male) was best suited or trained. In part, the objective was to use state intervention to overcome blockages in the labour market, particularly those resulting from the system of casual labour. But this was accompanied by a more positive conception in which the state was to secure both the maximization of the mobility of labour power and the cultivation of labour power of a particular quality. These policies necessarily involved not only the direct constitution of the market by the state but also the direct intervention of the state in the qualitative reproduction of social labour. The spectre of the casual poor as a stagnant pool of labour in the East End of London was the image which reverberated through these debates. Such blockages in the market could only be overcome by state agencies substituting direct regulation for the rule of the market in order to reconstitute the market as a whole. The immediate imperatives behind these schemes were not, as in the 1840s, to clear away specific, perceived inhibitions, but rather to ensure the survival of the market as such.

The transformation in state regulation was not merely quantitative but effectively produced a new idea of the 'social' (as in the term 'social reform'), a new discourse of social regulation, in which there arose new objects and targets for intervention. Thus, to continue with our earlier example, Beveridge saw his job as one of classification, determining the various causes of poverty and how these affected any particular group at any particular moment. The motive force of his investigations was to disaggregate what had previously been seen as the undifferentiated mass of the labouring poor. Within the enlarged sphere of action of the state, new categories and new social identities were produced in opposition to the generalized notions of poverty and pauperism: the unemployed man, the old age pensioner, the incorrigible loafer, the destitute alien, and so on. Each 'problem' needed a *specific* form of intervention and regulation.

This process of breaking down the 'social problem' into component parts, each corresponding to a specific practice of regulation by some apparatus of the state developed for the purpose, can be taken as an example of Foucault's 'proliferation of discourses' in which new social subjects appear as potential objects for state concern. Other examples in other domains of social reproduction can be cited – the common prostitute (in the moment of the contagious diseases legislation of the 1860s and 1870s) and slightly later the 'amateur prostitute'; the unfit mother; the male juvenile delinquent and the hooligan. Each social category required a whole battery of state and/or voluntary agencies in order to ameliorate the effects of each particular 'disorder'. As the state was progressively enmeshed in resolving, or attempting to resolve, these dysfunctions in the social system so specific bureaucracies and departments of state were adopted for their regulation. These apparatuses, together with the experts and administrators – the 'organic state intellectuals' of the period – assumed the positive role of producing and accumulating new knowledge about the specific subjects and categories which came under their disciplinary regimes. The formation, expansion and diversification of particular state departments and ministries, the arrival of the powerful state administrator-intellectuals like Hubert Llewellyn Smith or Robert Morant, and the use of a new philosophy of scientific administration were all institutional expressions of this process. In this way the machinery of state began to be transformed and reorganized.

Although the necessary emphasis here is on the particularity of each response, and of the theories and agencies constituted in each instance, there were certain common features. The emerging welfare and collectivist ideologies which came to be channelled most directly through the state were primarily organized around particular forms of knowledge: explicitly psychology and eugenics – the sciences of social engineering often summarized in the phrase 'social Darwinism'. The means by which the various categories of the 'unfit' could be identified was through the mechanistic utilitarianism of 'mental measurement'. Psychological and statistical criteria could pin-point those deemed to be a social burden. Eugenics was the means by which the socially unfit would be bred out of the nation. The discursive polarities separating the deficient from the efficient, the deprived from the depraved, the healthy from the unfit, became an organizing principle for many of the new collectivist projects. For the deficient, especially those categorized as the residuum, the sternest disciplinary measures were evolved within the expanding administrative arenas of state action.

Yet it would be misleading to attribute the impulse to collectivism within the state exclusively to this expansion of state practices and apparatuses. Collectivism had deep roots, too, in pressures from below. The labour movement, clearly, was an emergent organic social interest with which the state would have to deal. The broadening of the theories of social, as against individual rights, led not only the organized labour movement but other sections of the population – the poor, the homeless, the residuum, and, after the great feminist revival, women – to lay claims to a more equal share in the social goods to which citizenship entitled them. There was, by and large, only one force capable of intervening against the logic of the market and of individual interest in the cause of social reform, redistributive justice and the guarantee of social rights. That power was the state. This conception of rights was therefore of the utmost importance in the early struggles in this period for reform. These struggles from below constituted a powerful complementary force to that of disciplinary regulation in the growth of those forms of collectivist expansion which were implemented first in the period and which culminated in the welfare state. In combination these two streams – those which looked to the state for an organic solution to the crisis of reproduction, from 'above', and those which looked to the state to intervene in the name of the collective good against the imperatives of the free market – not only powered the transition to collectivism, but helped to form the contradictory parameters which, ever since, have enclosed modern welfare programmes.[7]

But collectivism, too, was linked to the struggles for mass democracy. If we put together the struggles for the extension of the male franchise, the great engagement around women's suffrage and the new forms of industrial and political representation, we can see that perhaps the most significant underlying social force threatening the delicate balancing-act of mid-century liberalism was the pressure for mass democracy. The emergence of mass democracy could not be contained within the limiting forms of representation of the liberal state. What the democratic challenge carried was nothing more nor less than a new set of claims on the state by the unenfranchised masses, a new conception of citizenship and, indeed, an expansion of the rights of citizenship from the sphere of legal and political to economic and social rights.

The Political Forces of Collectivism

Three of the dominant collectivist currents can be identified here: the imperialist, new liberal and Fabian – thus emphasizing the *political* and contingent constitution of these collectivist forces.

First, the social-imperialist position. There already existed a long Tory tradition of commitment to a strong state; in this period diehards inside the Conservative Party attempted to resist the 'capitulation' of their party to liberalism, arguing the essential continuity between Tory paternalism and the organic interventionist state. The alliance between Joseph Chamberlain's Unionists, and the eventual dominance in the party of a Unionist bloc which aimed to construct a vigorous imperial regime, resulted in the formation of an authentically Conservative and imperialist collectivism. The politics of imperialist collectivism were most characteristically of the radical right, envisaging drastic solutions, imposed from above, to resolve Britain's ills, and scarcely restrained by the constraints of parliamentary constitutionalism. The language was formed in the syntax of 'national efficiency' and 'social imperialism' – the former pinpointing liberalism's inadequacy in facing the task of national renovation, the latter designating a set of policies which, by combining imperialist development abroad with welfare and economic reforms at home, would build up the strength, efficiency and fitness of the British race as an imperial power. In this, the martial spirit of Prussia and Japan were held as ideals. Although deeply authoritarian in their drive for leadership and efficiency, and threatening to uproot many of the established constitutional practices of a parliamentary democracy, these collectivists of the right worked energetically to enlist a populist movement in the country. Social imperialism did not so much deny citizenship as recast it in a populist and activist idiom: the new citizen was to be a *participant* absorbed into the larger organic unities of race, empire and nation.

To the new liberals – our second current – this dirigisme was abhorrent. The new liberals, a group of highly gifted professional intellectuals, evolved a conception of collectivism which was constitutional and communitarian, ethical rather than utilitarian, and which aimed to preserve individual liberties through greater state intervention. New liberalism was a body of thought based on the determination to devise forms of collectivist control which could complement and extend, rather than negate, the inherited ethos of liberalism. Its trajectory was evolutionary, its driving-force idealist and ethical. In this respect and others, it played an inestimable role in the formation of British social democracy.

Its concept of citizenship was uncompromisingly constitutional, but principled in its desire to elevate the citizen as a full member of the political nation and the community, as a moral being, with duties as well as rights. The new liberal perspective shared the imperialist belief that citizenship not only conferred legal rights but signified a potential which could be realized in each individual through an educative political parti-cipation. To ensure that the majority could be educated in this way was therefore taken to be one of the moral functions of the state – hence the justification for state-sponsored public education. Yet, for all their formal adherence to constitutionalism, their attitude to democracy was ultimately rather more guarded. Democracy was a term which came frequently to their lips and they were often insistent on the need to democratize from top to bottom state and civil society. But this was often counterbalanced, even among the most generous of these theorists (like J.A. Hobson or John or Barbara Hammond) by a residual utilitar-ianism and by the fear of outright socialism. Socialism they conceived as representing a particular class interest as against the general interest of the 'common good'. This counterposition – liberalism not socialism – was a structural feature of their conception of citizenship.

The new liberal idea of democracy was subject to the persistent undertow of a fluctuating but recurrent spirit of inegalitarianism. The significance of the new position within the liberal tradition articulated by the new liberals lies most of all in their advocacy of the provision of *universal* social rights. But this was tempered and qualified by their identification of those whom they deemed were unfit for the purposes of citizenship – an exception to universalism within the discourses of new liberalism which was not perceived as contentious. However, the commitment to universalism was given a negative inflexion – the right, in other words, not to be impoverished, or ill-educated and so on. It was a negative conception of rights which left intact, as a system, the positive relations of private competition. In fact the new liberalism was premised on this assumption for, quite consistently, it aimed to compensate those who visibly suffered gross privation on account of their being unable, for whatever reason, to participate fully in market relations. The structural inequalities of class relations, however, did not come within the compass of new liberal investigations – not because they were forgotten, but because they were positively excluded. Their whole theorization was antipathetical to any analysis which privileged class relations for they reasoned that this was to succumb to the dictates of a singular social interest rather than elaborating a view of society which could accom-modate the full spectrum of different interests. This can be put more strongly, if polemically. The new liberals endeavoured to recast and rearticulate classical liberalism within the imperatives of a collectivist and democratic age. In so doing they preserved much of the liberal tradition and inheritance by partially transforming it. But it also represented precisely the response by humane and liberal social theorists to the combined threat of socialism and mass democracy. They attemptd to deal with that threat by appropriating and incorporating the language of universalism into their own discourse and making it their own.

The third and perhaps most intriguing collectivist grouping were the Fabians. The Fabians represented the contradictory thrust of collectivism at the very heart of socialism itself. Unlike those who adhered to a Tory imperialism or the new liberalism, the most prominent of the Fabians (like Bernard Shaw and Beatrice and Sidney Webb) were socialists: they wished to destroy the anarchy of the capitalist market and achieve a classless society. But there were many 'socialisms' contending for ascendancy within the working-class movement at this time and for decades there was no guarantee which current would prevail in English socialism. Fabian socialism was the reformist, bureaucratic, anti-democratic and illiberal variety. Their dream was of a fully regulated, fully administered collectivist society in which state surveillance would be an essential condition of civic conduct. Regulated collectivism should replace the regime of unregulated individualism. This variant of socialism was deeply at odds with other socialist currents and with the spirit of self-activism which animated the proletarian socialist organizations of the period. The drift of Fabianism even to the Labour Party was protracted and reluctant, and only finally accomplished on tactical grounds. Like the new liberals, with whom they had much in common in terms of their class position, the Fabians were not only members of a newly professionalized intelligentsia; they elevated the bureaucrat, the expert and the administrator to the position of the leading cadre of their struggle for a new society. Whereas the defining impulse of the new liberals was mainly ethical, the Fabians were utilitarian. If the new liberals played a key role in defining the character of the welfare state, it was Fabianism which fashioned the ideology of rational efficiency and administrative neutrality which characterized welfarism in practice.

It is important at this point to emphasize the authoritarianism of the collectivist project. There was the clear anti-constitutionalism of the imperialist and Conservative tradition. But more importantly, perhaps, was the statist nature of their vision – a common denominator of all the collectivist tendencies, including the new liberals. The new regime, it was supposed, would be imposed from above. The main agent of transformation would not be the masses but the agencies of the state itself. How would these agencies in turn be transformed? For Conservatives the main figures were the adventurist political leaders and charismatic imperial impresarios who hovered in the wings and on stage. For the new liberals and Fabians it was the state administrators and experts, the organic intellectuals who aligned themselves with the collectivist impulse, who would devise one blueprint after another according to rational and scientific procedures alone. The dominance of state over civil society inscribed in all these programmes gave a legitimate case to the uncompromising liberal critics of collectivism who argued convincingly that they could not imagine a collectivism which did not also result in an illiberal state.

The designation of the currents of collectivism sketched here is only preliminary, indicating the major intellectual tendencies. More important was how these ideological formations became organized politically. All the collectivist groupings opposed the established party labels to varying degrees; all hoped to construct alliances with other collectivist groupings or cells. This rejection of Victorian liberalism was often sufficient, in its own right, to promote alliances between groupings which, according to the more familiar, standard political classifications of today, appear to have little in common. The main institutional form for social imperialism was the Tariff Reform League; but a number of Fabians (not to mention a small but important coterie of Liberals) were also deeply committed to the imperial idea, a fact which created an enormous split in their ranks. Fabians and collectivist liberals, like many social imperialists, were doctrinaire supporters of national efficiency. On many political issues Fabians and new liberals were virtually indistinguishable: both had immense influence in defining socialism, in fixing the character of labourism, and in setting the targets of what could be achieved politically by the nascent Labour Party. Collectivism thus took no clear party or doctrinal form. On the contrary, it was instrumental in dismantling established party allegiances and formations. For a considerable number of politicians in this period, party labels came to appear an insubstantial and unnecessary irrelevance. As Beatrice Webb, writing in 1893, remarked: 'Collectivism will spread, but it will spread from no one centre.'[8]

Peculiarities of the British Case

'The crisis' and 'the transition' were *constituted* by political forces, and their outcomes were determined in the first instance by political struggle. Explanation needs to concentrate on the peculiarities of each particular social formation, and on the national features of a political culture. A number of such concepts from recent theories of the state have shaped and informed our empirical investigations in this respect. One such concept is the notion, again drawn from Gramsci, of 'passive revolution'.

In his fragmentary notes on 'Americanism and Fordism' Gramsci considered the problem of identifying 'the links in the chain marking the passage from the old economic individualism to the planned economy'. Two aspects of this question particularly concerned him. The first was whether the model of the United States as the most advanced capitalist society could be followed by the nations of Western Europe, and what cultural and political conditions would be necessary for this to occur. Second, if this were possible, what kind of social transformation would it involve? Gramsci proposed two alternatives to this question. On the one hand he saw the possibilities for 'a gradual evolution of the same type as the "passive revolution"'[8]; on the other, he foresaw a more cataclysmic transformation which he described as 'the molecular accumulation of elements destined to produce an "explosion", that is, an upheaval on the French pattern' – this last reference alluding to the revolutionary traditions of French political cultures.[9] These notes comprise little more than perceptive musings. But Gramsci's object of analysis is very close to our own. This accounts, in part, for our persistent return to his inquiries. His ideas on the relationship between a passive revolution and the formation of monopoly capitalism are especially fruitful in understanding developments in British society during this period.

By passive revolution Gramsci referred to historical occasions in which a 'revolution' was installed from above, in order to forestall a threat from below, but in which the popular masses did not take or win the political initiative. He thought of such transformations as marking both an important reordering of state and civil society and as a restoration of the fundamental social relations of production on a more stable basis for the future.

The defining feature of a passive transformation of this type is the success of the dominant groups in maximizing the exclusion of the masses from determining political affairs and the reconstruction of the state. Such a strategy constrains the scope and extent of the recomposition of the state, favouring overall those elements which contribute to restoration and continuity. This suggests methodologically the need to examine not only the measure of popular activity, but also the strategic position of mass movements in their relation to the state in this period.

In Britain the political strategies which predominated after the First World War formed a distinctive passive transformation. There were, however, organizations and parties which attempted to transcend these limits, drawing upon a radical popular movement in order to break the hold of the existing state. These political movements were of both the left and the right. The majority of socialist organizations, determined to overturn the state by pressure from below and create a more just and democratic alternative, imagined not a passive but an active remaking of society. But the populist organizations of the radical right – most notably the various currents inside the Tariff Reform League – also had as their objectives the construction of an alternative regime, albeit an authoritarian and imperial one. The ideal of the radical right was a state which would maximize, not the exclusion, but the incorporation of populist organizations into the composition of the state apparatuses. A clearer example of this harnessing of the masses in the reconstruction of the state during the formative moments of monopoly capitalism, in an explosive manner, were the mass fascist movements in Italy and Germany, in which the relation between popular organizations and the state was intensified and maximized to an unprecedented degree.

In Britain these radical movements were either defeated or marginalized. The mass movements of the time exerted pressure on the state, from a position outside the state. Characteristically, this resulted in the internal reconstitution of state institutions. To those on the radical right this often appeared no more than an appalling compromise failing to face the drastic consequences of the new global balance of forces and of the need for a complete overhaul of the machinery of the British state. Yet the compromises compounded the passive character of the transformation. From the predominance of these compromises derives the significance in the British state of the reforming state bureaucrats, the new breed of state intellectuals informed by the Fabian or new liberal ideals. Internal administrative reform became a key mechanism for transforming the state with the minimum upheaval and catastrophe. Challenges for reform from below were first defined in public discourse by new liberal or Fabian social theorists, taken up by progressive state administrators, reconstituted in a bureaucratic mould, installed as state policy and at that point presented back to the people. This was a process which lay at the very core of an administrative type of passive reform and led to the consolidation of statism. As a personification of this process the conservative administrative radical, Beveridge, stands out.

This suggests that the ideologies of new liberalism and Fabianism were in fact theorizations of passive transformation. The new liberal idea of citizenship, although never simply legalistic, was limited to the extent that it positioned political subjects either as public servants or as rational and discriminating participants in the electoral process. Any greater sense of collective political action, based on a more popular sense of social needs, or of a politics capable of transcending the limits of the lecture-room and the *Manchester Guardian,* appeared not only remote and a touch irrational, but also threatening. An even greater testimony to the depth and penetration of this passive transformation was the fact that this commitment to constitutionalism also came ultimately to define the objective and political practice of the Labour Party. It was on this ground, in the 1920s, that the renowned 'historic compromise' was elaborated between the major social classes. Within the limits of the deals concluded, the typical contours of British social democracy emerged. Of the many 'socialisms' which made themselves available in this period, it was this variant, with its commitments to statism and social engineering, which prevailed – not least because of the critical role played by the state itself in containing the more 'extreme' elements in the Labour formation, while educating the more accommodative elements into a safe place within the pale of the constitution.

The significance of new liberalism in these developments, as a political-intellectual formation, must lead us to qualify substantially the Dangerfield thesis. Classic mid-century liberalism was deconstructed. But liberalism did not 'die' in the years between 1910 and 1914. On the contrary, under the impact of the struggles which Dangerfield described there occurred the redeployment of liberal philosophy. An extensive labour of philosophical renovation was achieved to adapt it to a new democratic age. Yet many elements of the new ideology were recognizably those of classical liberalism, with constitutionalism and individual rights a prominent feature, transformed into the syntax of social democracy. It was the language of new liberalism which then effectively defined the collectivist, social-democratic project in Britain for the next four or five decades. The 'peculiarity' of the British case rests on these facts: on the passive transformation of liberalism and on the consequent elements of continuity and displacement. The fact that the dominant conception of collectivism remained within the discursive traditions of liberalism and constitutionalism should not conceal the profound crisis of Victorian liberalism and, in practice, the interruptions and breaks in social and political developments which followed in its wake. The transition to a collectivist regime was partial and uneven. But it remained (for the most part) within the constitutional boundaries. It is this underlying persistence which provides the staple argument for those dedicated to proclaiming the historic continuity of British political life. But this perception fails to see that what survived did so only at the cost of a sometimes frenzied reconstruction of constitutional liberalism and only through its displacement into a new and specific formation in the 1920s. Liberalism, as a system, was dismantled.

The Making of Contemporary Politics

The first steps in the creation of a mass democratic culture were made in the 1880s (the 1884 Reform Act, the 1885 Redistribution Act, the 1888 Local Government Act). They were followed in the next decades by the development of commensurate civic institutions (the provincial univer-

sities for example). This movement was cautious and protracted. Resistance to democratic progress – above all to the enfranchisement of
women – remained bitterly fierce. Nevertheless these early political
concessions, organized in the first moments of the crisis of liberalism,
formed the preconditions for the emergence of mass democracy before
the onset of the succession of crises which marked political developments until the mid-1920s. Undoubtedly the successive stages of incorporation within the democratic framework, however long resisted,
afforded the political system an increased flexibility and manoeuvr-
ability. It undermined the traditions of patronage and thereby broad-
ened, if only within very definite limits, the power centres of the state.
The breakup of the old alliances and the construction of a new political
system facilitated the movement towards a new type of democratic
political order. The long, defensive period of coalition governments
from 1915 to 1922 (including the exceptional circumstances of the war,
during which many of the new modes of state-collectivist regulation
were first pioneered) played a key role. It was in that period that the old
party formations finally dissolved and regrouped; the syndicalist
challenge was confronted and repelled; labour, its internationalism
broken by the war, was constitutionalized into the alternative party of
government; state intervention in the economy hastened the transition
to monopoly forms in some sectors; and the system of industrial conciliation, with the state as 'neutral' mediator between capital and labour,
was fully institutionalized. In the end the Conservatives could not live
with the vagaries of the architect of this transformation – Lloyd George.
But by the time they sent him and the coalition packing, their historic
mission had been achieved.

The major breakthrough in winning a system of universal suffrage
also came about in this moment, as a direct result of the war. The
Representation of the People Act of 1918 enfranchised all male adults
of twenty-one and over and all women aged thirty and over. Issues
which had caused the deepest passion before 1914 were quietly if reluct-
antly conceded by diehards in the course of the war. The Representation
of the People Act instituted the universalist state, formally representative of the totality of interests which composed the nation. It was within
this framework that its complement, 'universal' social provision, began
slowly to develop, if only as a formal commitment of state policy. With
universalism too came the triumph of the electoralist version of democracy: the individual voting subject became the lynchpin within all
official state discourses. In turn the act shaped the conditions which
made possible the strategic reassertion of the absolute centrality of parliament and constitutional politics. It provided the resources for the
emergence of a new political language based not on interest but on the

more expansive category of 'citizenship'. The precise forms of this language remained indeterminate and open until the period of the most intense industrial and class confrontations in 1925–6. In those years the democratic advances embodied in the act were finally absorbed into Baldwinite Conservatism and any hopes for a more assertive, radical and popular conception of democracy – either representative or direct – disappeared. Democracy was contained within the confines of electoralism and a very specific variant of national constitutionalism. The containment of labour and of other democratic forces also had international conditions of existence – the postwar proletarian upsurge and its large-scale defeats in Europe. In this context Britain continued in its role as European and global gendarme, a policy pursued with vigour and almost without interruption by Conservative and coalition leaders, from military intervention against the nascent Soviet Union to the appalling débâcle of Munich. In the turbulent years of insurgent socialist and anarchist movements in Europe from 1917 to 1923 the British formation could still be counted as the strongest link in the European chain, the one least vulnerable to the socialist offensive.

This constitutionalist framework remained intact for the next four or five decades, 'a continuum almost without precedence in post-Reformation history'.[10] The dominant features of the new organization of the state can be briefly summarized, indicating at the same time the discontinuity between the settlement of the 1920s and classic Victorian liberalism. First there was the universalist ordering of the institutions of political life, in terms both of legal and social rights, the latter giving rise to early welfare policies. It is this 'universalism' which underpinned Gramsci's understanding of the transformed conditions for the winning of hegemony 'in the period after 1870' and the new position of the masses in relation to the state.

Second, the Labour Party achieved the position of the political representative of the working class and, as 1924 showed, legitimately earned its constitutional credentials as the very junior partner in the new historic settlement. Alongside this there developed the constellation of corporatist institutions in which representatives of the collective interests of capital and labour were directly placed within the sphere of the state. To quote the major theorist of this process, 'what had been merely interest groups crossed the political threshold and became part of the extended state'.[11]

Third, the hesitant process of reforming the *imperial* state was initiated. The partition of Ireland in 1921 destroyed the unity of the old imperial regime. As a response to the sometimes insurgent movements for colonial liberation the majority of British politicians gradually came to the conclusion that, in order to save the empire as best they could, they had no option but to begin to constitutionalize the directive role of the imperial government. The first formal declaration of this recognition can be dated from the Montagu–Chelmsford reforms of 1919, anticipating a future of 'responsible government' for India, although it was not until the 1930s that the role of the imperial government itself was the object of legislation and not until the postwar period that decolonization as such was set in motion.

This political settlement represented an unequivocal victory for the forces of constitutionalism but a much more ambivalent outcome for democracy. Nevertheless, the significance of the defeat of the radical right as an organized movement must be stressed. The radical right cannot be consigned to the occasional footnote as simply an immoderate outburst of diehard spleen with no lasting significance. Its presence was a dominant component of the period and its logic, if unchecked, led directly to the possibility of an authentic proto-fascism. The marching and the counter-marching of the pro-consuls and other would-be 'Napoleons' waiting to be summoned to their destinies, the cynical manoeuvrings for power in the corridors of government, the sudden reappearances in Ulster of these figures at the head of an Orange troop, the repeated calls for a solution to be imposed from above, the very language of authoritarianism, were ingrained elements in the disintegrating political culture of those years. Despite widespread illusions to the contrary, the progression of English constitutionalism was not underwritten by some providential historical law. If the radical right had gained ascendancy there would have occurred not the redeployment but the destruction of liberalism. Even so, its characteristic ideologies have never disappeared as active dimensions of the political culture of Conservatism and have continued to shape its very project to this day.

The failure of the radical right and the fall of Lloyd George nevertheless ensured that by the 1920s the dominant political forces crystallized within a constitutionalized Conservatism, accommodated to the imperatives of mass democracy and universal suffrage. The only *legitimate* alternatives were the more actively assertive collectivisms of new liberalism and Fabianism, which transmuted into the 'middle opinion' of the 1930s and later into social democracy in the political debates of the 1940s; and an evolutionary socialist statism, whose organizational basis was the TUC and the Labour Party. This is how the configurations of a specifically contemporary set of political and ideological dispositions finally emerged from the crisis.

These were the currents in which a peculiarly British collectivism was articulated. Liberal opposition to collectivism, however, did not collapse. *Neo*-liberalism, the term which designates the continuing persistence within these other formations of the individualist critique of collectivism, had a submerged but critical presence in the political field. Neo-liberalism (not to be confused with new liberalism) was coextensive with the formation of collectivist ideologies, and its history also begins in the 1880s. Even in the moment of its formation it was not simply an ideology whose adherents advocated a return to classical liberalism; with the eventual dominance of collectivist forces it became progressively less so. On the contrary the project of neo-liberalism was systematically to contest and where possible to uproot the political conditions in which collectivism flourished. This called for a strong state (little resembling the Gladstonian model) and a particular kind of interventionism which could enforce free-market relations. State regulation of the market was defined as no more and no less than socialism and thus inimical in itself. The neo-liberal analysis was sound only in so far as commitment to state-organized welfare did impose great fiscal burdens on the state, leading to that 'overload' which neo-liberals of our own day are so keen to reverse. It was partial, however, to the extent that advanced capitalism could scarcely have continued without the existence of such state welfare programmes to compensate for the damaging social effects of the market. Neo-liberalism was nevertheless forced to adopt an increasingly radical posture at each moment of the consolidation of collectivism, as the limited forms of intervention and welfarism became established within all the major parties contending for government. As its objectives became increasingly defined not by particular pieces of legislation but by the very foundations of a regime which it hoped at some point to destroy, so its rhetoric became more strident. This too registers a strand in the dispersal of liberalism.

Resolutions and Contradictions

In rudimentary form two-party constitutionalism based on universalism, an institutional framework for corporatist bargaining and a system of state welfare were all in place by the mid-1920s. Each had a fragile existence, at times seeming to disappear altogether; for the most part, each was justified pragmatically rather than on grounds of principle. Only under the impact of the radical populism generated by the Second World War did these elements fuse into a developed political system capable of winning a broad degree of popular consent for a programme which temporarily deepened in democratic content. This was symbolized by the invocation of the date 1945.

The major elements which came together in 1945 were – we would argue – first formed in the conjuncture of events of the 1880s–1920s. This longer history is necessary in order to dispel the myths surrounding current interpretations and to contextualize and explain the profound ambiguities in the social-democratic experiment of the 1940s and 1950s. The ideologies of collectivism and citizenship which were predominant in the 1940s still carried in them all the contradictory features which had characterized the collectivist aspirations of the 1880s. Most of all, the persistently statist inflexion of these ideologies and practices on the one hand indelibly stamped the forms of social democracy, and on the other, sustained neo-liberal antagonism. After a period in which neo-liberals appeared to be all but politically extinct, they began to coalesce once more into an organic political tendency. They ultimately forced a breach in the collectivist defences, and won back the political ground they had lost for so long. Thus the solutions to the crisis of liberalism at the end of the nineteenth century restored a degree of political stability to the British social formation for a number of decades. But they also created the conditions for their own ultimate destruction.

In other respects too it seems as if the crisis of the late nineteenth century has been more protracted and continuous. In the 1880s British capitalism entered a period of secular decline from which in any fundamental sense it has never recovered. After the First World War Britain became for the first time a debtor nation, subordinate in global terms to the USA. Owing to its concentration in the financial markets of the world, its continued commitment to its traditional imperial role, and the adaptation of the dominant institutions of capital to the defence of sterling as an international currency, the British economy became peculiarly vulnerable to the exigencies of the world market. Even during the height of the consumer boom and 'consensus' politics of the 1950s this long-term economic decline was not structurally reversed.

Over the past century a constitutive dimension of British politics has been the return to the centre of the political stage of this antagonism between collectivists and their opponents. In a broad sense the dominance of the collectivist forces by the 1920s created the conditions for the consolidation of monopoly capitalism, the settlement of the new social order and the emergence of the 'consensus' politics of social democracy. The forms in which the crisis was resolved or contained are the forces which constituted the structures of modern British politics today. The neo-liberal resurgence today is testimony to the unfinished trajectory of the crisis of that earlier period. Social democracy was formed out of the crisis of liberalism between the 1880s and the 1920s. We are now living through its successor – the crisis of social democracy.

1985

Notes

1. George Dangerfield, *The Strange Death of Liberal England*, London 1984; and see E. Halévy, *Imperialism and the Rise of Labour* and *The Rule of Democracy*, London 1961.

2. It is worth recalling that in his characterization of the 'culture and society' tradition Raymond Williams marked the period between Morris and Lawrence as an 'interregnum': *Culture and Society, 1780–1950*, London 1971; and see too on this, Terry Eagleton, *Exiles and Emigrés*, London 1970.

3. A. Gramsci, *The Prison Notebooks*, London 1971, p. 243.

4. See especially C.B. Macpherson, *The Life and Times of Liberal Democracy*, Oxford 1977.

5. Gramsci, p. 210.

6. Jeffrey Weeks, *Sex, Politics and Society. The regulation of sexuality since 1800*, London 1981, p. 87.

7. For some interesting reflections, see Claus Offe, *Contradictions of the Welfare State*, London 1984.

8. Quoted in W.H. Greenleaf, *The British Political Tradition*, London 1983, 1, p. 43.

9. Gramsci, pp. 279–80. In a different language, this 'molecular accumulation of elements destined to produce an "explosion"' would be a crisis which was 'overdetermined'. The argument here is that the British crisis at the turn of the century was not one which was overdetermined in this way.

10. Keith Middlemas, *Politics in Industrial Society*, London 1979, p. 15.

11. Ibid., p. 373.

8

Popular-Democratic vs Authoritarian Populism: Two Ways of 'Taking Democracy Seriously'

I

The question of democracy ceases to be the subject of abstract speculation, and becomes concrete and politically compelling in the context of
the 'crisis of the British state' which now confronts us. Crisis has
appeared to be the very condition of existence of the social formation
for two decades – some would argue, for nearly a century. But few
would deny that, since the political débâcles of 1972 and 1974, and the
economic recession after 1975–6, the crisis has reached a qualitatively
new stage.[1] The Heath interregnum was a bold, contradictory bid to
'renovate', employing the twin instruments of the economic free-for-all
and legal compulsion. It ended in ruins, brought to a conclusion by its
internally contradictory twists and by a widening but defensive class
militancy. The Callaghan episode – a squalid and disorganizing interlude
– restored the now clasical repertoire of the social-democratic management of capitalist crisis, but on a markedly weakening political base. As
that social-democratic repertoire was progressively eroded and
exhausted, the fissures in British society became everywhere more manifest. The synchronization of the long-term crisis of the British economy
with a worldwide capitalist recession put paid to any prospects (and
there were few, even had conditions been more propitious) of the
'regeneration' of economic conditions. In this period, the economic
recession began really to bite in one sector after another of social life.
The sharp round of wage militancy in the opening months of 1979 was a

symptom of stalemate: a strategy of conservative containment confronted by a militant defence of declining living standards; the one unable to constitute the social and political conditions for recovery; the other able only to inflict instant damage in a losing battle against the erosion of real wages by inflationary pressures.

More pertinent to our concerns have been the political and ideo-logical conditions of 'crisis' which this interlude has revealed. The period has witnessed the de facto erosion of the two-party dominance of the parliamentary scene, and the opportunist construction of temporary parliamentary coalitions, alliances and pacts for the most short-term and pragmatic ends – that patching-up of cliques and cabals, that wheeling and dealing in the lobbies, which is a sign of the undermining of the repre-sentative parliamentary democratic system, and characteristic of the slow drift towards a 'government of national interest'.[2] There have also been the muffled but unmistakable signs of a fragmentation of the national state itself, in the movement towards devolution and regionaliz-ation; the first really significant shift of that kind since (excepting Ireland) the Act of Union.

The rotation of parliamentary fractions may not in itself be of struc-tural significance: but it provides symptomatic evidence of a general crisis of political representation. There have been important secular shifts and drifts in the relation between the classes and their traditional means of political representation: that process by which 'the great masses ... become detached from their traditional ideologies, and no longer believe what they used to believe' which, as Gramsci argued, 'consists precisely in the fact that the old is dying and the new cannot be born'.[3] Coupled with the new forces of the 'radical' right, and the frag-mentation of the traditional political ideologies of the social-democratic left, they point, if not to that 'force of non-party men linked to the government by paternalist ties of a Bonapartist–Caesarist type', then at least to a moment of what Gramsci called profound *transformism*, not unjustly referred to as creating the conditions for a 'parliamentary dictatorship'.[4] In this setting, the question of democracy becomes a principal site and stake in the struggle – the very object of the strategies of transformism, from right and left alike. Across this terrain, in the coming period, some of the most decisive engagements in the 'war of position' are destined to be joined.

Everything thus depends on how, in relation to the issue of demo-cracy, the present crisis is understood. It has gradually dawned on the left, face to face with the crisis, that – whatever the classical texts and revolutionary cookbooks prescribe – the possibility that the crisis may now be seized, and shaped so as to create favourable conditions for an advance towards socialism, is inextricably linked with the deepening of democratic life, and the widening of popular-democratic struggle. In that way alone lies the possibility of dividing society along the line of the exploited and the exploiters, which, in turn, alone might provide the conditions for a more sustained socialist advance. This is the only strategy – leaving theory alone for a moment – relevant to that 'Caesarist' moment, when 'the "lower classes" do not want the old and when the "upper classes" cannot continue in the old way'. About such an unstable equilibrium of forces, Lenin pertinently observed: 'This truth may be expressed in other words: revolution is impossible without a national crisis affecting both the exploited and the exploiters.'[5] Gramsci reminds us that 'A Caesarist solution can exist even without a Caesar.... The parliamentary system has also provided a mechanism for such compromise solutions. The "Labour" governments of MacDonald were to a certain degree solutions of this kind.'[6] This kind of alternative could be an extended process, in which 'various gradations of Caesarism succeeded one another, culminating in a more pure and permanent form.... Every coalition government is a first stage of Caesarism.' The 'morbid symptoms' which appear in such an interregnum are certainly no longer merely the figments of the fevered imaginations of the ideologues of the far right. The questions for the left here are of both the 'what' and the 'how' variety: in what forms can a popular democracy towards the left (one contrasted with a populist democracy, powerfully inflected towards the right) be advanced? How can an articulation to the right be checked? And (given its strategic weakness, in the face of this qualitatively new historical task) by what means?

This question has attained a new urgency because, perhaps for the first time in the postwar political history of the British state, the right is also convinced that it/we 'cannot continue in the old way'. This constitutes a quite different, qualitatively new, phase of the conjuncture. For now it is no longer a question of popular-democratic struggle from the left confronting social and political forces committed to the 'defence of the old'. The crisis has taken both right and left past its 'passive' point – that point where the political task for the ruling classes is merely to conserve the integrity of the state in conditions of economic recession.

The right has thoroughly renovated and 'reformed' itself.[7] It constitutes a political–ideological force of an altogether new kind. And, despite the gestures which the leadership occasionally makes to tradition, it must now be understood as an active political force, actively committed to the philosophy that, in order to conserve, it must reform, in order to preserve, it must revolutionize. It regards the current crisis as providing, not a passive status quo to be defended, but a strategic political field of force to be reconstructed: reconstructed, of course, to the right. What is more – like the left – it too regards 'democracy', in its populist aspect, as the site to be occupied, the stake to be seized. Mr Callaghan was quite correct – even though he did not understand the significance of what he was saying – what he described the trajectory of 'Thatcherism' as a force determined to 'tear the fabric of British society up by the roots'. In this sense, the disposition of political forces on the terrain of the state has been already significantly realigned. It is social democracy which seeks to conserve the state (as well as the 'state of play') and a failing monopoly capitalism. It aims to continue to preside, by pragmatic political engineering, over the political and economic crisis conceived as a permanent passive condition. It is the right – the 'radical' right – which knows that 'things cannot go on in the old way'. The latter has fashioned itself, even on the margins of actual governmental power, into an instrument capable of constructing a new equilibrium, preserving the system only at the cost of radically transforming it. What is more, the right knows that, in this process of restoration/revolution, the winning card is the democratic populist one. It aims to 'win the people' (and thus to conserve the representative form of the parliamentary democratic state) for policies and philosophies designed to transform the democratic content of the state in its actual mode of operation. It therefore inter-sects with the forces of the left exactly in the strategic field of 'popular-democratic struggle'.

It should be added that this is not exclusively a terrain of advantage created by the right, though it is the one on which it has operated most effectively in recent months. It is partly a legacy of the period of failing social democracy itself.[8] In its febrile efforts to master the economic and political struggle to the advantage of state-oriented big capital, social democracy has undertaken its own type of restructuring. This has itself entailed a far-reaching erosion of the democratic elements in political and social life. Social democracy has progressively assumed those postures of pragmatic and creeping authoritarianism, which had, as one of their effects, a gradual suspension of many of the traditional bases of democratic representation and countervailing power; but coupled with their formal preservation, as the means by which a passive popular consent is secured. This double movement – creeping authoritarianism masked by the rituals of formal representation – is what gives a peculiar historical specificity to the present phase of the crisis of the state/crisis of hegemony.[9] Poulantzas described this 'new form of state' as tending towards an 'authoritarian statism': 'namely, intensification of state control over every sphere of economic life combined with radical decline of the institutions of political democracy and with draconian and multi-form curtailment of so-called "formal" liberties whose reality is being discovered [presumably, he means, by the left] now that they are going overboard.'[10]

This is an all too recognizable scenario. What it omits is the steady and unremitting set of operations designed to bind or construct a popular consent to these new forms of statist authoritarianism. It is this element – which introduces into the equation the pivotal issue of 'popular consent to these new forms of statist authoritarianism. It is this present process as a movement towards 'authoritarian populism'.[11] The rest of this essay is concerned with analysing this phenomenon.

II

Scenarios of 'crisis' have an honoured place in the Marxist tradition but thinking them strategically, conjuncturally and politically, has not been a notable area of success. The most extensive work deals with economic conditions and tendencies, theorized across social formations at a very high level of abstraction. Even this work, with the fatalist twist it has so often been given, is now, rightly, regarded as contentious and problematic. In any case, a shift of theoretical perspective is required as soon as one moves from deductions based on an abstracted 'tendency of the rate of profit to fall', etc., to the complex, historically-specific terrain of a crisis which affects – but in uneven ways – a specific national-social formation as a whole.

Certain negative protocols can be established quite quickly. The economic aspects may provide a necessary level of determination, but they cannot provide the sufficient conditions for determining either the political/ideological forms which the crisis may assume, or the effects of these levels on one another – least of all, the character or overall tendency of their resolution.[12]

> It may be ruled out that immediate economic crises of themselves produce fundamental historical events; they can simply create a terrain more favourable to the dissemination of certain modes of thought, and certain ways of posing and resolving the entire subsequent development of national life.... The specific question of economic hardship or well-being as a cause of new historical realities is a partial aspect of the question of the relations of force, at the various levels.[13]

Gramsci here decisively repudiates that 'economism' which continues to shadow most materialist analyses of 'crisis', and defines the only tenable sense in which 'the economic' can be said to 'determine'. It sets fundamental economic 'tasks' historically – it cannot prescribe how those are resolved, or even whether they will be resolved. It is not a guarantee of the long-wished-for 'Winter Palace' showdown. This is because there are many more types of 'resolution' than the stark alternative between the collapse of the walls of Jericho and 'going on in the old way'. But it is also because the possible forms of resolution of a crisis fundamentally depend on the 'relations of force' – that is, they are subject to 'the limit of the class struggle *at the various levels'.*

In his sketch for an analysis of this aspect of the crisis, Gramsci insists on two fundamental points. First, that 'if the forces which are active in the history of a particular period are to be correctly analysed' then 'it is the problem of the relations between structure and superstructure which must be accurately posed and resolved ... and the relation between them determined'. Second, that the 'relations of force' are no simple backstop or final court of appeal. They have to be distinguished into their 'various moments or levels' (e.g. Gramsci's 'three moments').[14] There is no guaranteed order of progression between them. Moreover, they have to be thought in their relation to each other, and in their historical specificity. They 'imply each other reciprocally – horizontally and vertically, so to speak – i.e. according to the socioeconomic activity (horizontally) and to country (vertically) combining and diverging in various ways. Each of these combinations may be represented by its own organized economic and political expression'.[15]

There are a set of definite analytic protocols sketched here. Crises are 'over-determined in principle'.[16] They cannot be 'read off' from the economic. They are subject to a variety of possible forms of resolution, depending on how the relations of force develop and combine, in particular national societies, under specific conditions. But there is no fixed 'scheme' to be, as they say, applied. Lenin, speaking of 1917, insisted that its pace and trajectory was 'only due to the fact that, as a result of an extremely unique historical situation, absolutely dissimilar currents, absolutely heterogeneous class interests, absolutely contrary political and social strivings have merged in a strikingly "harmonious" manner ...'[17]

This approach underpinned Althusser's seminal – indeed, his most distinctive – theoretical contribution (the 'Contradiction and Overdetermination' essay in *For Marx*). This essay represents a theoretical threshold of the first order, deeply Gramscian and Leninist, in the best sense, in its conceptualization, which we cannot afford, now, to fall behind.

> If the general contradiction ... is sufficient to define the situation when revolution is the 'task of the day', it cannot of its own simple, direct power induce a 'revolutionary situation', nor a fortiori a situation of revolutionary rupture and the triumph of the revolution. If this contradiction is to become 'active' in the strong sense, to become a ruptural principle there must be an accumulation of 'circumstances' and 'currents' so that whatever their origin and sense ... they 'fuse' into a ruptural unity.'[18]

Lenin elsewhere remarked that 'History generally, and the history of revolutions in particular, is always richer in content, more varied, more many-sided, more lively and "subtle" than the best parties and the most class conscious vanguards of the most advanced class imagine'.[19] We must, he said, take into account 'the concrete peculiar features which this struggle assumes and inevitably must assume in each separate country in accordance with the pecular features of its economy, politics, culture, national composition (Ireland, etc.), its colonies, religious divisions, etc.' The task is 'To investigate, study, seek out, divine, grasp that which is specifically national in the concrete manner in which each country approaches the fulfilment of the single international task....'[20] What is true of revolutionary situations applies, *a fortiori*, for crises of a deep but 'peculiar' kind, where the little matter of the 'revolutionary guarantee' is a worryingly low item on the historical agenda.

We should beware of another tempting deviation. That is the tendency to deduce both the form and the outcome of a 'national crisis' from some general theory of the capitalist state, and its inherent general tendencies – of which the 'concrete peculiar features' are mere, marginal (i.e. ineffective) expressions. There is no 'general theory' of the capitalist state, specifiable outside its specific national and historical conditions of existence, from which a national crisis can be deduced or predicted. Of course, a general understanding of the differences, say, between the 'laissez faire' and the 'interventionist' type of state tells us something of importance: it would be purist to deny this. It tells us something because of its effects. But much depends on how we understand these 'effects'. These differences matter because they affect the role and position of the state. This in turn will have effects on how the political forces are organized and represented, on how the terrain of struggle is constituted, and where the strategic points of application are likely to arise. For example, the augmented role of the state in relation to economic strategies, in an 'interventionist' phase, must have effects for how the relations of force at the economic level are constituted, and for how the state intervenes in the economic class struggle. It tells us where to look for the pertinent sites in the terrain of struggle. But it cannot tell us what we are to find there. The key questions about the crisis of the British state and social formation in the 1970s are not deducible from some general theory: either of the interventionist state as the best 'shell for capital';[21] or (worse) from some a priori knowledge of its functional necessity. These general expectations are overridden – qualitatively transformed – as soon as we supply those further historical determinations which alone permit us to grasp the concrete conjuncture of historically specific societies at specific moments.

Thus the crisis is not usefully understood as the 'typical' crisis of the 'state of monopoly capital', deduced as to its British particulars. This type of state in Britain has a very specific national history. It was constituted through a set of particular histories. Especially in the transitional period between the 1880s and the 1920s, the 'representative' and the 'interventionist' aspects of the state were combined in distinctively new ways.[22] It has a long lineage, which has already included a whole series of 'crises' and partial 'recoveries', radically national in form. If the reconstruction of the 'peculiarity' of this historical route is now an urgent political and theoretical task, it will not be usefully conducted from a priori or transhistorical assumptions.[23] At best we can say that the present crisis is another 'exceptional moment' in the representative/ interventionist state; but it appears subject to those conditions of peculiarity which alone provide us with an accurate understanding of the British situation as the object of theoretical speculation and of political transformation. If we must give a date, we would offer the provisional periodization, 'early 1960s to the present'. If this seems a rather long time for a 'conjuncture', it is worth recalling that a conjuncture is not a slice of time, but can only be defined by the accumulation/condensation of contradictions, the fusion or merger – to use Lenin's terms – of 'different currents and circumstances'. It is a 'moment', not a 'period' – 'over-determined in its principle'.

III

Gramsci observed that there can be many 'current situations' within a strategic conjuncture: each marking a shift or a new stage in the relations of force: each 'represented by its own economic and political expression'. We seem to have arrived at precisely such a passage from one stage to another. More significantly, he observed that:

> A crisis occurs, sometimes lasting for decades. This exceptional duration means that incurable structural contradictions have revealed themselves ... and that, despite this, the political forces which are struggling to conserve and defend the existing structure itself are making every effort to cure them, within certain limits and to overcome them.[24]

The crucial point here is that it is not simply the given, passive conditions of crisis which the left has immediately to deal with, but the 'efforts' which different social and political and ideological forces are making to overcome the crisis, 'within certain limits'. Indeed, he goes on,

These incessant and persistent efforts ... form the terrain of the 'conjunct-ural', and it is upon this terrain that the forces of opposition organize. These forces seek to demonstrate that the necessary and sufficient conditions exist to make possible, and hence imperative, the accomplishment of certain historical tasks. ... The demonstration in the last analysis only succeeds and is 'true' if it becomes a new reality, if the forces of opposition triumph; in the immediate, it is developed in a series of ideological, religious, philosophical, political and juridical polemics, whose concreteness can be estimated to the extent to which they are convincing, and shift the existing disposition of social forces.[25]

Our argument turns on these two passages, from which a number of critical points follow:

1. Gramsci gives the widest scope and reference to the forces which form the basis of a 'conjunctural' terrain of struggle, and to the series of 'polemics', the 'incessant and persistent efforts', undertaken to shift the balance of forces in one direction or another. This could not be further from any residual 'economism'. It must be related to Gramsci's arguments that this is a type of struggle characterized as a 'war of posi-tion'. It takes place where the whole relation of the state to civil society, to 'the people' and to popular struggles, to the individual and to the economic life of society has been thoroughly reorganized, where 'all the elements change'. Such a transformation of the terrain of struggle depends on the following elements: (a) the 'internal and international organizational relations of the state become more complex and massive'; (b) the Forty-Eightist formula of 'permanent revolution' is expanded and transcended by the formula of 'civil hegemony'; (c) 'the massive structures of the modern democracies, both as state organizations and as complexes of associations in civil society, constitute for the art of politics as it were, the "trenches" and permanent fortifications of the front in the war of position'.[26]

2. It is critical to get the relationship between the 'organic' and the 'conjunctural' features right. Failure to do so leads 'to presenting [struc-tural, organic] causes as immediately operative ... or to asserting that the immediate causes are the only effective ones'[27] – in short, to that fatal oscillation, so characteristic of many positions of the left today – between 'economism' and 'ideologism'; the graveyard of many a sophis-ticated 'materialist' analysis, which veers between tactical opportunism and waiting for the 'last instance' to appear.

3. The nature of a 'success' in a war of position has to be thoroughly reworked. Victory does not consist of the appearance, newly minted, of some total 'world view', or some wholly evolved alternative 'social order', which has been slowly maturing, like a good cheese, in the vaults of the left, to be brought out at the right moment and propelled on to the field of struggle. It can only be understood as working on the

already-given disposition of social forces, through a wide series of 'polemics'.[28] The aim is to shift the balance of the relations of force into a new disposition; and thereby to begin to constitute a new result: Gramsci's 'new reality'. These 'polemics' must take the given situation, the present disposition of social forces, as their starting-point, the strategic field of their operations: 'an ever-changing terrain for the intervention of the working class'.[29]

4. However, what Gramsci here says, optimistically, of the 'forces of opposition' must also be applied to those social forces which are contending for the mastery of the current situation, but whose 'persistent and incessant efforts' are guided by the philosophy that, in order to conserve, they must reform. Gramsci elsewhere elaborates this idea through four related concepts. The first is that of the dialectical relation, in any real historical process, between 'revolution/restoration'. 'The problem,' he observes, 'is to see whether in the dialectic "revolution/ restoration" it is revolution or restoration which predominates; for it is certain that in the movement of history there is never any turning back, and that restorations in toto do not exist.'[30] The fixed logic of the left, so often tied to the scenario of confrontation/defeat/triumphal victory, is, he adds, 'useful for destruction but not for reconstruction already under way in the very moment of destruction. Destruction is conceived of mechanically, not as destruction/reconstruction'. In fact, as we know, every fundamental period of 'crisis' is also a period of 'restructuring'. The question is not why and how things stand still, but what are the prevailing tendencies of the forms of reform/resolution which are beginning to win support. 'Knowing how to find each time the point of progressive equilibrium (in the sense of one's own programme) is the art of the politician ... really of the politician who has a very precise line with a wide perspective of the future.'[31]

The second related concept is that of 'passive revolution'. This is not Gramsci's proposed programme for the left, but a 'criterion of interpretation' for deciphering the lines of direction and tendency in those epochs 'characterized by complex historical upheavals'. Simply put, the 'passive revolution' designates all those strategies designed to 'put through reforms in order to prevent revolution'. This casts an intense light on the political tendencies of both social democracy and the 'radical right'.

Third, there is Gramsci's attention to the process he called 'transformism'. Transformism describes 'the process whereby the so-called historic left and right parties which emerged from the Risorgimento tended to converge in terms of programme during the years which followed, until there ceased to be any substantive difference between them – especially after the "left" came to power'.[32] Molecular changes of this order 'progressively modify the pre-existing composition of forces, and hence become the matrix of new changes'.[33] This poses in a new way the manner in which the given space of power provides opportunities for intervention and recuperation by emergent political and social forces.

Fourth, there is the question of hegemony, the formation of equilibria and the process of compromises. It should by now be self-evident that, for Gramsci, the question of 'hegemony' is not a question of a permanent state of affairs, in which the action of the relations of force is suspended. It is neither a functional condition of ruling-class power, nor a matter, exclusively, of 'ideological consent' or 'cultural influence'.[34] What is in question, is the issue of the 'ethical state': the ceaseless work required to construct a social authority, throughout all the levels of social activity, such that a 'moment of economic, political, intellectual and moral unity' may be secured, sufficient to 'raise the level of the state to a more general plane'.[35] In societies of this type, this always requires the most intensive, extensive and unceasing intervention – 'persistent and incessant activities', the 'widest series of polemics', on every plane. It also requires that 'account be taken of those interests and tendencies of the groups over which hegemony is to be exercised' so that 'a certain compromise should be formed'. The formation of compromises, of moments of 'unstable equilibria', and the mobilization of political and social forces to secure and sustain them, is the material substance of political action and movement in such periods. This ought to abolish the delusion that the crisis is merely an inert reflection, in the mirror of politics, of a given set of economic conditions. The field of struggle is defined conjuncturally by all those strategies and interventions designed to 'put a new form of hegemony together'. Any countervailing strategy by the left, which has some lower, less ambitious set of objectives as its aim, is condemned to following in the wake of those which really aim to command the field. They are destined to be perpetually defending a position which is being already overrun, responding to last year's 'golden opportunities'. In the 'war of position', though the defensive–offensive tactics in relation to each position has an overall effect, it is overwhelmingly the question of strategic position and disposition – that is, the struggle for hegemony – which counts, 'in the last instance'.

IV

Against this background we can now turn to the consideration of three aspects of the crisis, not widely analysed in the annals of the left, each of which has a definite impact on the question of 'democracy'; each of which shapes the field of struggle as to limit the development of popular–democratic initiatives; each of which, however, constructs 'the people' and 'the popular' into the 'crisis of the state'. We may define these as: (1) the social-democratic 'solution'; (2) the law and 'social order'; (3) the emergence of 'authoritarian populism'.

The first deals with the effects, on the working class and on popular and democratic social forces, of the historical fact that, in the 1960s and 1970s, social democracy has been the 'natural governor' of the crisis. The second deals with the ways in which the popular classes have been constructed into a 'popular' ideological force, enlisted to the side of the defence of the 'social order', and the instrumentality of the law, as an 'educative' force, in this process. The third deals with the transformation of the field of practical and popular ideologies, so as to construct a 'popular' consent to an authoritarian regime.

1. The social-democratic solution

The heart of the question here may be summarized in two propositions. The formulation of economic policies and strategies requires a direct intervention by the state in the political class struggle. The form of state intervention has been, characteristically, of a distinctively 'social democratic' kind.

The key strategy employed has been the construction of corporatist forms of bargain and compromise, seeking to establish, within the logic and limits of capital, a 'partnership' between the representatives of capital (principally, in the form of the CBI), of labour (principally in the form of the TUC) and the state ('representative of the people'). The aim has been to incorporate these elements, through their means of representation, into the formation of strategies designed to find solutions to the crisis of capital accumulation.[36]

This process of incorporation has had a weak 'representative' and a strong 'interventionist' aspect. To have the working people 'represented' through their leaderships at the centre of policy formation has sometimes held out the hope of their imposing terms more favourable to working-class interests (as happened in the early days of the 'social contract', at the formation of the new Labour government in 1974). This has provided some justification for the ideological construction of the government as the kept mistress of 'overweening trade-union power'. But this has had little or no real effect, when the chips were down, on how economic policies were actually formulated or executed. The side which has been effectively accented has been the use of this corporatist strategy as a basis from which to discipline the class struggle.[37] The

Labour government – between 1966 and 1970, and again between 1974 and 1979 – has also played an active ideological role in constructing popular conceptions of the crisis, its causes and conditions, through a series of discourses which classically set 'the unions' against 'the nation', 'the people' against 'the classes', the 'consumer' against 'the producer', the 'sectional interests' of workers against the 'national interest' (and, a subsidiary but potent theme, 'the housewife' and 'the family' against the 'militant trade unionist' – the latter always, of course, a man).[38]

In 'corporatist' containment strategies of this kind, social democracy, organized through the trade unions and Labour Party forms of representation, exploits a classically social-democratic conception of the state as the neutral arbiter between the classes. It uses its historic position as the major form of political representation of the working classes. With the brief exception of Mr Heath's first two runaway years, it can also be said with truth – and Mrs Thatcher has not been loth to say it – that, whether 'Labour' or the 'Conservatives' have been at the helm, so far as the political management of the economic class struggle is concerned, it is 'social democracy' which has been effectively 'in command'. It is social democracy, with its Fabian and 'Webbian' traditions of equating socialism with statism,[39] which found itself in the best, most favourable position to 'win' the working classes for capitalist economic solutions. (Paradoxically, it has been the brief interludes of Conservative parliamentary rule in which a clearer, more oppositional role for 'labour' became possible.) It is also social democracy, with its commitment to particular forms of state collectivism, and its illusion that, through the mediation of 'Labour in power' it could win 'concessions' for the working class (without mobilizing the class) while representing the 'national interest' and defending the logic of capital, which has led the way in the bypassing of all the organs of popular-democratic power and struggle, including, often, that of the parliamentary institution itself, in the construction of quasi-governmental initiatives, directly linking the state apparatuses to economic strategies.

The 'corporatist' style of Labour governments is one real index of their dominant political tendency. The disorganizing effect on the political and economic struggle – the working classes and their allies reined in by the political representatives of 'labour' – has been incalculable. This is the heart of the social democratic 'passive revolution' from above: whereby 'through the legislative intervention of the state, and by means of corporatist organization – relatively far-reaching modifications are being introduced into the country's economic structure in order to accentuate the "plan of production" element; in other words, that socialization and cooperation in the sphere of production are being increased, without, however, touching (at least not going beyond the regulation and control of) individual and group appropriation of profit'.[40]

The monopoly of the state and its policies by social democracy, in alliance principally with the state-oriented fractions of 'big' capital, has opened an effective, alternative space of operations for the 'radical right'. Ditching the last vestiges of its commitment to 'centrist' forms of bargain and compromise with the overthrow of the Heath leadership, the new right has found room for manoeuvre. It has exploited the contradictions in social democracy. It has capitalized the disorganized discontents of the popular classes. It has constructed an alternative 'bloc' organized around the powerful themes of 'anti-statism', 'anti-collectivism', 'anti-creeping socialism' and 'anti-the power bloc' (i.e. social democracy in power). This has proved to be an effective and durable, indeed, a formidable political force and 'philosophy' – with, and this is the key point, the targetting of corporatism having wide popular appeal.[41]

II.   The law and 'social order': law and order

The second aspect relates to the increasing reliance on coercive authority and the repressive apparatuses of the state in disciplining the economic and the political struggle, in the context of crisis. The heart of the matter here is that, as social conflicts have sharpened, and the militant defence of living standards has intensified, so the state has come to rely increasingly on its coercive side, and on the educative and disciplining impact of the legal apparatuses.

We have in mind here the extension, over the period, of police power and surveillance of political groups and individuals; the use of police and legal apparatuses in a wide area of social conflicts; the role of the judicial forces in containing the economic and industrial class struggle; the employment of new judicial instruments – the Industrial Relations Act, legal constraints on picketing and strikes; the extension of the conspiracy charge and political trials; the abuse of habeas corpus under a loose definition of 'emergency'. Just as important have been the elaboration of legal and juridical ideas and discourses around the themes of the defence of the state, the protection of the political order from subversion, and their connection with crime as a 'symptom' of moral degeneration and the collapse of the social authority.

The role of the legal apparatuses in containing social and industrial conflict has been widely commented on by the left: but the way public and popular anxieties about 'the rising rate of crime' have been connected with the more 'political' aspects has largely escaped attention. Yet it is the latter which gives the former its 'popular' cutting-edge. There is a history here, which indeed predates the full appearance of the crisis.[42] The 'law-and-order' element made its appearance, first, in the early phases of political polarization in the mid-1960s, directed, in the first instance, towards targets of a 'non-political' kind, in the traditional sense: the student movements and counter-cultures of the mid-sixties, the so-called drift towards 'moral permissiveness', the hedonism of youth, the 'crisis' of authority and of social values. Gramsci, however, reminded us: 'That aspect of the modern crisis which is bemoaned as a "wave of materialism" is related to what is called the "crisis of authority". If the ruling class has lost its consensus, i.e. is no longer "leading" but only "dominant", exercising coercive force alone, this means precisely that the great masses have become detached from their traditional ideologies.' He added that this idea needed to be completed by some observations on 'the so-called "problem of the younger generation" – a problem caused by the "crisis of authority" of the old generations in power'.[43] What was at issue was, in effect, the fracturing and disruption of 'traditionalist' popular ideologies. This ideological crisis, however, assumed the form, not of a deepening critique of traditionalist values, but rather of a rallying of traditionalist social forces – a crusade in defence of the older order. The 'cry from below' for the restoration of moral regulation took, first, the immediate symptoms of disturbance – rising crime, delinquency, moral permissiveness – and constructed them, with the help of organized grassroots ideological forces, into the scenario of a general 'crisis of the moral order'. In the later phases, these were connotatively linked with the more politicized threats, to compose a picture of a social order on the brink of moral collapse, its enemies proliferating 'within and without'. This is 'the crisis' experienced at the popular level in the universal, depoliticized, experiential language of popular morality.

The themes of crime and social delinquency, articulated through the discourses of popular morality, touch the direct experience, the anxieties and uncertainties of ordinary people. This has led to a dovetailing of the 'cry for discipline' from below into the call for an enforced restoration of social order and authority 'from above'. This articulation forms the bridge, between the real material sources of popular discontent, and their representation, through specific ideological forces and campaigns, as the general need for a 'disciplined society'. It has, as its principal effect, the awakening of popular support for a restoration of order through imposition: the basis of a populist 'law-and-order' campaign. This, in turn, has given a wide legitimacy to the tilt of the balance within the operations of the state towards the 'coercive' pole, whilst preserving its popular legitimacy. In this more open recruitment of the legal apparatuses of control – 'the law' in the service of the moral order – popular ideological forces have played an active organizational role. We must include here the 'anti moral pollution' lobbies, the anti-abortion crusaders, the 'rising crime rate' lobby, the smaller but virulent 'restoration of hanging' propagandists, and above all the role of the police apparatus itself, as an openly organized ideological force – campaigning in ways hitherto unknown for the extension of police powers, for a stiffening of criminal justice procedures, for the suspension of legal rights, for harsher penalties, tougher sentencing policies and abrasive prison regimes. The key to this aspect of the crisis – a central plank in the drift towards 'exceptional' forms of control for 'exceptional' times – is the power which popular moral ideologies and discourses have in touching real experiences and material conditions, while at the same time articulating them as a 'cry for discipline' from below, which favours the imposition of a regime of moral authoritarianism 'in the name of the people'. It is therefore one of the principal ways in which the dominated classes 'live' the crisis – as a disruption of 'traditional' ways of life, as a breakdown of the traditional landmarks and social values. Its long-term effect, however, is to legitimate the swing towards a more authoritarian regime.

III. The emergence of 'authoritarian populism'

This brief discussion of the ways in which the field of popular morality has been rearticulated in a period of crisis around the themes of crime, discipline and social order bring us to the edge of 'authoritarian populism' itself – and to the proper terrain of popular ideological struggle.

Like other fronts in the 'war of position', popular ideologies constitute in time of crisis a peculiarly important and strategic terrain, an arena of active intervention by organized ideological forces. What is at issue here is the transformation of those 'practical ideologies' which make the conditions of life intelligible to the masses, and which exercise a practical and material force by organizing their actions. What is at issue is the production, in conditions of social upheaval, of new kinds of 'commonsense'. Gramsci insisted that 'this is not a question of introducing from scratch a scientific form of thought into everyone's life, but of renovating and making "critical" an already existing activity'.[44] Here Gramsci had the ideological interventions of the left in mind. But it must be applied *pari passu* to the ideological initiatives of those social forces struggling to conserve the existing state of things.

In another passage, Gramsci observes that ideological transformation in the field of practical common sense is 'a process of distinction and of change in the relative weight possessed by the elements of the old ideology ... what was secondary or even incidental becomes of primary importance, it becomes the nucleus of a new doctrinal and ideological ensemble. The old collective will disintegrate into its contradictory elements so that the subordinate elements amongst them can develop socially.'[45] This is to conceive the process of popular ideological struggle on the model of 'deconstruction/reconstruction' – or to put it another way, as the articulation of an ideological field through struggle.

This way of thinking about ideologies as a practical material force has been developed in a suggestive and original manner in two recent contributions by Laclau.[46] Briefly, Laclau argues that individual ideological elements have no necessary 'class-belongingness' or class ascription. What matters is (a) the particular ways in which these elements are organized together within the logic of different discourses; (b) the manner in which these discourses are effectively articulated to and by different class practices. Ideological discourses work through the process of 'recruiting' concrete social individuals, through the process of inter-pellating them as 'discursive subjects'. Different discourses can be organized into an effective hierarchy through their points of condensation, where one interpellated element in a discourse is able connotatively to condense the elements of other discourses into its 'logic' of arrangement. This condensation is accomplished through the connotative resonances between discourses. The internal principle of the articulation of ideological discourses is their connotative and interpellative constitution; but the principle of their active articulation is given by the class struggle, which therefore 'appears' in the field of ideology, not as the permanent class-colonization of a discourse, but as the work entailed in articulating these discourses to different political class practices. The discourses of 'populism' and of 'democracy', for example, do not belong intrinsically to any single class. They can, as the outcome of particular ideological struggles, be differently articulated in different conditions. The work of ideological struggle is therefore equivalent to the work of articulating/disarticulating discourses from their previously secured position in an ideological field. Laclau argues, further, that so far as 'popular-democratic' discourses are concerned, these are constructed around a contradiction between 'the people' and the 'power bloc'. If such discourses are to be won to the right, it follows that these contradictions must be effectively neutralized.

There are problems with this suggestive framework.[47] (1) The term 'interpellation' is used ambiguously by Althusser (from whom Laclau derives it), and can be given either a more classical Marxist or a more revisionist psychoanalytic inflexion.[48] Following Lacanian psychoanalysis (from which Althusser himself borrowed the term, though he was himelf ambiguous about the nature of the 'loan'), interpellation is fundamentally the result of the psychoanalytic process by which the 'social subject' is constituted in a series of contradictory subject-positions. In this perspective, the work of ideological interpellation is accomplished in 'ideology in general' through the same process by which the subject as such is constituted. Laclau appears however to use the term to designate how what we might call 'already-formed' social subjects are recruited into subject-positions in the historically specific discourses of specific social formations. (2) If ideologies do not belong to classes but are articulated to them through ideological struggle, it remains a difficulty to understand what ideologically free 'class practices' are and how they function. (3) The thesis of the 'non-class belongingness' of ideological elements effectively exploits the theory of the multi-accentuality of signs in discourse, and the fact that, as Volosinov expressed it, 'everything that belongs to ideology has a semiotic value'. But some of Laclau's formulations may lead us to expect the constant formation and reformation of discourses across the ideological field. This takes too little into consideration the fact that the articulation of certain discourses to the practices of particular classes has been secured over long periods. And that, though there is no 'necessary correspondence' between them, 'in all ideological domains' – as Engels once put it – 'tradition forms a great conservative force'.[49] (4) The arena of intervention towards which Laclau's argument points is, especially, that of 'popular-democratic' struggle. Indeed, almost all ideological discourses which do not relate to economic struggles appear to be too easily subsumed by him into the 'popular democratic' category (are patriarchal ideologies, for example, instances of the 'popular-democratic'?).

The 'people/power bloc' contradicton, which appears at the centre of these discourses, forms, for Laclau, a more inclusive field of struggle than those which relate to the capital/labour contradiction, and this is the point: here a struggle wider than that of class-against-class can be developed (people/power bloc, oppressed/oppressors), and that way a wider alliance of popular-democratic forces can be 'won' towards socialism. But Laclau's thinking, especially about the 'popular' side of that couplet, sometimes appears to reflect the Latin American context in relation to which it was first formulated: it does not take sufficiently into account the role which 'populist' (rather than popular) discourses have played in securing the 'people', through an effective interpellation, to the practices of the dominant classes.

Despite these reservations, the theory lends considerable sophistication to the rudimentary schemas which we earlier derived from Gramsci's work on 'national-popular' and 'common sense'. It follows from this thesis, however, that, in the arena of ideological struggle – to put it facetiously – two can play at the game. Our argument is that the fracturing of many traditional ideologies in the period of the crisis has provided a golden opportunity for the political right, in its 'Thatcherite manifestation' – without benefit of theory, but by instinct (as we are told all good and true Conservatives operate) – to intervene precisely in this area, and to rework and neutralize the people/power bloc contradiction effectively in the direction of an 'authoritarian populism'. As an organized ideological force, 'Thatcherism' has played – long before its actual succession to power – a formative role, articulating the field of popular ideologies sharply to the right. Some of the keys to this success lie in its wide appeal and 'common touch'; its inclusive range of reference (for example, its ability to condense moral, philosophical and social themes, not normally thought of as 'political', within its political discourse); its proven capacity to penetrate the traditional ideological formations of sections of the working class and petty bourgeoisie; its unremitting 'radicalism' (for instance, it buried the competing positions of the Heathite 'respectable' right without ceremony); its taking up of themes much neglected in competing ideologies.

Its success stands in contrast with its failure to generate a credible economic programme for 'big' monopoly capital, with its built-in reliance on state initiatives and support. However, ideologically, this has given it greater credibility as the champion of 'independent' small capital and the party of the 'little man' against the big battalions of the state. This archetypal petty-bourgeois 'shopkeeper' figure has a well-constituted space in traditional conservative ideologies, if not as a real social category, then certainly as a discursive subject: the enunciative subject of a whole series of conservative 'philosophies'. This interpellation represents the 'respectable' working class, at the centre of the 'Thatcherite' discourses in its traditional petty-bourgeois disguise. It is a rhetorical and discursive operation much employed by the reactionary sections of the popular press, who also seek to interpellate their working-class readers through this construction – and with which Mrs Thatcher and her allies have forged a formidable alliance.

The success of this venture must be seen in the context of what it is replacing and displacing: the fragmentation of many of the traditional 'us/them' discourses of the working class (which sustained the people/ power bloc contradiction, although in a corporatist form) as a consequence of the disorganizing impact of the 'social-democratic solution' (discussed earlier); the displacement of the alternative Tory 'philosophy' – that associated with the failures of Mr Heath's administration, which played for a time with radical 'populist' themes, but was forced back on to more centrist ideological territory.

It is possible, now, to see the links between the revivalist style of 'authoritarian populism' and the other themes discussed above – the 'social-democratic solution' and the 'law-and-order' crusades. The monopoly by social democracy of the bureaucratic state has enabled the discourses of Thatcherism to condense at the negative pole statism, bureaucracy, social democracy, and 'creeping collectivism'. Against this representation of the 'power bloc' are counterposed various condensations of possessive individualism, personal initiative, 'Thatcherism' and freedom, as the positive pole. It is possible, then, to represent Labour as part of the 'big battalions', ranged against the 'little man' (and his family) oppressed by an inefficient state bureaucracy. Thus, social democracy is aligned with the power bloc, and Mrs Thatcher is out there 'with the people'. This has enabled Thatcherism to neutralize the people/power bloc contradiction.

In the arena of law and order, Thatcherism has effectively exploited a traditional space in popular ideologies: the moralism endemic in conservative 'philosophies'. The language of popular morality has no necessary class-belongingness: but it is also true that traditional and uncorrected common sense is a massively conservative force, penetrated thoroughly – as it has been – by religious notions of good and evil, by fixed conceptions of the unchanging and unchangeable character of human nature, and by ideas of retributive justice. These are by no means the only moral concepts embedded in popular common sense: for, within its contradictory structure, there are also the ideas of the injustice, of the oppression and exploitation which arise from the 'us/them' distribution of power, wealth and prestige.

'Common sense', in this respect, is a contradictory ideological structure, which, though thoroughly formed as a 'product of history',[50] presents itself to popular experience as transhistorical – the bedrock, universal wisdom of the ages. It is 'disjointed and episodic....' It contains 'Stone Age elements and principles of a more advanced science, prejudices from all past phases of history at a local level and intuitions of a future philosophy'. The 'criticism of all previous philosophy ... has left stratified deposits in popular philosophy'.[51] Traditional commonsense can only be raised to a more coherent level through a political intervention, especially in unusual times, when the 'embryonic' conception of a group 'manifests itself in action': otherwise 'this same group has, for reasons of submission and intellectual subordination, adopted a conception which is not its own but is borrowed from another group; and it affirms this conception verbally and believes itself to be following it, because this is the conception which it follows in "normal" times'.[52]

Social democracy, as a political force, has, however, long since abandoned (if it ever had any conception of) a moral-social leadership of this kind over the classes it claims to represent. It has long ago ceased to work the 'good sense' of the class, its 'spontaneous' class instinct, its sense of the world as unjustly divided into the oppressed and the oppressing classes: it has limited itself to making tactically pragmatic accommodation with the most traditionalist and conservative elements in popular morality. It has no conception of the educative and formative function of 'parties' in relation to the 'classes' which they aim to represent – and which, in order to represent, they must first form, politically and ideologically.[53] Indeed, the left as a whole, in its one-sided rationalism, has utterly failed to comprehend the necessity to educate the commonsense of the common people, in order to constitute a popular bloc, a practical material force, against traditionalist ideas.

But Thatcherism, with its refined populist instinct, has made no such strategic error. Indeed, it has the force of history – that is, the secured correspondences between 'the people' and the 'traditional wisdom of the nation' – to rely on: a field of popular conceptions, in which it has made a series of strategically effective interventions. Those representations of 'the people', of 'the nation', of 'our culture and way of life', of the 'instincts of the ordinary British people', etc., which it ideologically constructs, it can claim not to have forged through ideological intervention, but simply to have 'rediscovered', awakened from their deep national slumber.

The point about popular morality is that it is the most practical material-ideological force amongst the popular classes – the language which, without benefit of training, education, coherent philosophizing, erudition or learning, touches the direct and immediate experience of the class, and has the power to map out the world of problematic social reality in clear and unambiguous moral polarities. It thus has a real concrete grasp on the popular experiences of the class. In periods of social upheaval and change, it provides a moral reference point, which organizes experience and sorts it into its evaluative categories. Under the right conditions, 'the people' in their traditionalist representation can be condensed as a set of interpellations in discourses which systematically displace political issues into conventional moral absolutes.

Crime is precisely a theme of this kind, which is present in the real experience of the dominated classes as a threat from within to their already limited material resources and 'sense of order'. And when crime is mapped into the wider scenarios of 'moral degeneration' and the crisis of authority and social values, there is no mystery as to why some ordinary people should be actively recruited into crusades for the restoration of 'normal times' – if necessary through a more-than-normal imposition of moral-legal force. That is why the 'law-and-order' theme is not a mere side issue, not a question relating essentially to the control of crime and the system of criminal justice exclusively: why it has become a vibrant, general social theme in the discourses of Thatcherism:

and why it has served so effectively in generalizing amongst the silent majorities a sense of the need for 'ordinary folk' to stand up in defence of the social order.

'Thatcherism' has worked directly on the terrain of popular ideologies. It has worked their more traditionalist elements systematically in an authoritarian direction. It has constituted not a discourse, but a field of discourses in which the interpellations of the one summon up and condense a series of others. In the field of education, it has made itself the guardian of the 'return to standards' and of authority in the classroom. Here it has constructed at the centre of its interpellative structure, the figure of the worried parent, facing the harsh realities of a competitive world which does not 'owe his children a living', aiming to secure, not a decent education for all children but an education which will help his or her child to 'get on and compete' (here, the condensation with the figure of the possessive individualist): against this figure is set the 'permissive' or radical teacher, the indisciplined school experimenting with the child, the willing employer who constantly discovers that 'children nowadays can't read and write'.

As in the area of crime, these discourses have been elaborated, and gained a hold in the popular universe, by the tactical exploitation of a series of 'moral panics' in which these ideological oppositions are dramatized, set in motion, winning public attention: for example, the intervention at Thameside (Manchester), dramatizing 'the parents' against the state; the well-engineered débâcle at William Tyndale (London), stage-managing the 'parent and the traditional teacher' against the 'radical teacher and the permissive school'. The measure of the success of these and the campaigns of related social forces (for example, the vigorous campaign on discipline waged annually by the conservative wing of the teachers' union) may be found in the fact that whereas, ten years ago, parent-power and parental involvement in the school belonged securely to the discourses of 'permissive education', deschooling and the libertarian wing, it has now been effectively rearticulated into one of the most potent themes of the 'radical' right – a guarantee that parents will help to restore discipline, authority, traditional values and educational standards in the classroom. Whilst Mr Rhodes Boyson range-rides these populist crusades on the educational frontier, Mr St John Stevas gives them a 'moderate' and respectable voice in the councils of the nation. Once again the link is forged.

On the theme of 'welfare' the outcome of a parallel ideological intervention hardly needs repeating here. The discourse of the 'spendthrift state', recklessly giving away wealth the nation has not earned (here, the shopkeeper 'subject' is condensed), and thereby undermining the self-reliance of ordinary people (here, the possessive individual makes his reappearance), produces as its discursive opposite the 'welfare scrounger', living off society, never doing a day's work (here, the Protestant Ethic makes a late return) – with more than a hint that this negative he or she is often a 'person from an alien culture' who does not share 'our values' (here, the discourses of race and nation are condensed). But this discourse also intersects and replicates many of the positions already built into those discourses, which have women, mothers and the family at the centre of their interpellative structure.

Women, mothers and the family have by no means been restricted, in the discourses of Thatcherite populism, to those themes which directly touch on questions of welfare. For women, represented as 'guardians' of the family, are also, by that position, connotatively identified with the keeper of traditional wisdoms, and guardian of conventional popular morality; but this composite 'she' is, at the same time, the 'practical one' – the one who knows the 'value of money' and the 'impact of rising prices in the shops': that is, the figure through which the economic and monetarist themes of Thatcherism can be made to connect with the empirical experience of the everyday life of ordinary folk. 'She' is, of course, the same parent we saw earlier, concerned for the educational chances of her child: the woman alone on the streets at night, who can no longer go about her ordinary business unmolested: the housewife whom the state and the permissive educators would seek to detach from her traditional role and 'force' to 'abandon' her children and hearth and go out to work: and, properly addressed, she is the wife of the militant trade unionist on strike, who brings home to him the harsh realities and consequences of living without the weekly wage, and urges a 'speedy return to work' – for the sake of the children, of course. Needless to say, she is the emblematic mother of conventional sexual ideology, for whom abortion is a 'crime against nature'. 'She' has played a quite critical ideological role in the construction of popular moralities in the recent period.

In the area of race, 'Thatcherism' has had an even more striking success. It has recuperated to the 'legitimate' terrain of parliamentary politics the extremist racism of the National Front, many of whose basic themes were merged into the official party position on race in an intensive campaign in the early months of 1979, whilst being distanced from their more disreputable associations of street fascism. The history of race and the forging of the political forces of the radical right would bear expanded consideration on their own: the story would have to include the successful 'conforming' of Powellism without Powell, followed by the effective coopting of an anti-immigrant populism bypassing National Front extremism. Here, the interpellations of 'nation', of 'national cultures/alien cultures', of 'our people', are the respectable signifiers of a new cultural racism. Indeed, there is more than a superficial similarity in the discursive structure of the two discourses. For the rhetoric of the National Front is also working not to neutralize, but to disarticulate, some of the same contradictions as 'Thatcherism'; and its appeal to 'ordinary, hard-pressed' people against the conspiracies of the liberal state occupies something of the same space. The point can be usefully encapsulated in the report of the anti-fascist slogan (in the business to build alliances), 'Against the bosses, For the blacks', altered by a simple National Front amendment to 'Against the bosses, Against the blacks'. The relatively recent decline in the electoral fortunes of the Front should not be too rapidly welcomed until the full consequences of that dialectic between the racism of the 'extremist' and the 'radical' right have been considered.

In selecting these three areas of response to the crisis from the political centre and the right, we have been trying to show that the crisis is not a given state of things, but an actual field of struggle, on which the forces of the right have been actively intervening. They are indeed waging a remorseless struggle, precisely as Gramsci described – through 'a series of ideological, religious, philosophical, political and juridical polemics' – whose aim is not simply to conserve and preserve, but to 'shift the previously existing disposition of social forces'. This is a form of 'passive revolution'; but if the exercise of social democratic politics through the exercise of the state had all the makings of a 'passive revolution' from above, the rigorously populist character of the interventions of the radical right give it the unmistakable stamp of a passive revolution from below. What gives it this character are its unceasing efforts to construct the movement towards a more authoritarian regime from a massive populist base. It is 'populist' because it cannot be 'popular-democratic'. This is what, in the conditions of crisis, the social forces of the right now mean by 'taking democracy seriously'.[54]

1980

Notes

1. For an analysis of this period see S. Hall, J. Clarke, C. Critcher, T. Jefferson and B. Roberts, *Policing The Crisis*, London, 1978.
2. For an original analysis of these and related trends, see Tom Nairn, *The Break-Up of Britain*, London, 1977; and 'The Future of Britain's Crisis', *New Left Review*, 113–14, 1979.
3. A. Gramsci, *Selections From The Prison Notebooks*, London, 1971, p. 276.
4. Gramsci, 'Prison Notebooks', p. 227.

5. V.I. Lenin, *'Left-Wing' Communism: An Infantile Disorder*, The Little Lenin Library, vol. 16, London, 1934, p. 65.

6. Gramsci, 'Prison Notebooks', p. 220.

7. For an analysis of the reconstruction of the 'radical right' under the Thatcher leadership, see S. Hall, 'The Great Moving Right Show'.

8. This question is analysed further below, in the section on 'The Social-Democratic Solution'. But it is worth saying that it still constitutes the problem of and for the left. It cannot be ignored, since social democracy is the political-ideological force which organizes and represents the majority of the working class. Democratic-popular struggles require the formation of strategic alliances, and hence the question of the character of 'left' social democracy is critical. The disasters of the period of 'social fascism' are too well known to rehearse, or repeat. Yet, without falling into an essentialist conception of social democracy, it condenses within itself all the problems which 'reformism' constitute for any radical transformation. This is accentuated in the period when social democracy in power becomes, effectively, the 'natural' manager of the capitalist crisis.

9. It is also what distinguished this phase of the crisis from any simple reduction to 'fascism'.

10. N. Poulantzas, *State, Power, Socialism*, London, 1978, pp. 203–4.

11. For a definition of 'authoritarian populism', see S. Hall, 'The Great Moving Right Show'.

12. The neglect of this 'necessary sufficient' distinction has confused many of the recent debates concerning 'determination by the economic'. Despite Marx's observation that the concrete is the result of 'many determinations', and Althusser's concept of 'over-determination', it continues to be argued that logically the economic must either determine, or not; but it cannot be 'relatively determinate'. But relations in the 'logic of historical process' are never so either/or as this logical binary suggests.

13. Gramsci, 'Prison Notebooks', p. 184.

14. Ibid., pp. 177ff.

15. Ibid., pp. 180–2.

16. L. Althusser, 'Contradiction and Overdetermination', *For Marx*, London, 1969, p. 101.

17. Lenin, *Letters From Afar*, No. I, pp. 35–6; quoted in Althusser, *For Marx*, p. 99.

18. Althusser, ibid., p. 99.

19. Lenin, *Left-Wing Communism*, p. 75.

20. Ibid., pp. 72–3.

21. For a lucid discussion of this formulation, see B. Jessop, 'Capitalism And Democracy: The Best Possible Shell?' in Littlejohn, Smart, Wakeford and Yuval-Davis, eds, *Power and the State*, London, 1978.

22. In this version of the paper, I have omitted a long discussion of the relation between the 'representative' and 'interventionist' elements of the modern capitalist state, especially in the new forms of their combination in the 1880–1920 period. It suffices to say here that these two aspects must now be distributed as between their 'good' and 'bad' side: they are complementary and contradictory features of many variants of state and of specific political regimes after the 'transition to monopoly' begins.

23. The reconstruction of the emergence of this state form in British conditions is indeed an urgent theoretical-political task now for the left.

24. Gramsci, 'Prison Notebooks', p. 178.

25. Ibid.

26. These elements of the phase of 'war of position' form part of Gramsci's seminal discussion, in 'Prison Notebooks', pp. 242–3.

27. Ibid., p. 178.

28. It is sometimes thought that to speak of 'working on the already-given disposition of social forces' is next-door to succumbing to a reformist strategy. This is the product of that 'optimism/fatalism' oscillation, which besets the left in periods of containment, which Gramsci has so pertinently analysed. In fact, nothing could be farther from the truth.

29. For this quote, and a thoughtful and suggestive outline of Gramsci's political thinking, see Anne Sassoon, 'Hegemony and Political Intervention', in S. Hibbin, ed, *Politics*,

Ideology and The State, London, 1978.
    30. Gramsci, 'Prison Notebooks', p. 219.
    31. Quoted from Gramsci's *Quaderni*, p. 1825, in Sassoon, 'Hegemony and Political Intervention', p. 24.
    32. Gramsci, 'Prison Notebooks', p. 58.
    33. Ibid., p. 109.
    34. For an extended argument on this point, see Hall, Lumley and McLennan, 'Politics and Ideology in Gramsci', in *On Ideology*, London, 1978.
    35. Gramsci, 'Prison Notebooks', pp. 181–2.
    36. Perhaps it needs to be stressed that the 'means of political representation' do not automatically reflect an already-formed, homogeneous class, with ascribed 'class interests' and a formed coherent 'world view', outside the representation process. Representation is an active and formative relation between 'parties' and 'classes': they form and constitute 'the class' politically and ideologically by representing it. However a propos the argument that there can only be 'means of representation' and 'what is represented', we would argue that there must be something there to be 'represented', even if it is altered and transformed in the process.
    37. See the discussion in *Policing The Crisis*, Part IV.
    38. The heart of the social-democratic representation of the working class and its allies is the displacement of the 'representative' relation (in the articulation 'class-party') into the disciplinary-interventionist articulation, 'party-nation'. For a discussion of this aspect, see S. Hall, 'Newspapers, Parties and Classes', in J. Curran, ed., *The British Press: A Manifesto*, London, 1978; and Finn, Grant and Johnson, 'Social Democracy, Education and the Crisis', in *On Ideology*.
    39. The complex relations between 'Liberal Collectivism' and Fabian social-democratic statism is currently the subject of an extensive reworking by the 'new liberal' school of historians, but is of the utmost importance to a Left analysis of the character of British Social Democracy and of the British state. See Emy, *Liberals, Radicals and Social Politics*, Cambridge, 1973; P. Clarke, *Liberals and Social-Democrats*, Cambridge, 1979.
    40. Gramsci, 'Prison Notebooks', p. 120.
    41. See S. Hall, 'The Great Moving Right Show'.
    42. For the history of the slow drift to a 'law and order' state, see *Policing The Crisis* and extract in this volume, pp. 19–38.
    43. Gramsci, 'Prison Notebooks', pp. 276–7.
    44. Ibid., p. 330.
    45. From Gramsci, *Quaderni*, III, p. 1875, quoted in the context of a lucid and exemplary discussion of Gramsci's conception of ideology, in the introductory essay by Chantal Mouffe to her *Gramsci and Marxist Theory*, London, 1979.
    46. Ernesto Laclau, *Politics and Ideology in Marxist Theory*, London, 1977; an elegant and original contribution to Marxist theory.
    47. I am indebted, in formulating some of these criticisms, to the paper 'Laclau and Interpellation' by Alan O'Shea: Centre for Cultural Studies, Birmingham mimeo, 1978.
    48. In Althusser's influential essay, 'Ideology and Ideological State Apparatuses', *Lenin and Philosophy and Other Essays*, London, 1971. These were originally two essays, revised into a single text: but the two parts are still visible: the first relates ideology to the reproduction of the relations of production and to hegemony; the second argues that ideology requires the constitution of 'subjects', through interpellation. The term is borrowed from Lacan, and is the theoretical warrant for much subsequent theorizing attempting to combine Marxism with Lacanian psychoanalysis. Althusser's usage here is, however, highly ambiguous – and one is tempted to think not unconsciously so, for the volume also contains the important 'Freud and Lacan' essay. Althusser's tentative formulation, that 'the eternity of the unconscious is not unrelated to the eternity of ideology in general' (p. 152) has since lost all qualifications in the assertion that ideology is structured like, and acquired in the same process that constitutes the unconscious. For some continuing problems with this assertion, see S. Hall, 'Some Problems with the Ideology/Subject Couplet' and the Editorial Reply, in *Ideology and Consciousness*, No. 3, spring 1978.
    49. Engels, 'Feuerbach and the End of Classical German Philosophy', in *Marx–Engels*

Selected Works, vol. 2, London, 1951, p. 362.
50. Gramsci, 'Prison Notebooks', p. 325.
51. Ibid., p. 324.
52. Ibid., p. 327.
53. See above, footnote 36.

54. In its recent conversion to the strategy of 'alliances' and 'popular-democratic' struggle, the left – freed of the essentialism of some of its old, sectarian, 'reformism/ revolution' binarism – sometimes acts and talks as if only it is in a position to seize the 'democratic-popular' initiative. This article is written in the conviction that the right also knows how to 'take democracy seriously', and may have been more effective than the left in doing so – in a certain way. It is now also sometimes argued that, in the search for 'openings' the left should cease asking the question about 'reformism'. This seems to me a damaging evacuation. There is no necessary, permanent, inevitable and essential content to be ascribed to 'reformism': it can only be defined in the conjuncture, in relation to the balance of forces. But the crucial question, as to whether any strategy is working on a pertinent contradiction (in such a way that it cannot be resolved without transformation) or so as to 'permit reforms which do not touch the essential structure', remains in my view an extremely pertinent political question to ask – of any intervention or any alliance. We may have abandoned the fixed ascription of reformism as a pejorative label. Unfortunately, the political problem of reformism is still very much present.

9

Authoritarian Populism:
A Reply to Jessop et al.

Jessop, Bonnett, Bromley and Ling contributed a long and important article 'Authoritarian Populism, Two Nations and Thatcherism', to New Left Review 147. This article took issue with 'authoritarian populism' (hereinafter, alas, AP) and the use of that concept in my work on Thatcherism; and proposed some wide-ranging alternative theses. I should like to take issue with some aspects of their argument, not so much to defend my work as, through mutual discussion and debate, to advance our understanding of the phenomenon of Thatcherism.

My view, briefly, is that in their genuine desire to produce a *general* and definitive account of Thatcherism as a global phenomenon, Jessop et al. have been led to mistake my own, more delimited project for their own, more ambitious one. In so doing, they obscure or misread many of my arguments. They produce, in the end, a rather confused tangle of important arguments and spurious debating points. Let me say categorically that 'authoritarian populism' (AP) has never been intended to, could not possibly have been intended and – I would claim – has never been used in my work, to produce a general explanation of Thatcherism. It addresses, directly, the question of the forms of hegemonic politics. In doing so, it deliberately and self-consciously foregrounds the political-ideological dimension. Thatcherism, however, is a multifaceted historical phenomenon, which it would be ludicrous to assume could be 'explained' along one dimension of analysis only. In that basic sense, I believe the Jessop et al. critique to have been fundamentally misdirected. The misunderstanding begins, so far as I can see, with their partial and inadequate account of the genealogy of the concept.

AP first emerged, as they acknowledged, from the analysis of the political conjuncture, mid-1960s to mid-1970s, advanced by myself and others in *Policing The Crisis*.[1] That analysis accurately forecasted the rise of Thatcherism, though it was researched in the mid-1970s and published in 1978. It pointed, inter alia, to a shift taking place in the 'balance of social and political forces' (or what Gramsci calls the 'relations of force'), pinpointed in the disintegration of the social-democratic consensus under Callaghan and the rise of the radical right under Thatcherite auspices. It argued that the corporatist consensus – the form of politics in which Labour had attempted to stabilize the crisis – was breaking up under internal and external pressures. However, the balance in the relations of force was moving – in that 'unstable equilibrium' between coercion and consent which characterizes all democratic class politics – decisively towards the 'authoritarian' pole. We were approaching, it argued, a moment of 'closure' in which the state played an increasingly central 'educative' role. We noted, however, the degree to which this shift 'from above' was pioneered by, harnessed to, and to some extent legitimated by a populist groundswell below. The form of this populist enlistment – we suggested – in the 1960s and 1970s often took the shape of a sequence of 'moral panics', around such apparently non-political issues as race, law-and-order, permissiveness and social anarchy. These served to win for the authoritarian closure the gloss of populist consent.[2]

Development of the Concept

The actual term 'authoritarian populism', however, only emerged in 1978 after I read the concluding section to Nicos Poulantzas's courageous and original book, *State, Power, Socialism*, which was also – tragically – his last political statement. There, Poulantzas attempted to characterize a new 'moment' in the conjuncture of the class democracies, formed by 'intensive state control over every sphere of socio-economic life, combined with radical decline of the institutions of political democracy and with draconian and multiform curtailment of so-called "formal" liberties, whose reality is being discovered now that they are going overboard'.[3] (I especially relished that final phrase, since it put me in mind of how often the fundamentalist left is scornful of civil liberties until they find themselves badly in need of some.) More seriously, I thought I recognized in this account, and in my brief conversations with Poulantzas at the time, many similarities between his characterization and those I had been struggling to formulate in *Policing the Crisis*, 'Drifting into a Law-and-Order Society', and so on.

Poulantzas called this the moment of 'authoritarian statism' (AS). He added, inter alia, that it was linked with 'the periodization of capitalism into distinct stages and phases'; that it existed 'in the form of regimes that vary according to the conjuncture of the country concerned'; that it covered, specifically, both 'the political crisis and the crisis of the state'; that it was intended to help us periodize 'the relationship between the state and the political crisis'. He insisted it was neither the birth pangs of fascism nor an 'exceptional form of the capitalist state' nor even 'the fulfilment of the totalitarian buds inherent in every capitalist state'. Indeed, the importance of AS was that it represented a new combination of coercion/consent, tilted towards the coercive end of the spectrum, while maintaining the outer forms of democratic class rule intact. It did, he argued, relate to 'considerable shifts in class relations'. But also, it coincided with the generalization of class conflict and other social struggles to 'new fronts'. It thus represented a fundamental shift in the modalities through which ruling blocs attempt to construct hegemony in capitalist class democracies. That was its explicit field of reference.

Poulantzas's concept seemed to me extremely useful – but weak in two major respects. It misread the emerging strategy, since one of the fundamental things which seemed to me to be shifting was precisely the abandonment of the 'corporatist' strategy central to Labourism, and its replacement by an 'anti-statist' strategy of the 'new right'. (An 'anti-statist' strategy, incidentally, is not one which refuses to operate through the state; it is one which conceives a more limited state role, and which advances through the attempt, ideologically, to *represent itself* as anti-statist, for the purposes of populist mobilization.) I assumed that this highly contradictory strategy – which we have in fact seen in operation under Thatcherism: simultaneously, dismantling the welfare state, 'anti-statist' in its ideological self-representation *and* highly state-centralist and dirigiste in many of its strategic operations – would inflect politics in new ways and have real political effects.

Secondly, I believed that Poulantzas had neglected the one dimension which, above all others, has defeated the left, politically, and Marxist analysis, theoretically, in every advanced capitalist democracy since the First World War: namely, the ways in which popular consent can be so constructed, by a historical bloc seeking hegemony, as to harness to its support some popular discontents, neutralize the opposing forces, dis-aggregate the opposition and really incorporate some strategic elements of popular opinion into its own hegemonic project.

These two arguments led me to build on Poulantzas's insights, but to shift the characterization of the conjuncture from 'authoritarian statism' to 'authoritarian populism'. I hoped by adopting this deliberately contradictory term precisely to encapsulate the contradictory features of the emerging conjuncture: a movement towards a dominative and 'authoritarian' form of democratic class politics – paradoxically, apparently rooted in the 'transformism' (Gramsci's term) of populist discontents. This was further elaborated in my article 'Popular-Democratic versus Authoritarian Populism', where I drew on the seminal work of Laclau, and his notion of 'populist rupture'. But I distanced my more delimited use of the term 'populism' from his more inclusive one, attempting thereby to distinguish the genuine mobilization of popular demands and discontents from a 'populist' mobilization which, at a certain point in its trajectory, flips over or is recuperated into a statist-led political leadership.

Levels of Abstraction

I grant that this genealogy is nowhere fully laid out; though I would claim that it is plain enough from the context and sequence of my work. I also grant that there was too little rigorous or logical 'construction of concepts' here. The concepts, I am afraid, were generated in the heat of conjunctural analysis – I was trying to comprehend the shift towards Thatcherism as it was taking place, So, admittedly, the theorization is a bit rough and ready. I explored the idea of 'passive revolution', for example; and I still believe it has something to contribute to our understanding of populist (as opposed to popular) strategies. But I could not at the time bring off the link and have not been able to do so since. Like many of Gramsci's most fruitful concepts, AP remains 'overdescriptive'. Perhaps I have caught his disease. I suspect that a more fundamental disagreement divides my position from that of Jessop et al. here. I do not believe that all concepts operate at the same level of abstraction – indeed, I think one of the principal things which separates me from the fundamentalist marxist revival is precisely that they believe that the concepts which Marx advanced at the highest level of abstraction (i.e. mode of production, capitalist epoch) can be transferred directly into the analysis of concrete historical conjunctures. My own view is that concepts like that of 'hegemony' (the family or level of abstraction to which AP also belongs) are of necessity somewhat 'descriptive', historically more specific, time-bound, concrete in their reference – because they attempt to conceptualize what Marx himself said of 'the concrete': that it is the 'product of many determinations'. So I have to confess that it was not an error or oversight which determined the level of concreteness at which AP operates. It was quite deliberately and self-consciously not pitched at that level of 'pure' theoretical-analytic operation at which

Jessop et al. seem to assume all concepts must be produced. The costs of operating at this level of abstraction are clear. But to me – in the wake of the academicizing of Marxism and the theoreticist deluge of the 1970s – so are the gains.

I would argue, therefore, that I have only used AP at the level of abstraction and with the range of reference outlined above. I have never claimed for it the general explanatory sweep which Jessop et al. attempt to graft on to it. I am therefore not at all surprised to find that AP is only a partial explanation of Thatcherism. What else could it be? It was an attempt to characterize certain strategic shifts in the political/ideological conjuncture. Essentially, it refers to changes in the 'balance of forces'. It refers directly to the modalities of political and ideological relationships between the ruling bloc, the state and the dominated classes. It attempts to expand on and to begin to periodize the internal composition of hegemonic strategies in the politics of class democracies. Theoretically – if anyone is interested – it is part of a wider project to develop and expand on the rich but too condensed concept of hegemony. It is a sort of footnote to Gramsci's 'Modern Prince' and 'State and Civil Society'. It references, but could neither characterize nor explain, changes in the more structural aspects of capitalist social formations. I do not understand how, even grammatically, AP could have been misunderstood as a concept operating at the latter level. 'In this field, the struggle can and must be carried on by developing the concept of hegemony', Gramsci observed, in *The Prison Notebooks*. AP is a response to that fateful injunction.

Jessop et al. are certainly in need of no further instruction from me about the concept of hegemony. However, I cannot resist pointing out, at this stage in the argument, that I have never advanced the proposition that Thatcherism has achieved 'hegemony'. The idea, to my mind, is preposterous. What I have said is that, in sharp contrast to the political strategy of both the Labourist and the fundamentalist left, Thatcherite politics are 'hegemonic' in their conception and project: the aim is to struggle on several fronts at once, not on the economic-corporate one alone; and this is based on the knowledge that, in order really to dominate and restructure a social formation, political, moral and intellectual leadership must be coupled to economic dominance. The Thatcherites know that they must 'win' in civil society as well as in the state. They understand, as the left generally does not, the consequences of the generalization of the social struggle to new arenas and the need to have a strategy for them too. They mean, if possible, to reconstruct the terrain of what is 'taken for granted' in social and political thought – and so to form a new common sense. If one watches how, in the face of a teeth-gritting opposition, they have steadily used the unpopularity of some aspects of trade union practice with their own members to inflict massive wounds on the whole labour movement, or how they have steadily not only pursued the 'privatization' of the public sector but installed 'value for money' at the heart of the calculations of every Labour council and every other social institution – health service, school meals, universities, street cleaning, unemployment benefit offices, social services – one will take this politico–ideological level of struggle somewhat more seriously than the left currently does. That is the project of Thatcherism – from which, I am sufficiently in apostasy to believe, the left has something to learn as to the conduct of political struggle. But I do not believe and have nowhere advanced the claim that the project has been delivered.

Indeed, I have several times pointed out the yawning discrepancy between Thatcherism's ideological advances and its economic failures. I have consistently argued against the view that Thatcherite neo-monetarism could provide solutions to Britain's structural economic crisis. As the authoritarian face of Thatcherism has become – in line with my analysis – more and more pronounced, it seems to me self-evident that Thatcherism remains dominant but not hegemonic. It must impose – because it cannot lead. But I have also tried quite carefully to define what we might mean by its 'success'. In 'Thatcherism – A New Stage?' I said inter alia: 'It is beset by internal contradictions and subject to real limits. It won a measure of electoral support ... It cannot deliver on them all ... It is not touching the structural economic problems at home ... and it is powerless to ward off the savage effects of a global capitalist recession.' But I also warned that Thatcherism had won power on 'a long leash' and would not be blown off course 'by an immediate crisis of electoral support'. I added that it would be perfectly possible for Thatcherism to 'fail' in delivering a solution to Britain's economic crisis, and yet to 'succeed' 'in its long-term mission to shift the balance of class forces to the right'. Big capital, I suggested, has supported Thatcherism because it sees in it 'the only political force capable of altering the relations of forces in a manner favourable to the imposition of capitalist solutions'. In that sense, I argued, 'the long-term political mission of the radical right could "succeed" even if this particular government had to give way to one of another electoral complexion.' To that extent, I concluded, 'Thatcherism has irrevocably undermined the old solutions and positions'.[4] That analysis was offered in 1980, but I believe it to have been fundamentally correct and to have been confirmed by subsequent developments. In the face of that, it is ludicrous to suggest that I have argued that Thatcherism has already achieved hegemony.

'Ideologism?'

This brings us to the charges advanced by Jessop et al. of 'ideologism'. This is so impacted that it is hard to disentangle. First of all I think they are themselves at fault in eliding the levels of political and ideological struggle, and in suppressing what they must know well – the need for concepts which define their specificity. They may be right in saying that AP does not sufficiently distinguish between these two dimensions of struggle. However, I do hold to the position that, in my own work, I have consistently struggled against any definition of hegemony which identifies it as exclusively an ideological phenomenon. On the contrary, I have repeated ad nauseam Gramsci's argument about hegemony being impossible to conceptualize or achieve without 'the decisive nucleus of economic activity'. It is therefore particularly galling to be accused of advancing an explanation of Thatcherism as exclusively an ideological phenomenon, simply because I have drawn attention to features of its ideological strategy which are specific and important.

It seems well-nigh impossible on the left to affirm the importance and specificity of a particular level of analysis or arena of struggle without immediately being misunderstood as saying that, because it is important, it is the only one. I have tried in my own work not to make that easy slide. I work on the political/ideological dimension (a) because I happen to have some competence in that area, and (b) because it is often either neglected or reductively treated by the left generally and by some Marxists. But the idea that because one works at that level, one there-fore assumes economic questions to be residual or unimportant is absurd. I think the ideological dimension of Thatcherism to be critical. I am certain the left neither understands it nor knows how to conduct this level of struggle – and is constantly misled by misreading its importance. Hence I was determined to bring out this level of analysis – and AP in part served to do just that. But since AP was never advanced as a general or global explanation, it entailed no prescriptions whatsoever as to the other levels of analysis. The fact is that until these other dimen-sions are in place alongside the concept of AP, the analysis of Thatcher-ism remains partial and incomplete. But the 'foregrounding' involved in AP was quite deliberate: 'bending the stick' towards the most neglected dimension, against the drift of current discussion, Althusser once called it. Jessop et al. have, I think, missed my tactical purpose; they have thereby robbed themselves of insights from which their own analysis might have profited.

When they do turn to the question of ideological foregrounding, I think they misrepresent the work done with AP. Even on the ideological front, Thatcherism has adopted other strategies – like the construction of an intellectual leadership, the formation of a new stratum of 'organic' intellectuals, the level of the organization of theoretical ideas in certain strategic academic, research and other intellectual sites – to which I have also drawn attention, but which have nothing whatsoever to do with the AP strategy and the construction of the popular consent to power. Thatcherism also has a distinct political strategy for the internal recomposition of the power bloc and the state machine which is not 'purely' ideological – whatever that means – and has little to do with AP. It is true that, when I turn to describing the ideological mechanisms I use the insights of 'discourse theory'. That is because I believe that discourse theory has much to tell us about how Thatcherism accomplishes the condensation of different discourses into its contradictory formation, and how it 'works' so as to recruit people to its different, often contradictory, subject positions: even though it has only had partial success in its project to construct a new kind of political 'subject'. But I have long ago definitively dissociated myself from the discourse theoretical approach to the analysis of whole social formations, or even from the idea that the production of new subjectivities provides, in itself, an adequate theory of ideology (as opposed to a critical aspect of its functioning).[5] I have characterized that as a species – long familiar to the tradition of 'Western Marxism' – of neo-Kantianism. In doing so, I have also tried carefully to demarcate the immensely fruitful things which I learned from Ernesto Laclau's *Politics and Ideology in Marxist Theory* from the dissolution of everything into discourse which, I believe, mars the later volume, *Hegemony and Socialist Strategy*, despite its many insights.[6] These distinctions were widely debated in the so-called 'Hegemony Group' in 1980–83, in which Jessop himself took a leading role, so I find it difficult to be now mis-identified by Jessop et al. with the latter position.[7]

I believe from what I have already said that it is also quite difficult to sustain the charge that I treat Thatcherism as an 'uncontradictory monolith'. The entire thrust of my work on the ideology of Thatcherism has been to try to show how Thatcherism has managed to stitch up or 'unify' the contradictory strands in its discourse – 'the resonant themes of organic Toryism – nation, family, duty, authority, standards, traditionalism, patriarchalism – with the aggressive themes of a revived neo-liberalism – self-interest, competitive individualism, anti-statism', as I put it in 'The Great Moving Right Show'.[8] In the same piece, I pointed to the highly contradictory subject-positions which Thatcherism was attempting to condense. I deliberately adopted Gamble's brief but telling paradox – 'free market, strong state'. How all this could be described as representing Thatcherism as an uncontradictory ideological monolith beats me. Nor do Jessop et al. score points by showing that many of these elements in Thatcherism are not new. 'Some of these,' I said in the very next sentence, 'had been secured in earlier times through the grand themes of one-nation popular Conservatism: the means by which Toryism circumnavigated democracy'. I thought this of particular importance in giving substance to Gramsci's argument that, often, ideological shifts take place, not by substituting one, whole, new conception of the world for another, but by presenting a novel combination of old and new elements – 'a process of distinction and of change in the relative weight possessed by the elements of the old ideology'. I don't see how all that could conceivably be construed as endowing Thatcherism with an 'excessively unified image'.

The Keynesian Welfare State

For the reasons I have already advanced, there are many things which Jessop et al. argue in the succeeding sections of their article with which I wholeheartedly agree. Their analysis and mine are only, I am afraid, in competition with one another in the rather spurious atmosphere of polemical contestation which they quite unnecessarily generated. Nevertheless, I believe that the failures they show in understanding how AP works carry over into their own substantive analysis. Thus they repeat the now-familiar, lefter-than-thou, argument that the breakup of the postwar consensus could not be of much political significance because the 'Keynesian Welfare State' (KWS) was never 'socialist'. This is supposed to inflict further damage on the concept of AP. However, I am perfectly well aware that the KWS was not socialist. In *Policing the Crisis* I spent a great deal of space analysing the limits of the KWS and spelling out the contradiction of Labour in power, which I quite specifically characterized as 'social democratic' not socialist in political content. The argument has, so far as I know, never been that the KWS was 'socialist' and that we should therefore now go back to it. That is a figment of the fundamentalist left imagination. What I have argued and do argue is that the KWS was a contradictory structure, a 'historic compromise', which both achieved something in a reformist direction for the working class and became an instrument in disciplining it. Why else should anyone on the left be now campaigning for the restoration of the cuts in the welfare state if it did nothing for the working class? I have also argued that, if we cannot mobilize a full-scale popular agitation around the limited demands of maintaining and expanding 'welfare state reformism', on what grounds could we conceivably conceptualize the political conjuncture as one likely to lead to an 'irreversible shift of power' towards immediate working-class power? I keep not getting an answer to this conundrum, and must presume this is because the symbolics of who can swear loudest at the reformism of Labour governments is more important on the left than hard analysis. It seems to be convenient to answer not the question I post but another, fictional one because the latter usefully demonstrates the degree of my apostasy! I am surprised to find Jessop et al. allowing themselves to drift into that vulgar exercise.

I have other problems with the analysis they advance, though on these I can be briefer. I do not find the 'two nations' hypothesis at all convincing. 'Good citizen' and 'hard worker' seem to me poor characterizations of the critical points of reference in the Thatcherite strategy. Thatcherism deliberately – and from its viewpoint, correctly – eschews all reference to the concept of citizenship. 'Worker' is also a difficult one for it to negotiate, and it constantly prefers 'wealth creator'. Jessop et al. pose the 'hard' question of the relation of Thatcherism to 'specific class interests'. But they fail to provide the non-class-reductionist articulation to class positions they call for. 'An uneasy and unstable alliance of interests'? Amen – but we all got as far as that long ago. I also think that Jessop et al. are still too mesmerized by a problem which has long ago disappeared, in the sociological form in which it was carefully tended in the 1970s, into the oblivion. That is the question of 'corporatism'. The problems to which 'corporatism' was a response in the 1970s remain. The corporatist strategy is in abeyance – one of Thatcherism's accomplishments: though a healthy dose of Kinnockism will undoubtedly revive its deeply undemocratic features and endow it with a life after death.

On many other aspects of the Jessop et al. analysis I do not substantially differ. But on the central thrust of the argument, I think their article sophisticated but mistaken. They have badly skewed their own analysis and our general understanding of the Thatcherism phenomenon by entering into a misconceived confrontation with my work and with the concept of AP. They have profoundly misread the entire Gramscian terrain in which, from beginning to end, the whole AP discussion has been rooted. I am afraid they have sometimes had their eye cocked more towards scoring points than deconstructing Thatcherism. Nevertheless, they have contributed substantially to our understanding of many of its perplexing aspects. Perhaps, now that the sound of conceptual gunfire has died away, we might all get back to the far more important task of understanding the real complexity of the Thatcherism phenomenon, the better to defeat and destroy it.

1980

160 The Hard Road to Renewal

Notes

1. Stuart Hall et al., *Policing the Crisis*, London 1978.
2. On the conceptual distinction between 'popular' and 'populist' mobilization, which Jessop et al. seem to ignore, see S. Hall 'Popular-Democratic versus Authoritarian Populism', from Alan Hunt, ed., *Marxism and Democracy*, London 1980, reprinted in this volume pp. 123–149.
3. Nicos Poulantzas, *State, Power, Socialism*, NLB, London 1978, p. 203. For Stuart Hall's review of this book, see *New Left Review*, 119.
4. *Marxis Today*, February 1980.
5. See, inter alia, 'Recent Developments in Language and Ideology', in Hall et al., *Culture, Media, Language*, London 1980.
6. E. Laclau, *Politics and Ideology in Marxist Theory*, NLB, London 1977; E. Laclau and C. Mouffe, *Hegemony and Socialist Strategy*, Verso, London 1985.
7. An informal discussion group, convened in the 1982–84 period by Ernesto Laclau and others, around the broad themes of expanding the concept of 'hegemony' and the analysis of the present conjuncture.
8. In S. Hall and M. Jacques, eds, *The Politics of Thatcherism*, London 1983. Reprinted in this volume, pp. 39–56.

10

Gramsci and Us

This is not a comprehensive exposition of the ideas of Antonio Gramsci, nor a systematic account of the political situation in Britain today. It is an attempt to 'think aloud' about some of the perplexing dilemmas facing the left, in the light of – from the perspective of – Gramsci's work.

I do not claim that, in any simple way, Gramsci 'has the answers' or 'holds the key' to our present troubles. I do believe that we must 'think' our problems in a Gramscian way – which is different. We mustn't use Gramsci (as we have for so long abused Marx) like an Old Testament prophet who, at the correct moment, will offer us the consoling and appropriate quotation. We can't pluck up this 'Sardinian' from his specific and unique political formation, beam him down at the end of the twentieth century, and ask him to solve our problems for us: especially since the whole thrust of his thinking was to refuse this easy transfer of generalisations from one conjuncture, nation or epoch to another.

The thing about Gramsci that really transformed my own way of thinking about politics is the question which arises from his *Prison Notebooks*. If you look at the classic texts of Marx and Lenin, you are led to expect a revolutionary epochal historical development emerging from the end of the First World War onwards. And indeed events did give considerable evidence that such a development was occurring. Gramsci belongs to this 'proletarian moment'. It occurred in Turin in the 1920s, and other places where people like Gramsci, in touch with the advance guard of the industrial working class – then at the very forefront of modern production – thought that, if only the managers and politicians would get out of the way, this class of proletarians could run the world, take over the factories, seize the whole machinery of society, materially transform it and manage it economically, socially, culturally, technically.

The truth about the 1920s is that the 'proletarian moment' very nearly came off. Just before and after the First World War, it really was touch and go as to whether, under the leadership of such a class, the world might not have been transformed – as Russia was in 1917 by the Soviet revolution. This was the moment of the proletarian perspective on history.

What I have called 'Gramsci's question' in the *Notebooks* emerges in the aftermath of that moment, with the recognition that history was not going to go that way, especially in the advanced industrial capitalist societies of Western Europe. Gramsci had to confront the turning back, the failure, of that moment: the fact that such a moment, having passed, would never return in its old form. Gramsci, here, came face to face with the revolutionary character of history itself. When a conjecture unrolls, there is no 'going back'. History shifts gears. The terrain changes. You are in a new moment. You have to attend, 'violently', with all the 'pessimism of the intellect' at your command, to the 'discipline of the conjuncture'.

In addition (and this is one of the main reasons why his thought is so pertinent to us today) he had to face the capacity of the right – specifically, of European fascism – to hegemonise that defeat.

So here was a historic reversal of the revolutionary project, a new historical conjuncture, and a moment which the Right, rather than the left, was able to dominate. This looks like a moment of total crisis for the left, when all the reference points, the predictions, have been shot to bits. The political universe, as you have come to inhabit it, collapses.

I don't want to say that the left in Britain is in exactly the same moment; but I do hope you recognize certain strikingly similar features, because it is the similarity between those two situations that makes the question of the *Prison Notebooks* so seminal in helping us to understand what our condition is today. Gramsci gives us, not the tools with which to solve the puzzle, but the means with which to ask the right kinds of questions about the politics of the 1980s and 1990s. He does so by directing our attention unswervingly to what is specific and different about this moment. He always insists on this attention to difference. It's a lesson which the left in Britain has yet to learn. We do tend to think that the right is not only always with us, but is always exactly the same: the same people, with the same interests, thinking the same thoughts. We are living through the transformation of British Conservatism – its partial adaptation to the modern world, via the neo-liberal and monetarist 'revolutions'. Thatcherism has reconstructed Conservatism and the Conservative Party. The hard-faced, utilitarian, petty-bourgeois businessmen are now in charge, not the grouse-shooting, hunting and fishing classes. And yet, though those transformations are changing the political terrain of struggle before our very eyes, we think the differences don't have any real effect on anything. It still feels more 'left-wing' to say the old ruling class politics goes on in the same old way.

Gramsci, on the other hand, knew that difference and specificity mattered. So, instead of asking 'what would Gramsci say about Thatcherism?' we should simply attend to this rivetting of Gramsci to the notion of difference, to the specificity of a historical conjecture: how different forces come together, conjuncturally, to create the new terrain on which a different politics must form up. That is the intuition that Gramsci offers us about the nature of political life, from which we can take a lead.

I want to say what I think 'the lessons of Gramsci' are, in relation, first of all, to Thatcherism and the project of the new right; and, second, in terms of the crisis of the left.

Here, I'm foregrounding only the sharp edge of what I understand by Thatcherism. I'm trying to address the opening, from the mid-1970s onwards, of a new political project on the right. By a project, I don't mean (as Gramsci warned) a conspiracy. I mean the construction of a new agenda, the constitution of a new force, in British politics. Mrs Thatcher always aimed, not for a short electoral reversal, but for a long historical occupancy of power. That occupancy of power was not simply about commanding the apparatuses of the state. Indeed, the project was organized, in the early stages, in opposition to the state which in the Thatcherite view had been deeply corrupted by the welfare state and by Keynesianism and had thus helped to 'corrupt' the British people. Thatcherism came into existence in contestation with the old Keynesian welfare state, with social democratic 'statism', which, in its view, had dominated the 1960s. Thatcherism's project was to transform the state in order to restructure society: to decentre, to displace, the whole postwar formation; to reverse the political culture which had formed the basis of the political settlement – the historic compromise between labour and capital – which had been in place from 1945 onwards.

The depth of the reversal aimed for was profound: a reversal of the ground-rules of that settlement, of the social alliances which underpinned it and the values which made it popular. I don't mean the attitudes and values of the people who write books. I mean the ideas of the people who simply, in ordinary everyday life, have to calculate how to survive, how to look after those who are closest to them.

That is what is meant by saying that Thatcherism aimed for a reversal in ordinary common sense. The 'common sense' of the English people had been constructed around the notion that the last war had erected a barrier between the bad old days of the 1930s and now: the welfare state had come to stay; we'd never go back to using the criterion of the market as the sole measure of people's needs, the needs of society. There would always have to be some additional, incremental, institutional force – the state, representing the general interest of society – to bring to bear against, to modify, the market. I'm perfectly well aware that socialism was not inaugurated in 1945. I'm talking about the taken-for-granted, popular base of welfare social democracy, which formed the real, concrete ground on which any English socialism worth the name had to be built. Thatcherism was a project to engage, to contest that project, and, wherever possible, to dismantle it and to put something new in place. It entered the political field in a historic contest, not just for power, but for popular authority, for hegemony.

It is a project – this confuses the left no end – which is, simultaneously, regressive and progressive. Regressive because, in certain crucial respects, it takes us backwards. You couldn't be going anywhere else but backwards to hold up before the British people, at the end of the twentieth century, the idea that the best the future holds is for them to become, for a second time, 'Eminent Victorians'. It's deeply regressive, ancient and archaic.

But don't misunderstand it. It's also a project of 'modernisation'. It's a form of *regressive modernization*. Because, at the same time, Thatcherism had its beady eye fixed on one of the most profound historical facts about the British social formation: that it had never, ever, properly entered the era of modern bourgeois civilization. It never made that transfer to modernity. It never institutionalized, in a proper sense, the civilization and structures of advanced capitalism – what Gramsci called 'Fordism'. It never transformed its old industrial and political structures. It never became a second capitalist-industrial-revolution power, in the way that the US did, and, by another route (the 'Prussian route'), Germany and Japan did. Britain never undertook that deep transformation which, at the end of the nineteenth century, remade both capitalism and the working classes. Consequently, Mrs Thatcher knows, as the left does not, that there is no serious political project in Britain today which is not also about constructing a politics and an image of what *modernity* would be like for our people. And Thatcherism, in its regressive way, drawing on the past, looking backwards to former glories rather than forwards to a new epoch, has inaugurated the project of reactionary modernization.

There is nothing more crucial, in this respect, than Gramsci's recognition that every crisis is also a moment of reconstruction; that there is no destruction which is not, also, reconstruction; that historically nothing is dismantled without also attempting to put something new in its place; that every form of power not only excludes but produces something.

That is an entirely new conception of crisis – and of power. When the left talks about crisis, all we see is capitalism disintegrating, and us marching in and taking over. We don't understand that the disruption of the normal functioning of the old economic, social, cultural order, provides the opportunity to reorganize it in new ways, to restructure and refashion, to modernize and move ahead. If necessary, of course, at the cost of allowing vast numbers of people – in the North East, the North West, in Wales and Scotland, in the mining communities and the devastated industrial heartlands, in the inner cities and elsewhere – to be consigned to the historical dustbin. That is the 'law' of capitalist modernization: uneven development, organized disorganization.

Face to face with this dangerous new political formation, the temptation is always, ideologically, to dismantle it, to force it to stand still by asking *the* classic Marxist question: who does it really represent? Now, usually when the left asks that old classic Marxist question in the old way, we are not really asking a question, we are making a statement. We already know the answer. Of course, the right represents the ruling class in power. It represents the occupancy, by capital, of the state which is nothing but its instrument. Bourgeois writers produce bourgeois novels. The Conservative Party is the ruling class at prayer. Etc, etc ... This is Marxism as a theory of the obvious. The question delivers no new knowledge, only the answer we already knew. It's a kind of game – political theory as a Trivial Pursuit. In fact, the reason we need to ask the question is because we really don't know.

It really is puzzling to say, in any simple way, whom Thatcherism represents. Here is the perplexing phenomenon of a petty-bourgeois ideology which 'represents,' and is helping to reconstruct, both national and international capital. In the course of 'representing' corporate capital, however, it wins the consent of very substantial sections of the subordinate and dominated classes. What is the nature of this ideology which can inscribe such a vast range of different positions and interests in it, and which seems to represent a little bit of everybody? For, make no mistake, a tiny bit of all of us is also somewhere inside the Thatcherite project. Of course, we're all one hundred per cent committed. But every now and then – Saturday mornings, perhaps, just before the demonstration – we go to Sainsbury's and we're just a tiny bit of a Thatcherite subject ...

How do we make sense of an ideology which is not coherent, which speaks in our ear with the voice of freewheeling, utilitarian, market-man, and in the other ear with the voice of respectable, bourgeois, partriarchal man? How do these two repertoires operate together? We are all perplexed by the contradictory nature of Thatcherism. In our intellectual way, we think that the world will collapse as the result of a logical contradiction: this is the illusion of the intellectual –that ideology must be coherent, every bit of it fitting together, like a philosophical investigation. When, in fact, the whole purpose of what Gramsci called an organic (i.e, historically effective) ideology is that it articulates into a configuration different subjects, different identities, different projects, different aspirations. It does not reflect, it constructs a 'unity' out of difference.

We've been in the grip of the Thatcherite project not since 1983 or 1979, as official doctrine has it, but since 1975. 1975 is the climacteric in British politics. First of all, the oil hike. Secondly, the onset of the capitalist crisis. Thirdly, the transformation of modern Conservatism by the accession of the Thatcherite leadership. That is the moment of reversal when, as Gramsci argued, national and international factors come together. It doesn't begin with Mrs Thatcher's electoral victory, as politics is not a matter of elections alone. It lands in 1975, right in the middle of Mr Callaghan's political solar plexus. It breaks Mr Callaghan – already a broken reed – in two. One half remains avuncular, paternalist, socially conservative. The other half dances to a new tune.

One of the siren voices, singing the new song in his ear, is his son-in-law, Peter Jay, one of the architects of monetarism in his missionary role as economic editor at *The Times.* He first saw the new market forces, the new sovereign consumer, coming over the hill like the marines. And, harkening to these intimations of the future, the old man opens his mouth; and what does he say? The kissing has to stop. The game is over. Social democracy is finished. The welfare state is gone forever. We can't afford it. We've been paying ourselves too much, been giving ourselves a lot of phoney jobs, been having too much of a swinging time.

You can just see the English psyche collapsing under the weight of the illicit pleasures it has been enjoying – the permissiveness, the consumption, the goodies. It's all false – tinsel and froth. The Arabs have blown it all away. And now we have got to advance in a different way. Mrs Thatcher speaks to this 'new course'. She speaks to something else, deep in the English psyche: its masochism. The need which the English seem to have to be ticked off by Nanny and sent to bed without a pudding. The calculus by which every good summer has to be paid for by twenty bad winters. The Dunkirk spirit – the worse off we are, the better we behave. She didn't promise us the giveaway society. She said, iron times; back to the wall; stiff upper lip; get moving; on your bike; dig in. Stick by the old, tried verities, the wisdom of 'Old England'. The family has kept society together; live by it. Send the women back to the hearth. Get the men out on to the Northwest Frontier. Hard times – to be followed, much later, by a return to the good old days. She asked you for a long leash – not one, but two and three terms. By the end, she said, I will be able to redefine the nation in such a way that you will all, once again, for the first time since the Empire started to go down the tube, feel what it is like to be part of Great Britain Unlimited. You will be able, once again, to send our boys 'over there', to fly the flag, to welcome back the fleet. Britain will be great again.

People don't vote for Thatcherism, in my view, because they believe the small print. People in their minds do not think that Britain is now a wonderfully booming, successful, economy. Nobody believes that, with 3³/₄ million people unemployed, the economy is picking up. Everyone knows Lord Young's figures are 'economical with the truth'. What Thatcherism as an ideology does, is to address the fears, the anxieties, the lost identities, of a people. It invites us to think about politics in images. It is addressed to our collective fantasies, to Britain as an imagined community, to the social imaginery. Mrs Thatcher has totally dominated that idiom, while the left forlornly tries to drag the conversation round to 'our policies'.

This is a momentous historical project, the regressive modernization of Britain. To win over ordinary people to that, not because they're dupes, or stupid, or because they are blinded by false consciousness. Since, in fact, the political character of our ideas cannot be guaranteed by our class position or by the 'mode of production', it is possible for the right to construct a politics which does speak to people's experience, which does insert itself into what Gramsci called the necessarily fragmentary, contradictory nature of common sense, which does resonate with some of their ordinary aspirations, and which, in certain circumstances, can recoup them as subordinate subjects into a historical project which 'hegemonises' what we used – erroneously – to think of as their 'necessary class interests'. Gramsci is one of the first modern Marxists to recognize that interests are not given but always have to be politically and ideologically constructed.

Gramsci warns us in the *Notebooks* that a crisis is not an immediate event but a process: it can last for a long time, and can be very differently resolved: by restoration, by reconstruction or by passive transformism. Sometimes more stable, sometimes more unstable: but in a profound sense, British institutions, the British economy, British society and culture have been in a deep social crisis for most of the twentieth century.

Gramsci warns us that organic crises of this order erupt not only in the political domain and the traditional areas of industrial and economic life, and not simply in the class struggle, in the old sense; but in a wide series of polemics and debates about fundamental sexual, moral and intellectual questions, in a crisis in the relations of political representation and the parties – on a whole range of issues which do not necessarily, in the first instance, appear to be articulated with politics in the narrow sense at all. That is what Gramsci calls the crisis of authority, which is nothing but 'the crisis of hegemony or general crisis of the state'.

We are exactly in that moment. We have been shaping up to such a 'crisis of authority' in English social life and culture since the mid-1960s. In the 1960s, the crisis of English society was signalled in a number of debates and struggles around new points of antagonism, which appeared at first to be far removed from the traditional heartland of British politics. The left often waited patiently for the old rhythms of 'the class struggle' to be resumed, when in fact it was the forms of 'the class struggle' itself which were being transformed. We can only understand this diversification of social struggles in the light of Gramsci's insistence that, in modern societies, hegemony must be constructed, contested and won on many different sites, as the structures of the modern state and society complexify and the points of social antagonism proliferate.

So one of the most important things that Gramsci has done for us is to give us a profoundly expanded conception of what politics itself is like, and thus also of power and authority. We cannot, after Gramsci, go back to the notion of mistaking electoral politics, or party politics in a narrow sense, or even the occupancy of state power, as constituting the ground of modern politics itself. Gramsci understands that politics is a much expanded field; that, especially in societies of our kind, the sites on which power is constituted will be enormously varied. We are living through the proliferation of the sites of power and antagonism in modern society. The transition to this new phase is decisive for Gramsci. It puts directly on the political agenda the questions of moral and intellectual leadership, the educative and formative role of the state, the 'trenches and fortifications' of civil society, the crucial issue of the consent of the masses and the creation of a new type or level of 'civilization', a new culture. It draws the decisive line between the formula of 'Permanent Revolution' and the formula of 'civil hegemony'. It is the cutting-edge between the 'war of movement' and the 'war of position': the point where Gramsci's world meets ours.

That does not mean, as some people read Gramsci, that therefore the state doesn't matter any more. The state is clearly absolutely central in articulating the different areas of contestation, the different points of antagonism, into a regime of rule. The moment when you can get sufficient power in the state to organize a central political project is decisive, for then you can use the state to plan, urge, incite, solicit and punish, to conform the different sites of power and consent into a single regime. That is the moment of 'authoritarian populism' – Thatcherism simultaneously 'above' (in the state) and 'below' (down there with the people).

Even then, Mrs Thatcher does not make the mistake of thinking that the capitalist state has a single and unified political character. She is perfectly well aware, as the left is not, that, though the capitalist state is articulated to securing the long-term, historical conditions for capital accumulation and profitability, though it is the guardian of a certain kind of bourgeois, patriarchal civilization and culture, that it is, and continues to be, an arena of contestation.

Does this mean that Thatcherism is, after all, simply the 'expression' of the ruling class? Of course Gramsci always gives a central place to the questions of class, class alliances and class struggle. Where Gramsci departs from classical versions of Marxism is that he does not think that politics is an arena which simply reflects already unified collective political identities, already constituted forms of struggle. Politics for him is not a dependent sphere. It is where forces and relations, in the economy, in society, in culture, have to be actively worked on to produce particular forms of power, forms of domination. This is the production of politics – politics as a production. This conception of politics is fundamentally contingent, fundamentally open-ended. There is no law of history which can predict what must inevitably be the outcome of a political struggle. Politics depends on the relations of forces at any particular moment. History is not waiting in the wings to catch up your mistakes into another 'inevitable success'. You lose because you lose because you lose.

The 'good sense' of the people exists, but it is just the beginning, not the end, of politics. It doesn't guarantee anything. Actually, he said, 'new conceptions have an extremely unstable position among the popular masses'. There is no unitary subject of history. The subject is necessarily divided – an ensemble: one half Stone Age, the other containing 'principles of advanced science, prejudices from all past phases of history, intuitions of a future philosophy'. Both of those things struggle inside the heads and hearts of 'the people' to find a way of articulating themselves politically. Of course, it is possible to recruit them to very different political projects.

Especially today, we live in an era when the old political identities are collapsing. We cannot imagine socialism coming about any longer through the image of that single, singular subject we used to call Socialist Man. Socialist Man, with one mind, one set of interests, one project, is dead. And good riddance. Who needs 'him' now, with his investment in a particular historical period, with 'his' particular sense of masculinity, shoring 'his' identity up in a particular set of familial relations, a particular kind of sexual identity? Who needs 'him' as the singular identity through which the great diversity of human beings and ethnic cultures in our world must enter the twenty-first century? This 'he' is dead: finished.

Gramsci looked at a world which was complexifying in front of his eyes. He saw the pluralization of modern cultural identities, emerging between the lines of uneven historical development, and asked the question: what are the political forms through which a new cultural order could be constructed out of this 'multiplicity of dispersed wills, these heterogeneous aims'? Given that that is what people are really like, given that there is no law that will make socialism come true, can we find forms of organization, forms of identity, forms of allegiance, social conceptions, which can both connect with popular life and in the same moment, transform and renovate it? Socialism will not be delivered to us through the trapdoor of history by some deus ex machina.

Gramsci always insisted that hegemony is not exclusively an ideological phenomenom. There can be no hegemony without 'the decisive nucleus of the economic'. On the other hand, do not fall into the trap of the old mechanical economism and believe that if you can only get hold of the economy, you can move the rest of life. The nature of power in the modern world is that it is also constructed in relation to political, moral, intellectual, cultural, ideological, and sexual questions. The question of hegemony is always the question of a new cultural order. The question which faced Gramsci in relation to Italy faces us now in relation to Britain: what is the nature of this new civilization? Hegemony is not a state of grace which is installed forever. It's not a formation which incorporates everybody. The notion of a 'historical bloc' is precisely different from that of a pacified, homogeneous, ruling class.

It entails a quite different conception of how social forces and movements, in their diversity, can be articulated into a set of strategic alliances. To construct a new cultural order, you need not to reflect an already-formed collective will, but to fashion a new one, to inaugurate a new historic project.

I've been talking about Gramsci in the light of, in the aftermath of, Thatcherism: using Gramsci to comprehend the nature and depth of the challenge to the left which Thatcherism and the new right represent in English life and politics. But I have, at the same moment, inevitably, also been talking about the left. Or rather I've not been talking about the left, because the left, in its organized, labourist form, does not seem to have the slightest conception of what putting together a new historical project entails. It does not understand the necessarily contradictory nature of human subjects, of social identities. It does not understand politics as a production. It does not see that it is possible to connect with the ordinary feelings and experiences which people have in their everyday lives, and yet to articulate them progressively to a more advanced, modern form of social consciousness. It is not actively looking for and working upon the enormous diversity of social forces in our society. It doesn't see that it is in the very nature of modern capitalist civilization to proliferate the centres of power, and thus to draw more and more areas of life into social antagonism. It does not recognize that the identities which people carry in their heads – their subjectivities, their cultural life, their sexual life, their family life and their ethnic identities, are always incomplete and have become massively politicized.

I simply don't think, for example, that the current Labour leadership understands that its political fate depends on whether or not it can construct a politics, in the next twenty years, which is able to address itself not to one, but to a diversity of different points of antagonism in society; unifying them, in their differences, within a common project. I don't think they have grasped that Labour's capacity to grow as a political force depends absolutely on its capacity to draw from the popular energies of very different movements; movements outside the party which it did not – could not – set in play, and which it cannot therefore 'administer'. It retains an entirely bureaucratic conception of politics. If the word doesn't proceed out of the mouths of the Labour leadership, there must be something subversive about it. If politics energises people to develop new demands, that is a sure sign that the natives are getting restless. You must expel or depose a few. You must get back to that fiction, the 'traditional Labour voter': to that pacified, Fabian notion of politics, where the masses hijack the experts into power, and then the experts do something for the masses: later . . . much later. The hydraulic conception of politics.

That bureaucratic conception of politics has nothing to do with the mobilization of a variety of popular forces. It doesn't have any conception of how people become empowered by doing something: first of all about their immediate troubles. Then the power expands their political capacities and ambitions, so that they begin to think again about what it might be like to rule the world . . . Their bureaucratic politics has ceased to have a connection with this most modern of all revolutions – the deepening of democratic life.

Without the deepening of popular participation in national cultural life, ordinary people don't have any experience of actually running anything. We need to reacquire the notion that politics is about expanding popular capacities, the capacities of ordinary people. And in order to do so, socialism itself has to speak to the people whom it wants to empower in words that belong to them as late twentieth century ordinary folks.

You'll have noticed that I'm not talking about whether the Labour Party has got its policy on this or that issue right. I'm talking about a whole conception of politics: the capacity to grasp in our political imagination the huge historical choices in front of the British people today. I'm talking about new conceptions of the nation itself: whether you believe Britain can advance into the next century with a conception of what it is like to be 'English' which has been entirely constituted out of Britain's long, disastrous, imperialist march across the earth. If you really think that, you haven't grasped the profound cultural transformation required to remake the English. That kind of cultural transformation is precisely what socialism is about today.

Now a political party of the left, however much it is centred on government, on winning elections, has, in my view, exactly this kind of decision before it. The reason why I'm not optimistic about the 'mass party of the working class' ever understanding the nature of the historical choice confronting it is precisely because I suspect Labour still does secretly believe that there's a little bit of leeway left in the old, economic-corporate, incremental, Keynesian game. It does think it could go back to a little smidgeon of Keynesianism here, a little bit more of the welfare state there, a little bit of the old Fabian thing ... Actually, though I don't have a cataclysmic vision of the future, I honestly believe that that option is now closed. It's exhausted. Nobody believes in it any more. Its material conditions have disappeared. The ordinary British people won't vote for it because they know in their bones that life is not like that any more.

What Thatcherism poses, in its radical way, is not 'what we can go back to?' but rather, 'along which route are we to go forward?' In front of us is the historic choice: capitulate to the Thatcherite future, or find another way of imagining it. Don't worry about Mrs Thatcher herself; she will retire to Dulwich. But there are lots more third, fourth and fifth generation Thatcherites, dry as dust, sound to a man, waiting to take her place. They feel themselves now on the crest of a wave. They are at the forefront of what they think is the new global expansion of capitalism. They are convinced that this will obliterate socialism forever. They think we are dinosaurs. They think we belong to another era. As socialism slowly declines, a new era will dawn and these new kinds of possessive men will be in charge of it. They dream about real cultural power. And Labour, in its softly-softly, don't-rock-the-boat, hoping-the-election-polls-will-go-up way, actually has before it the choice between becoming historically irrelevant or beginning to sketch out an entirely new form of civilization.

I don't say socialism, lest the word is so familiar to you that you think I mean just putting the same old programme we all know about back on the rails. I am talking about a renewal of the whole socialist project in the context of modern social and cultural life. I mean shifting the relations of forces – not so that Utopia comes the day after the next general election, but so that the tendencies begin to run another way. Who needs a socialist heaven where everybody agrees with everybody else, where everybody's exactly the same? God forbid. I mean a place where we can begin the historic quarrel about what a new kind of civilisation must be. That's what it's about. Is it possible that the immense new material, cultural and technological capacities, far outstripping Marx's wildest dreams, which are now actually in our hands, are going to be politically hegemonized for the reactionary modernization of Thatcherism? Or can we seize on those means of history-making, of making new human subjects, and shove them in the direction of a new culture? That's the choice before the left.

'One should stress', Gramsci wrote, 'the significance which, in the modern world, political parties have in the elaboration and diffusion of conceptions of the world, because essentially what they do is to work out the ethics and the politics corresponding to these conceptions and act, as it were, as their historical "laboratory" ...'

1987

PART THREE

◆

Crisis and Renewal
on the Left

11

The Battle for Socialist Ideas in the 1980s

I want to say something about the importance of ideological struggle. Thinking about the place and role of ideas in the construction of socialism, I would particularly emphasize the notion of struggle itself: ideology is a battlefield and every other kind of struggle has a stake in it. I want therefore to talk about the ideological preconditions for socialist advance: the winning of a majority of the people – the working people of the society and their allies – to socialist ideas in the decades immediately ahead. I stress the centrality of the domain of the ideological – political ideas and the struggle to win hearts and minds to socialism – because I am struck again and again by the way in which socialists still assume that somehow socialism is inevitable. It is not coming perhaps quite as fast as we assumed: not trundling along in our direction with quite the speed and enthusiasm we would hope; but nevertheless, bound sooner or later to take command. Socialism, it is felt, remains the natural centre of gravity of working-class ideas, and only a temporary, magical spell could divert working-class consciousness from its natural aim.

One can recognize a certain kind of Marxist 'traditionalism' behind this notion of the 'inevitable triumph of socialist ideas'. But, actually, it is even more deeply rooted in the non-Marxist, 'labourist' traditions. Vulgar economism comes in many disguises. Socialist ideas, having taken root in the culture, will never die; socialism is the true, the 'objective consciousness' of the class; material conditions will always make working people think 'socialism'; once a Labour voter, always a Labour voter; the welfare state is here to stay. And so on. If the 'laws of history' do not, then familial habit and electoral inertia will make 'correct ideas' win through in the end.

I have to confess I no longer subscribe to that view. I think perhaps I once did; but I believe now that if socialism is not *made* by us, it certainly will not be made *for* us, not even by the laws of history. The alternative which Marx offered, namely 'socialism or barbarism', sometimes seems to be more powerfully tilted, at the end of the twentieth century, towards barbarism than socialism. The capacity of a nuclear-filled world to destroy itself in the defence of some frozen social system, or some lofty ideal, is as much on the cards as the triumph of socialism in the advanced industrial capitalist world. We have to abandon the notion that socialism will somehow come in spite of how effectively we struggle for it; and I think that is also true for socialist ideas. Since it is possible to conceive of a world without human life, it is possible to envisage a world without socialism.

I want to say something about what lies behind the untenable notion of the inevitable triumph of socialist ideas, and suggest some of the reasons why that is not a socialism in which we can any longer indulge ourselves. There is a strong assumption that, in a class society like ours, where the vast majority of working people are continuously at the negative, the receiving end of the system, the social and material conditions in which working people themselves live will inevitably predispose them towards socialism. And I think that this proposition contains a profound materialist truth – despite the reconstruction job we have had to do on the classical materalist theory of ideology. Marx once remarked that you do not literally have to *be* a shopkeeper all your life to have petty-bourgeois ideas – an observation demonstrated by our own prime minister. It is true that if you live constantly in a corner shop and try to squeeze a living under advanced capitalism from that particular corner of it, you will be strongly inclined to *think* that that is actually how the world works. Similarly, if you are always at the exploiting end of an economic, social and political system, there is a built-in tendency, in the very material conditions in which the class has to live and survive, to think of socialist ideas as most effectively capturing the interests of the working class and the stake of working people in the future of their own society.

Still, there is no inevitable or guaranteed link between class origin and political ideas. What matters, Marx suggested, was whether or not in your thinking you go beyond the horizon of thought typical of the petty bourgeois – the sort of spontaneous thinking which arises when one tries to live one's relation to an advanced capitalist economy as if it were simply the old corner shop writ large. This might be called the

'Grantham' world-view. Undoubtedly, living at the exploited end of a system creates a powerful tendency to see the world in terms of 'us' and 'them': the governing and the governed, the powerful and the powerless, the possessing and the possessed. 'Us' and 'them' is the spontaneous consciousness of all exploited classes and oppressed people everywhere: what Gramsci called their 'good' sense. And, though social struggles have their roots deep in the structural contradictions of a system, they cannot become politically active unless they become articulated through this oppressor/oppressed form of consciousness.

The problem is that even this tendency cannot provide socialism with a permanent guarantee. 'Us' and 'them' can be represented through a number of different political ideologies. It underpins reformism or 'Labourism' just as much as it does more revolutionary positions. Even working-class deference can feed off this built-in sense of class difference. So there may be good materialist reasons why, in some circumstances, socialist ideas do win support among the working class. But there is certainly no materialist guarantee that *only* socialism can represent the interests of the working class and their stake in the future. And the addition of 'true' to the word 'interests' only begs the question: it is an attempt to save our historical face. Interests may be the motor of political action. But interests frequently conflict: the 'interest' in defending one's standard of living against the interest in remaining in employment – a contradiction which Mrs Thatcher, Mr Tebbitt and Mr Michael Edwardes – to name but three – have not hesitated to exploit. Moreover, working-class interests do not exist outside of the political space in which they are defined, or outside of the ideological discourses which give them sense, or outside the balance of forces which define the limits of the possible in which they have to be realized. Materialism remains active. But its tendency is not unidirectional. Socialism carries no absolute guarantees.

We have to confess that socialist ideas have come and gone among working people in our own society throughout recent history. A significant proportion of the British working class has consistently voted the other way. The deference vote amongst that class is not an insignificant proportion and it is not historically transient. We have to acknowledge that though, of course, material conditions may predispose working people to think in the direction of the reform and reconstruction of a system which exploits them in so many ways, they do not guarantee that economic and social position will always be translated into a political project or will and of itself – without political organization and education – give birth spontaneously to socialist ideas.

The working class, as we know it, is powerfully divided and stratified internally. It is not always unified in its origins, though it may *become* so through its political practice. In itself, it is sectorialized; impregnated by ideas, interests and outlooks from elsewhere. It is marked by the contradictory conditions in which it came to maturity: for instance, by the uneven impact of the social and sexual division of labour under capitalism. The unity of working-class political movements, activities and ideas around a common socialist core would not be a reflection of what the class already is 'in-itself' but the effect of the involvement of a 'class-in-itself' in a 'politics-for-itself'. That shift involves something more than merely translating one's everyday, lived experience into the socialist project. It means qualifying, criticizing and interrogating working-class 'experience'. It means, often, breaking the mould of working-class common sense.

I know this idea runs right against the grain of libertarian–socialist received wisdom in the 1980s. Socialists who work as intellectual people have come to understand the costs of their profound separation from the lived, everyday experience of working people under capitalism. They are also deeply, and correctly, suspicious of setting themselves up as a vanguard to bring socialism to the masses 'from the outside'. In the light of the Bolshevik experience, we know what happens when the party is substituted for the class, and the leadership for the party, and so on. But, in the post-1968 period, such people have been driven to the opposite and equally untenable alternative: Narodnikism. This is the view that 'the people' are *already* really socialist; and this will come through if we only allow them to speak. The role of socialists is therefore simply to be the 'voice' of this already adequate experience: to flatter the 'authenticity' of working-class experience and its spontaneous consciousness by simply affirming it.

But this cannot be correct, either. If socialism were simply the flowering of what already exists, and nothing more, why hasn't it defeated its enemies before now? Even more worryingly, if under capitalism the working class is able to live its relation to its conditions of existence transparently and 'authentically', why does it have need for socialism at all? The division of labour has inscribed itself indelibly across the body of the working classes, and nowhere more damagingly than in the division between mental and manual, physical and intellectual labour. But you don't overcome the capitalist division of labour by denying that it exists – only by going beyond it, in reality, in practice. By breaking down some of the divisions, through political education and organization; by setting – slowly, painfully – in their place, an alternative division of labour. That is why, in spite of all the traps which lie in wait for the attempt to restore the question of 'party' to socialist politics today, the fragmented political scene continues to be haunted by the absent ghost of – not *the* Party (there are plenty of those), but of 'party' in Gramsci's sense. For it is only in the course of political organization and practice ('party') that the damaging divisions of status between manual and intellectual labour, between the intellectual function (all of us, since we all think) and those who do intellectual work for a living (a very small number of us) can actually be overcome, so that the conditions for genuine political education – learning and teaching beyond the hierarchies of 'teacher' and 'taught', 'vanguard' and 'mass' – can be created. This failure to find an alternative basis for political education – alternative to either the 'vanguardist' or the 'Narodnikist' solutions – is part of a larger political crisis: the crisis of political organization which has afflicted the left since Leninism lost its magic in 1956, and since 1968 when to be 'radical' meant, by definition, to be 'radically against *all* parties, party lines and party bureaucracies': the 'inside but not beyond the fragments' problem. This problem of 'party' represents an unsurpassed limit in the politics of the left today: a line we seem able neither to return to nor pass across. But we shouldn't mistake this dilemma for a solution!

It is true that working-class experience – the experience of exploitation and of 'secondariness' – is the soil in which socialism takes root. Without it we may have all manner of 'radicalisms' – including the spurious extremisms of 'armed struggle' – but we will not have socialism. On the other hand, if working-class 'experience' is the necessary, it is not the sufficient condition for socialism or for socialist ideas today. First, because working-class 'common sense' under capitalism *must* be fragmentary and contradictory. It is inscribed with the traces of heterogeneous ideas. It contains in the same thought, as Gramsci remarked, modern and archaic, progressive and stone-age elements. Experience, as such, is historically shaped. It is constituted through ideological categories. How could we feel and reason entirely outside the categories of our own culture? It cannot, despite its appearance of immediate authenticity, escape its own history. Second, because the lived experience of class exploitation is not the only brand which socialism in the twentieth century must incorporate; it is not the only variant of exploitation which socialism must address, though it may be the modal one, the one with which all the other social contradictions are articulated, the paradigm instance. Therefore, other types of social experiences will have to be drawn on and built into socialism if it is to become a politics capable of condensing the variety of social struggles into a single, differentiated one, or – to put the metaphor the other way – if it is to become a politics capable of fighting and transforming life on a variety of different 'fronts'. Once we abandon the guarantee that working-class ideas will 'inevitably tend towards socialism' as their given, teleological end, and the assumption that everything else follows once socialism begins, it has to be acknowledged that sexist and racist and jingoist ideas have deeply penetrated and naturalized themselves in sectors of working-class thinking. Such ideas – frequently drawing exactly on 'immediate experience', and simply mirroring it – are not consonant with socialism. In the name of socialism itself (not in the name of some superior wisdom) they will have to be interrogated, corrected, transformed, *educated.* And, without falling back into vanguardism, we must – for all our sakes – find a way of undertaking this far-reaching political and ideological struggle *against* 'working-class common sense' inside the class itself.

Experience has many dimensions, many structures. The 'experience' of the British working class is also the massive historical experience of corporateness, and of the struggle against incorporation. The moment one says this it is likely to be pounced on by the keepers of revolutionary purity as living proof of one's lack of faith in the capacities of the class. This is polemical rubbish. Corporateness is simply an acknowledgement of where, under capitalism, the majority of working people are *positioned.* Otherwise, why would one need the Marxist concept of 'exploitation' at all? Within that, the British working class is also the most 'experienced' industrial class in the history of capitalism, rich in political traditions and culture. It has generated organization capable of defending class interests and advancing its cause. It is a   class wisdom of the infinite negotiations and resistances necessary for survival within the culture of capitalism. It has immense *depth* in defence. And yet socialism – of course – requires something more, something that does not arise spontaneously: a class which can transform itself from the secondary to the *leading* element in society. A class which aspires to refashion the world in its image. A class capable of conducting a struggle in areas of civil society, moral and intellectual life and the state, *outside* of its 'immediate' class experience; a class capable of winning the 'war of position' in relation to a whole complex of social movements which do not spontaneously cohere around *the* 'class experience'. We do not yet have a class which is driving to make itself the hegemonic element in society: which sees its purpose not to defend but to *lead.* Experience of exploitation, alone, will not create a 'class-for-itself' in this sense, though socialism in the twentieth century requires one.

We also have to acknowledge that working people are not 'unified' around *any* single political philosophy or ideology, let alone socialism. There are different kinds of socialist ideas and the labour movement in this country has gravitated, for often quite understandable reasons, towards reformism. Political reformism represents a strong, indigenous British political tradition: as authentic a working-class tradition as the revolutionary one. It represents a different, more adaptive, negotiated way of struggling for survival inside a system. But it is not an illusion. It is not false consciousness. It is not that working people do not understand the nature of the game in which they are involved. In part, all politics is a form of political calculation; and some people, under certain circumstances, will calculate for themselves, their children, and the people they love and work with, that it is better to take advantage of whatever advance you can make rather than cutting off the head of the goose that sometimes – occasionally – lays a golden egg. In a system that usually yields *something* under pressure at the eleventh hour, reformism has its own kind of 'rationality'. All the same, reformism is not the same as socialism. I do not want to make a kind of absolute divide or fetish of the distinction between them. But in the year of the Social Democratic Party one has to distinguish in a very sharp way between the two. It is certainly important not to fall into the trap of repeating the formal, abstract opposition between reform and revolution – a specious piece of left formalism. Still, we must understand the clear line that divides socialists from people who would like to see society more humanely governed, who are more open to progressive ideas and who would like to see people who have not had much out of life getting on a little. Those are all sound, worthy, reformist ideas They are what you might call socialism without tears. Socialism without all that bother about the working class. They are political change without political power: the great liberal illusion in twentieth-century fancy dress. Well, reformism is not only a long and important tradition. Actually, it has always been the dominant tradition inside the Labour Party itself. But it is not socialism. I do not want to rely on the rhetoric or received wisdom of the past, because one of the requirements of a socialism without guarantees must be to rethink what socialism might mean in the 1980s and 1990s. But nevertheless, one thing it *has* always meant is a fundamental reshaping of the social relations and the institutions in which men and women live.

Socialism has, in its past, learnt a good deal from progressive people who have contributed in important ways to the labour movement. I expect it always will try to show that only socialism can create the condi-tions in which *reform* can make a fundamental difference rather than introducing minor modifications. But progressivism can never provide the lure of socialist ideas. Between good reformism and the will to socialism runs what William Morris once called the 'river of fire'. Of course, when socialism touches the imagination, people do still go on living just as they did before, trying to survive, coming to terms with a society in which they have to make an existence. But their imaginations have been fired by the possibility of an alternative way of making life with other people, and nothing less will do. Socialism may be just half the turn of a screw away from reformist and progressive ideas but it is this final twist that counts. It is what makes the difference between good and humane people and committed socialists: between the logic of one principle of social organization and another.

Now when that gulf opens, the river of fire dissects people's lives, and they glimpse the possibility not of having the existing set of social relations improved a bit, but of beginning the long, dangerous, historical process of reconstructing society according to a different model, a different logic and principle that do not come 'spontaneously'. It does not drop like manna from the skies. It has to be made, constructed and struggled over. Socialist ideas win only because they displace other not so good, not so powerful ideas. They only command a space because they grip people's imagination, or they connect with people's experience; or they make better sense of the world they live in; or they are better at analysing what is happening; or they provide a language of difference and resistance; or they capture and embody people's hopes. Apart from their effectivity there is no guarantee that socialist ideas must and will prevail over other ideas. In that sense, I believe that the struggle for socialist ideas is a continuous one. It is something which will have to go on under 'actual existing socialism' itself. I am even quite tempted by the thought of that much discredited leader of the people, Chairman Mao, that the period of socialist construction might be the moment of greatest intensity in the battle for socialist ideas.

Why, then, is the terrain for socialist ideas so stony in the 1980s? One can think of many good reasons, but I refer here to only three. The first I can deal with quickly, though it may surprise you. I think that one of the reasons why the terrain for socialist ideas is so stony is the fact, the legacy, the experience of Stalinism. By this I mean something quite different from the usual simple minded anti-communism. Nevertheless, I do think that when they speak to people drawn and attracted to socialism, socialists today have something to explain, to account for: why the attempt to transform some societies in the image of socialism has produced this grim caricature. I know that the transform-ation of relatively backward societies is a much more difficult and prolonged process than most of us imagine; that 'socialism in one country' is not a particularly good way to have to start; that all is not lost in these societies, that the struggle for socialism is not terminated in them. All the same, people are willing to contemplate pulling up what they know by the roots *only* if they can have some rational hope, some concrete image of the alternative. At the beginning of the century, the language of socialism was full of hope, indeed of a perhaps too naive scientific guarantee about the future. But the actuality of Stalinism and its aftermath has added the tragic dimension to the language of social-ism: the stark possibility of failure. The socialist experiment *can* go wildly and disastrously wrong. It *can* produce a result which is both recognizable as 'socialism' and yet alien to everything intrinsic in our image of what socialism should be like. It can deliver consequences against which socialists may have to stand up and be counted. This is a deep and wounding paradox – and a damaging weakness which every socialist has first to dismantle before he or she can persuade people in good faith to come to our side and assume positions alongside us in the struggle. In our struggle to realise a proper kind of socialism, we have first to explain – not explain away – the *other* kind: the kind where, in the name of the workers' state, the working class is actually shot down in the streets, as is happening at this very moment to Polish Solidarity in Gdansk.

Second, there is a problem about the resilience and buoyancy of socialist ideas in our time because of the exhaustion which has overtaken the labour movement, especially under the management of Labour governments in the past two or three decades. I do not want to talk about the record of those governments in detail. But I want to communicate my overwhelming sense that the collapse of the last Labour government in 1979 was not simply the rotation of political parties in government but the end of a particular political epoch. It was the culmination of a period in which, although there were actually Conservative governments in power some of the time, the framework of ideas being drawn on, the dominant ideas, the consensus, was taken precisely from the social-democratic repertoire. Those were ideas to which people had become acclimatized; the taken-for-granted welfare state, mixed economy, incomes policy, corporatist bargaining and demand management. If you stood up at that time, in a debate on the national economy, and tried to justify neo-classical economics, or indeed monetarism, you would have been laughed out of court. Everyone who mattered was one kind of Keynesian or another. Good ideas belonged to the 'left'. In the sixties and early seventies the right refused to use the word 'capitalism' at all. Bad old capitalism, they insisted, had long gone past. In its place we had something else to help people to, as it were, survive through the dark ages of creeping collectivism. This was the epoch of social-democratic hegemony. That is no longer the case. People again talk quite openly about 'free-market capitalism'. When the Institute for Economic Affairs first started pumping out simple-minded monetarism for the one or two experts in the civil service who still read books, they glossed the capitalist ethic by calling it 'social market values'. They could not actually pronounce the word 'market' in its full, bare, capitalist form. They had to colour it over a bit, to soften the blow, by calling it 'social market values'. They don't talk about social market values or the mixed economy any longer. They talk about *the market* – the good old hidden hand, Adam Smith's market. There are civil servants in Sir Keith Joseph's ministry who are busy reading *The Wealth of Nations* for the first time. They actually believe in the invisible hand which draws us all involuntarily into the market, produces what everyone needs and pays us what we all deserve. These ancient, preindustrial, prehistoric ideas are capitalist ideas making a later twentieth-century reprise to displace those outdated social-democratic nostrums about the benevolent state, the national interest and the 'caring society'. Calculating everything according to its pure market value and measuring the national interest in terms of gross self-interest are back in fashion. Even Mr Roy Jenkins and the SDP can't resist the 'new brutalism'.

I don't deny that social democracy helped to make life more humane and tolerable for many in its heyday in the 1960s and 1970s. We have only to bring to mind the alternative – say, Mr Tebbit or Mr Heseltine in full flow – to find it relatively easy to think kind thoughts about Mr Callaghan, squalid though his last political hours proved to be. But however we assess the differences, it is clear now that those social-democratic ideas which seemed to define the age were trapped in their own contradictions. They proved hopelessly inadequate to the crisis which was already confronting the country and whose dimensions have rapidly increased. They were thin ideas in front of a fat, long historical crisis – some, including me, would say a crisis which began in the closing decades of the last century, the post-imperialist crisis from which Britain has never in fact recovered. The central illusion – the social-democratic illusion, Mark I – to which Labour leaders good, bad and indifferent were attached was that the social-democratic bandwagon could be hitched to the star of a reformed capitalism: and that the latter would prove capable of infinite expansion so that all the political constituencies could be 'paid off' at once: the TUC and the CBI, labour and capital, public housing and the private landlord, the miners and the Bank of England. Why worry about the size of your slice relative to the next person's if the size of the cake is constantly expanding?

This social-democratic illusion was undermined by the fundamental weaknesses in British industrial capitalism and by the logic of capitalism itself. There simply was not enough expansion in the system, after a time, to pay off everybody. Besides, it was always an illusion that by taking the industrial infrastructure into the public economy, you had somehow transformed the logic of profitability and accumulation. This illusion was caught in the scissors of capitalist reality. When the goodies stop rolling in and you have to choose – under the helpful guidance of the International Monetary Fund – between maintaining living standards and restoring profitability and the managerial prerogative, which is it to be? At that point, an incomes policy ceased to be a recipe for 'planned growth' and instead became a strategy by which a government 'of' the working people polices and disciplines the working class. In the end, under capitalism, the interests of capital and restoring the conditions of expanded accumulation must count first, ahead of the wages and living standards of the people.

When caught in the *logic* of a system, there is no need for conspiratorial theories about leadership sell-outs. If you are inside a declining capitalism, there are no extra funds in the kitty to pay off the working class. That is a logic which catches governments of the left, right and centre. That is why I made such heavy weather, earlier on, about the distinction between socialist ideas and other ideas. It is not a distinction between the good and the bad. It is the distinction between two logics. R.H. Tawney – one of those truly progressive minds whom the Social-Democratic Party are trying to hijack – once said that capitalism is not an onion, but a tiger: 'You can peel an onion layer by layer; but you cannot skin a tiger stripe by stripe.' Not a particularly SDP sentiment, you may think. Social democracy – I mean Mark I, when the Labour Party was in power – was no doubt committed, broadly speaking, to improving society in a social-democratic way. It chose to reform but not to transform. But British capitalism required not greater humanity but the kiss of life. And, trapped by that remorseless logic, those ideas of reform have gone to the wall. They have disintegrated on us. People are not attracted or powered by them any more. People may be driven back to them because of the horrendous alternative offered by the other side, but that is not a victory for socialist ideas. That is a revulsion against reactionary ideas, which is a very different thing. We could certainly have another Labour government or even a social democratic Mark II government next. But whether there will be a government on the basis of a popular and positive mandate for advancing towards socialism is open to doubt. The problem is that the positive commitment to the serious, dangerous and difficult task of unpacking the oldest capitalist system in the world, and beginning to construct some other system – without triggering off 'barbarism' – will require a great deal of popular will, mobilization, commitment and nerve. And one of the essential prerequisites for this is the transformation of popular consciousness in a socialist direction. I am not concerned, at the moment, with prophecies about the exact character and political colouration of the next government. But there is a qualitative difference between advancing towards socialism and achieving another Labour government which comes in on the mandate of the exhausted political ideas of the last two decades.

I have talked about two barriers standing in the way of the advance of socialist ideas. One is the legacy of actual existing socialism. The second is the historic record of the exhaustion and collapse of the ideas and programmes on which majority Labour governments have taken legitimate power in the state during the postwar period.

But I want to say something about a third inhibition. This is the advance of the right itself. Since the accession of the Thatcherites to power in the Conservative Party in the mid-1970s, I have taken a more gloomy view of the advance of the right than most other socialists. It may be that I am overstating the case, in which case I may stimulate you into deeper socialist commitment. I think that the radical right under Thatcherite leadership is very different from any other conservative power base we have seen in the post war period. I think its ideological penetration into society is very profound. It has shifted the parameters of common sense. It has pioneered a considerable swing towards authoritarian populism and reactionary ideas. It goes deep into the heartland of traditional labour support: skilled workers; working women; young people. Its success is partly the result of the right, not the left, *taking ideas seriously*. The radical right is not hung up on some low-flying materialism which tells them that, of course, ideas are wholly determined by material and economic conditions. They actually do believe that you have to struggle to implant the notion of the market; and that, if you talk about it well enough, effectively and persuasively enough, you can touch people's understanding of how they live and work, and make a new kind of sense about what's wrong with society and what to do about it.

That is, of course, precisely the nature of ideology. It provides the frameworks within which people define and interpret social existence. Not necessarily in a very learned or systematic way, but in terms of everyday, practical social reasoning, practical consciousness. Events and their consequences can always be interpreted in more than one ideological framework. That is why there is always a struggle over ideology: a struggle as to which definition of the situation will prevail. This is a struggle over a particular kind of power – cultural power: the power to define, to 'make things mean'. The politics of signification. What matters is which frameworks are in play, which definitions fill out and articulate the 'common sense' of a conjuncture, which have become so naturalized and consensual that they are identical with common sense, with the taken-for-granted, and represent the point of origin from which all political calculation begins. It has become unfashionable to quote the French Marxist philosopher, Althusser, in polite socialist company in Britain, so since this is a virtual repository of unseasonable thoughts, let me do so now:

> The realities of the class struggle are 'represented' by ideas which are 'represented' by words. In scientific and philosophical reasoning, the words (concepts, categories) are 'instruments' of knowledge. But in political, ideological and philosophical struggle, the words are also weapons, explosives or tran-

quillisers and poisons. Occasionally, the whole class struggle may be summed up in the struggle for one word against another. Certain words struggle amongst themselves as enemies. Other words are the site of an ambiguity: the stake in a decisive but undecided battle.'[1]

To this struggle the radical right have devoted themselves with conspicuous success. In the categories of common sense, 'freedom' has not only been separated from, but has effectively *displaced* 'equality'. The state, as representative of the 'caring society' and the 'national interest', has attracted to it all the negative connotations of the spend-thrift, bureaucratic totalitarian machine. In its place there flames once more that spark of hope, freedom and individual choice: free enterprise.

Socialists tend to dismiss the idea that such thoughts could ever really take root again in popular consciousness. They are false, an illusion. But organic ideologies, which are deeply rooted in real practices (as the market, after all, is in our society), which represent the interests of fund-amental classes, which have been historically developed and refined and which have mobilized masses of men and women into action, are very rarely pure fabrications in this sense. They may be hideously wicked; but they do touch reality, even if they misrepresent its meaning; they have some rational core. The first thing to ask about an organic ideology is not whether it is false but what is true about it. After all, under capital-ism, men and women *do* live their lives and sell their labour, every day, in the market. It has its own materiality; it imposes its gross reality on everyone, whether we like it or not. What Marx suggested was that we cannot unlock the secret of capitalist production starting from that point: and we cannot supercede the laws of capitalist exploitation until we can surpass the imperatives of market exchange. But he never argued that it does not exist, or that it has no reality or effectivity of its own, or that it is the figment of someone's imagination. Quite the contrary. He showed how – without the concept of surplus value, which had to be introduced into the analysis of capitalism since it did not appear on its surface – the laws of market exchange appeared to work only too well. Also, how simple, succinct and elegant a 'mechanism' it was. Also, how men and women came to live their whole relation to capitalism within the categories, the spontaneous consciousness, of market relations: 'Freedom, Equality, Property and Bentham.' And before you jump to the conclusion that this exhausts its 'rationality' as an effective organizer of demand and supply, we had better ask the Hungarians or the Czechs or the Poles whether or not the idea still has some purchase, some rationality, to it; and how it stands up against the superior rationality of 'The Plan' in actual existing socialist societies which have attempted to plan everything from tractors to hatpins.

Of course, it is possible to reconstruct the market as an ideological construct. Provided – as is always the case in ideology – you play up the good side and repress the negative; provided, that is to say, you do not ask who precisely does, and who does not, benefit from this kind of 'freedom'. Provided you do not ask who brings unequal power into the equivalences of market exchange, you can set in motion a powerful cluster of ideas which trigger off a postive chain of associations – the market = free choice = freedom and liberty = anti-statism = 'put an end to creeping collectivism'! Even in the era of corporatism and state capitalism, of giant corporations and multinationals, it is still possible for people to 'make sense' of their experience within the categories of market 'freedom and choice'.

One of the most important features of the radical right in the period between 1975 and 1979 was the degree to which its protagonists grasped the argument that there was no point taking political power with a radical, reactionary programme unless they had already won the ideological terrain. And they set about doing just that. One could contrast that with the Labour policy towards, for example, immigration. Labour's conscience may be in the right place, if a little faint, about immigration. But without a preparatory politics which confronts indigenous working-class racism, without the means of ideological struggle which allow you to set your own agenda vis-á-vis racism, without a politics which confronts racism and prepares – educates – people for legislation which will positively favour an anti-racist policy, without these Labour simply 'takes office' – a different thing from 'taking power'. Then it sticks the political thermometer into peoples' mouths and its social-democratic conscience is shocked and astonished to discover that the fever of racism is actually running quite high in society, not least in local Labour clubs and parties. There is nothing for it but to cut the problem off at the source: thus, immigration controls. If you do not prepare ideologically for political power, you will find the weight of popular ideas stacked against change and your freedom of action constrained by the nature of the existing terrain.

Between 1975 and 1979 an effective ideological crusade was waged by the radical right. This was not a simple 'Vote for Mrs Thatcher' propaganda campaign. It was an attempt to penetrate to some of the core and root social ideas in the population. They seized on the notion of freedom. They marked it off from equality. They contrasted it to a dim and dingy statism which they chained to the idea of social democracy in power. 'Freedom' is one of the most powerful, but slippery ideas in the political vocabulary: it is a term which can be inserted into several different political discourses. The language of freedom is a rivetingly powerful one, but it contains many contradictory ideas. And somehow the right persuaded ordinary people that, rather than everyone sinking into a morass of social-democratic mediocrity, it might be better for them to take their chances, as the British people have before now, and make a break for it. Take your chance in the market for education; don't let your children fall behind. Take your chance in the free market for housing; don't wait until the housing list slowly goes down. Take your chance in the market for jobs. The slow wait, the long queue, the people who don't count, the people who don't care, the people behind desks who know how to fill out forms but are uninterested in human problems – that's socialism. Where is the ancient instinct for human freedom which the British psyche has long nourished? The instinct to compete and survive, to get up and go? This ancient instinct is called possessive individualism. I am not so sure that it is printed in the genes of free-born Anglo-Saxons but is certainly one of the root-ideas of capitalism. Without the ethic of possessive individualism, capitalism would never have taken off. But old ideas weigh like a nightmare on the brains of the living. At the end of the twentieth century, there still are political languages which can bring ordinary working people out into the streets in favour of that notion of possessively and individually choosing their own future. Some of these connections have been made active again in the language of the radical right. They have seized on a number of powerful ideas, indeed positive slogans which touch deep historical chords. They have transformed them to their own political purposes. They are ideas which have once more gained a powerful currency in our society.

I have talked very negatively, so far, about what is making it so difficult for socialist ideas. Let me now look briefly at some of the areas in which it seems to me a battle for socialist ideas has to be joined. By socialist ideas here you may be surprised to find I am not going to talk about programmatic ideas, like nationalization and public ownership and so on, important though they are. I am talking about *root* ideas: the social ideas on which the socialist programme or socialist politics must be based. Let me, for instance, talk about the idea of the nation, the people, the British people. No political counter has proved so effective, such a guarantee of popular mobilization as being able to say 'the people think ...' Conjuring yourself into 'the people' is the true ventriloquism of populist politics. Political leaders who claim to have no ideas of their own: they just reflect what 'the people', out there, think ... 'The people' out there are, of course, varied; different; divided by gender, sex, class and race. They are free-traders, ratepayers, low taxers, wild Trotskyists and flat-earth monetarists: they are wife and mother, lover, part-time worker and madonna of the sink all in one and the same person. The politics of *populism* is to construct all of them into a composite political identity so that the divisions of class and interest, or the divisions of role and person, count for less than the unity, the undifferentiated, unclassed, unsexed, unraced unity of 'the people'. Then you must perform the second ideological trick: which is to project 'the people' back as far as they can go, in a bid for the history of the British people. 'The people', you will find, have really always existed since at least Anglo-Saxon times, or Magna Carta, and perhaps before that. These reactionary ideas constitute the essence of 'Englishness'. The British people have *always* been like that. God made them like that and for that purpose, with an instinct for possessive individualism, private property, a respect for authority, the constitution, the law and the nuclear family and so on. One cannot go against the grain of history. This ideological construct – 'the people' – has been much in evidence since 1975. It was in evidence during the 'winter of discontent' when the discourse of the radical right successfully counterposed the working class *against* the people. Within this ideological framework the politicized sectors of the working class are represented as nothing more than a narrow interest group. While, out there, are the people – who may well, of course, be the sectional group 'holding the nation up to ransom' in some *other* dispute. Nevertheless, they come to see themselves, to position them-selves, as simple, uninvolved, depoliticized commuters: 'the people' who can't get home, who can't bury their dead, who can't shop, can't catch any trains or get hospital treatment. Who is causing all this? The workers. The unions. The leadership. Or the left. The Marxists. The Trots. Somebody. Some other, tiny group of politically motivated militants is standing in the way of 'what the people want': or, as Mr Heath once felicitously called them, 'The Great Trade Union of the Nation'. Now the astonishing political fact that the people can be colon-ized by the right has in part to do with the fact that there is no alter-native vision of what or who the people *are*. On the left and in the labour movement, we have lost our sense of history: when something like the Falklands crisis blows up, history belongs to the right. Freedom of speech, assembly and the franchise, the things amongst others that we took to the high seas to defend, have only been won in our society as a result of the prolonged struggle of working people. That is what demo-cracy actually is. But how is it represented in popular history, in popular memory? As the gift of the rulers. Somehow, democracy 'came'. It descended from heaven. It is part of the great Anglo-Saxon inheritance or the Magna Carta decrees or something. There are thousands of young people who do not know that without a civil war and a king walking around with his head lopped off, there would be no so-called parlia-mentary tradition to speak of, no constitutionalism for Mr Foot to nail his colour to. Without people besieging Hyde Park and Trafalgar Square in a thoroughly extraparliamentary fashion there would be no such thing as the right of public assembly. Without the radical press there would be no such thing as Mr Murdoch's right to report what was said about him in parliament let alone to command the channels of public communication. Democracy is what working people have made it: neither more or less. Yet the people can only speak and act in history through their representative from Grantham. The Grantham corner shop has become the sum and crystallization of the whole, so-called democratic process. That is because we have evacuated our own history. We are going to fight Mr Tebbit's anti-trade union bill without the vast majority of workers knowing when the right to strike was won, or how, or who stood against it, and for how long.

It is not only people in the labour movement who do not know their own history. But certain absolutely root ideas without which socialism cannot survive have been allowed to wither and atrophy in the past two decades. Consider the notion of equality. What we have at the moment is a phoney argument between freedom and equality which the right has effectively posed as a choice: if you want everybody to be equal, then that will be at the expense of their liberty. And since, as I have said, we are a freedom-loving people at least from Magna Carta onwards, we will not tolerate that; we have to sacrifice equality in order to defend freedom. Either/or. Against that, where does the notion of equality stand as an unqualified, basic socialist idea with a sense behind it of the deep, persistent and ineradicable inequalities of life in our society? Who speaks today of the way in which capital, wealth, property, status, authority, social power and respect are riven by the divisions between the 'haves' and the 'have nots'? There may be problems about everybody being absolutely equal in the future. I leave that discussion to the future of socialism. But I want to reaffirm that to be ardent for socialism and lukewarm about the notion of equality is a living contradiction. Yet very few people these days speak the radical language of the politics of equality: the politics not just of the redistribution of goods and resources, but of the fundamental equality of condition. The language of equality used to be an absolutely root vocabulary for socialists. Different socialists of different schools spoke it in different ways, but socialism was unthinkable without this notion of destroying the bastions of accumulated privilege of a social and political and cultural kind. The assumption that we could advance the ideas of socialism without rethinking what equality now means in an advanced industrial society is, I think, untenable.

Let me talk about another rather different idea – one that now belongs as it were, to the other side: the idea of tradition and traditionalism. I remember the moment in the 1979 election when Mr Callaghan, on his last political legs, so to speak, said with real astonishment about the offensive of Mrs Thatcher that 'She means to tear society up by the roots.' This was an unthinkable idea in the social-democratic vocabulary: a radical attack on the status quo. The truth is that traditionalist ideas, the ideas of social and moral *respectability*, have penetrated so deep inside socialist consciousness that it is quite common to find people committed to a radical political programme underpinned by wholly traditional feelings and sentiments.

This is a movement without a strong, republican, secularist tradition, of socialists without a strong commitment to the ending of the obfuscations of monarchical privilege and ritual. This is a socialist movement which has not committed itself – in general, metaphorical terms, of course – to Voltaire's fond ambition to strangle the last king with the entrails of the last priest. I am not suggesting a witch hunt of Christian socialists or indeed of socialists who believe in the monarchy. But it amazes me that the thrust of the socialist movement should not be pitted unremittingly against a society whose forms are held in place by the rituals of rank, respect and deference. Because our definition of 'the political' is so narrow, restricted and constitutionalist, we do not seem capable of understanding the ideological cement in the crevices of the social system represented by those lines of deference and authority. Already at the end of the eighteenth century, always in the forefront of the programme of the bourgeois revolution – let alone of socialism – was the notion of 'the bourgeois republic'. Yet here we are, socialists at the end of the twentieth century, jacking ourselves up occasionally, when we are feeling particularly bold, into the odd republican remark. Traditionalism, in the *social* sense, has a deep and profound hold inside the socialist movement, inside the labour movement, inside the working class itself. That is why and where racism and sexism lurk. Traditionalism provides these with the roots on which they continue to feed inside the minds and consciousness and allegiances of working people. But a socialism which hopes to construct itself on the back of a class committed to the secondary position of blacks and the secondary position of women in the scheme of things will not transform society. It may reform it, modernize it, and improve it in some ways. But it cannot pick society up by the roots and change the relations in which people live. Indeed, a socialism which has a political programme but does not include in its perspective the questioning of those social and moral ideas and relationships, which does not understand the connection between how people live in families, how men and women relate to one another and what kinds of societies they build, is a socialism which will remain 'backward'. It will remain captured, caught, in the net of the respectability and traditionalism of ancient ideas. For politics are rooted in social relations, not just in a programme of political targets. Socialists must penetrate to the ground, the place, where radical *social* ideas can be brought into connection with the traditional institutions of the labour movement and transform them into a new kind of politics. That is a different sort of struggle for socialist ideas than the labour movement has traditionally had on its agenda.

Let me conclude. I talked first of all about what I think are some of the principal inhibitions to the advance of socialist ideas. The problems that stand in the way of getting socialist ideas rolling again as a popular force in society. I think they are profound. I think one has to confront them head on – but with *a socialism which is without guarantees*, that is to say a socialism which does not believe that the motor of history is inevitably on its side. One has to fasten one's mind, as Gramsci said, 'violently' on to things as they are: including, if things are not too good, the fact that they are not too good … So that is why I started with the negative. In the more positive section, I have tried to talk about where socialism needs to begin to grow again. Not yet in terms of programmatic demands, but in terms of the root values, the root concepts, the root images and ideas in popular consciousness without which no popular socialism can be constructed. If you have working people committed to the old ways, the old relations, the old values, the old feelings, they may vote for this and that particular reform but they will have no long term commitment to the hard graft of transforming society. And unless socialists understand the *strategic* role of this level of struggle – the struggle to command the common sense of the age in order to educate and transform it, to make common sense, the ordinary everyday thoughts of the majority of the population, move in a socialist rather than a reactionary direction, then our hearts may be in the right place but our relation to the task of putting socialism back on the historical agenda is not all that different from that of the besieging armies at the city of Jericho who hoped that seven times round the city wall, a blast on the trumpet and a quick prayer to the gods would bring that ancient 'Winter Palace' tumbling to the ground.

1981

Notes

1. L. Althusser, 'The Politics of Philosophy', *New Left Review*, 64, 1970.

12

The Crisis of Labourism

There are worrying signs that the labour movement is simply not willing to grasp, or is incapable of grasping, the seriousness of the position into which it has fallen. Crises are not reversed simply by thinking about them. But to recognize that they exist – and to try to analyse why they are occurring – is the first, essential requirement for overcoming them. Simply to deny their existence is to exhibit the political nous of the ostrich.

In place of the radical reappraisal which this seems to require, however, what one hears is the troubling noise of a great deal of whistling in the dark: the solid affirmation, against all the evidence, that 'we can still win', 'things will turn our way', 'unemployment will deliver the vote to us in the end' or, at best, 'we are going through a difficult patch, but Labour is going to form the next government'. As Gramsci once observed, you must turn your face violently towards things as they really are. The reality for Labour is that it is only just holding its own in popularity with the electorate, in circumstances which ought to be favourable. More seriously, it does not seem capable of forming a credible alternative or making a decisive political impact on the electorate. And without a major revival, there can be no realistic possibility of another Labour government this decade, let alone of socialism this century.

'Things' are not automatically turning Labour's way. The short-term electoral indicators point the other way – in a situation of extreme political volatility. The two-party electoral mould has been shaken by the 'unthinkable' Labour/SDP split; and the party's morale has clearly been deeply affected by it. These short-term reversals only compound the long-term political and ideological trends which have how been moving steadily against Labour for some years, as shown in the erosion of its popular base and solid class character, especially since the mid-1970s.

Many people will say this is gross exaggeration, founded on an inexcusable pessimism. With scandals and banana skins liberally strewn everywhere, surely the Tory magic is at last dispersing? The authoritarian face of Mrs Thatcher, now more or less permanently on view, lacks a great deal of its former immediate populist appeal. Postponing elections, taking away basic civil rights, demolishing councils because you do not like their political complexion is not the most obvious route to sustained popularity in a democracy. For a time Mrs Thatcher and her government seemed virtually error-proof, swimming with every tide. If the tides have not turned, have they not, at least, manifestly ebbed?

On the Labour side, there has been a partial upturn in the opinion polls. Some of the splits and divisions have been healed. The left in the constituency parties is both more vigorous and in much better heart. The Benn victory at Chesterfield was a welcome bonus. There is a new, younger, more vigorous leadership, with a young, vigorous, boyish, freckle-faced leader, who has an infectious grin, a passion for rugby and a fondness of the too well sculptured question at Question Time. His ascent to power, bringing with it the promise of an end to splits and divisions, was itself constructed on the back of a damaging split on the left. Face to face with the only credible parliamentary leader of the left – Tony Benn – the Tribune left resorted to the comfort of its traditional role, 'having a word . . .'. (It has always just 'had a word' with someone – Harold or Barbara or Jim or Michael . . .) Of such stuff is leadership made.

Still Mr Kinnock harnessed to his side in the 'dream ticket' the legitimate heir of the centre, thereby ensuring unity. Labour's policies, so the official version goes, are okay: only the way they're put across needs a little attention. If one listens hard, one can almost hear the ranks of Labour closing – not always a pretty sound in the labour movement. Is the crisis over, then? Perhaps it never existed. Is Labour poised for political revival? Is it ready to run the country? Is it once more *the* alternative party of government? Does it show evidence of once more becoming a popular political force?

These are dubious propositions. First, despite the revival, Labour is still a very long way behind. To win a majority it would have to capture every seat where it lay second in the 1983 election: a formidable challenge. The SDP may not be the threat it was, but the split in the anti-Thatcher forces is exceedingly damaging structurally and wears a look of permanence. It is a situation designed to provide a structural bloc

against movement to the left – which is why Dr Owen (who has gravitated so far rightward he has virtually disappeared over the western
horizon altogether, powered by an insatiable political envy) takes such
fiendish delight in it. And 1988 is a long time away in British politics.
Meanwhile the Thatcherites, by their sheer bloody-minded determination to press on, will continue to set the terms, define the parameters,
establish the benchmark of 'political reality'.

Then there is the new Kinnock–Hattersely leadership. It wears a more
attractive face but it is still untested. So far, it lacks political weight and
authority. And it shows little sign as yet of becoming a popular political
force, as opposed to a (not very successful) electoral machine. Apart
from the issue of the health service, the leadership has shown little
understanding of the need to confront the real basis of Thatcher populism in the country at large. Its perspective is still narrowly confined to
the terrain of the labour movement and the daily accommodations of
policy which its contradictory structure requires.

More significantly, the new Labour leadership still lacks a really
sound grasp of the parameters of Labour's crisis or the ascendancy of
Thatcherism, which should be rooted in a searching analysis of Labour's
own record over the past two decades. Neil Kinnock is solidly in touch
with the well-springs of Labourist culture – and that is important. But he
has no feel for the language and concerns of the new social movements –
and that is dangerous. He has embraced Eric Hobsbawm's analysis, give
or take the ambiguities about alliances with the Alliance.[2] But he does
not understand the politics of putting together a new historical bloc of
forces, which is very different from an electoral marriage of convenience
with the Alliance (in my view, a much more questionable proposition).

I make no prejudgements, but I offer a benchmark: no one who
thinks feminism and the women's movement is a bit of a joke will lead
Labour towards socialism in this century. Everybody loves a Welshman.
But the Labour vote in Wales is down to 37 per cent and, as Hobsbawm
pointed out, 'in a country in which everything combined to create a
Labour and socialist stronghold'.

What the ranks are closing against is precisely the kind of searching
and agonizing analysis which is necessary before anyone can chart a new
course. There is a manifest hardening of Labour hearts against 'the
pessimists'. Resentment is growing like rising damp against those inside
and outside the ranks 'telling us what to do'. Only those insulated from
the grassroots, it is said, could be so disloyal as to believe that the crisis
is *inside* the labour movement as well as out there in the real world.

These aspects constitute important enough problems of strategy and
development for Labour. But, essentially, the problem has not gone
away because it did not in the first place consist of a temporary loss of

electoral popularity. That was symptom, not cause. What is at issue is the disintegration of the historic social democratic programme of Labour, pursued in and out of government since the war. What has 'turned' is that underlying consensus in the political culture around the historic compromise struck in the postwar years, which has underpinned British politics and which gave Labour its legitimate claims of office as the alternative party of government. Gone are the conditions which enabled Labour governments in office to convince the electorate that they could keep the capitalist economy alive *and* pay off their social and industrial constituencies: Labour's historic compromise with labour. It cannot be done in times of economic recession. What 'went' was the solidity of the political formations around that compromise – Labourism as a particular constellation of social forces. We may or may not agree on how far that social basis for Labourist politics has eroded, or what new constituencies there are for radical political change. But there cannot be serious argument about the scale of the problem. It is not simply attributable to the misplaced pessimism of a few free-floating intellectuals.

The complacent view of Labour's crisis is held in place by the consoling illusion that it all happened with the Falklands and, therefore, that 1983 was the backwash of a brief but passing phase. This view is historically incorrect and hence politically misleading. Strategically, the election of 1979 was a more significant turning point than 1983, though the scale of the disaster was less manifest. 1979, in turn, was the product of a major reversal culminating in the middle of the Callaghan government – the 1975–9 period. *Those* were the years when the basis of postwar reformism was destroyed. There, the first turn into monetarism occurred – led by Labour, not by the Tories. It was then that the oil hike exposed the vulnerability of the British economy. By that time trade-union unpopularity was far advanced – and nowhere was it so unpopular as inside the Labour cabinet. That was where the savaging of public expenditure began. Those were the conditions in which the re-education of the Labour leadership in the 'new realism' of managing a capitalist crisis was completed.

They were also the circumstances in which Mrs Thatcher emerged – to capitalize on the crisis, put her finger on the experiences of the people and disperse Labour's exhausted programme to the four corners of the political wilderness. Against that backcloth, she engineered the fatal coupling of the anti-Labourist, anti-statist, anti-equality, anti-welfare spirit with the revitalized gospel of the free market. Thus the qualitatively new and unstable combination of 'Thatcherism' – organic national patriotism, religion of the free market, competitive individualism in economic matters, authoritarian state in social and political affairs –

began to cohere as an alternative social philosophy. It was then that the seepage of Labour's popular support quickened into a torrent. In its wider sense the crisis is not of Mrs Thatcher's making alone. Historically, Labour is deeply implicated in it.

Take the question of politics and class. The left is convinced that too much 'analysis' will lead to the growth of a post-class politics in which Labour abandons its historic mission to represent the working class. But no one can pretend that the British class structure still mirrors the portrait drawn by Engels in 1844 or that, then and now, the relationships between class, party and political representation have ever been simple or one-way. The relevance of the class issue to British politics does not require us to say that class formations do not change, since palpably they do. And when they do, the strategies and dynamics of class politics will also shift, leaving those organizations transfixed in earlier structures to one side like beached whales. After all, such shifts have occurred before within the history of British capitalism. Labour, 'Labourism' as we know it and modern trade unionism are all the product precisely of one such shift in the 1880-1920 period. We may again be at a similar watershed.

No one, looking around Britain today, would deny the pertinence of class relations. No one seriously concerned to analyse the nature of present class formations could fail to recognize the changing class composition of our society: the decline of certain traditional sectors and the growth of new sectors; the shift in patterns of skill; radical recomposition as a result of the new gender and ethnic character of labour; the new divisions of labour resulting from changing technologies, and so on. Likewise, no one would deny the enormous variety of class circumstances and experiences, the internal divisions and sectionalisms and the differential cultures which contemporary British society exhibits; the emergence of new social forces leading to what Marx once called 'the production of new needs.' But nor can we afford to ignore the many pressures and forces emerging from contradictions in social life which are, like everything in Britain, inscribed within class but do not have a simple class vs class origin.

This range of political questions are issues which often touch us as social consumers rather than as producers; are more pertinent to domestic life, the neighbourhood or locality than the 'point of production'; are democratic questions, which affect us as citizens rather than class subjects; are issues of personal and sexual politics which influence the structures of our everyday life; these now constitute the social politics of our era. They are backed by strong constituencies and movements in which, of course, working people have a stake but which do not necessarily move according to the tempo of the industrial class struggle. The articulation of these arenas of struggle with the changing rhythm of traditional class politics is the political challenge confronting Labour and the labour movement today. What an increasing majority of people feel is not that all these lines converge naturally in and around Labour but – quite the reverse – that there is now the most massive disjuncture between where the real movements, issues and subjects of politics are and the ways in which they are traditionally represented in the political marketplace.

There is not – and never has been – *the* given unity of *the* working class in Britain, which Labour could simply 'reflect' in its programmes. There have always been the divisions and fracturings we would expect under an advanced capitalist division of labour. Underlying these are certain shared conditions of exploitation and of social and community life which provide the contradictory raw materials from which the complex unity of a class could possibly be constructed; and out of which a socialist politics *could* be forged but of which there was never any guarantee. How else are we to unite the very different needs, demands and ideas within the class and constitute those necessary bridges and alliances with other sectors which are currently essential to any popular political ascendancy? Where, for example, would a socialist strategy be without having at its centre the needs and demands of the many disadvantaged groups and communities at the receiving end of the Thatcher recession? Yet Labour can neither win elections nor lead the country into the next decade as the party of disadvantaged minorities alone. They have to become part of a wider popular strategy.

Now, what is the common political programme which resonates with both these experiences and outlines a political strategy capable of uniting them within a programme for socialism? Could we develop such a programme on the basis of the current division between waged and unwaged? Or without addressing the contradiction between the defence of the working conditions of the employed and the need of the unemployed for jobs? Could we retain the leapfrogging between high- and low-paid workers on which the whole economistic trade union strategy of the 1960s and 1970s depended, or attempt to construct a political alliance between the two extremes without disturbing the divisions between black and white or men and women?

People sometimes speak as if all we have to do to construct a new social alliance is to add up incrementally the demands of everybody who happens to be in the room at the time. The fact is that because of the variety of social experiences and the uneven consequences of a capitalist development, these different needs and demands are often genuinely contradictory. They have to be subsumed and 'reconciled' within some larger programme, which only a party aiming to become a popular political force is capable of putting together. They also have to retain their integrity, their autonomy and their difference within that programme if the alliance is to be anything more serious than a marriage of electoral convenience. This is a totally different conception of how to form a 'historical bloc' which recognizes its difference from an electoral marriage of convenience – a much more dubious proposition. These are the strategic political questions which lie behind Labour's so-called 'recovery'. They require a strategy of renewal, a fundamental and permanent recasting which is certainly not yet on the labour movement's agenda.

Take the debate on council housing. Suppose that instead of adopting instantly fixed positions 'for' or 'against' the existing form of public housing provision, we proceeded in the following way: first, define what it is the private market in housing *cannot do*. Besides identifying the variety of needs it cannot actually meet, this approach will develop the broader socialist critique of the distortions produced by pursuit of the private property ethic. It will look at the inadequacy of 'the market' as the measure of human need – and thereby question the very roots of Thatcherism.

Next, proceed to the massive changes which have actually taken place in the patterns of residential and family life, the new needs that have arisen, the variety of demands – whether from working-class families who cannot afford to buy; young homeless blacks adrift in the city; single-parent families; unmarried working women or gay men living on their own with the need for decent and secure places to live, and so on. In short, expose the socialist principle behind the provision of housing as a social need for a diverse society and *then* try to design a housing policy which reflects both the venerable tradition of public housing and the real world of the 1980s and 1990s.

The conclusion of such a discussion may well be to reaffirm the present thrust of Labour's housing policies. But it would be a programme which had withstood the pressure of 'socialism in our time'.

Unemployment is another key issue. The problem here is that very few people put much faith in Labour's capacity to reverse the trend. On this, as on so many other questions, Mrs Thatcher so far continues to win the battle for hearts and minds; and those who command the definitions command the credibility. A deep fatalism has, therefore, settled over the country in this respect, which is part of the fashionable collapse before the Thatcherite would view that goes under the name of the 'new realism'. The new realism is really a capitulation to the belief that, after all, market forces *are* economic reality and there is no point arguing with or seeking to modify or influence market forces. Unemployment is, therefore, the responsibility of world trends, outside our capacity to influence. The problem is that this ideologically motivated 'explanation' contains a tiny, rational core. Some part of unemployment is indeed the consequence of a deep, capitalist world recession. Some of it is also structural; located in the endemic structural weakness of the British economy and in the restructuring of our economic base which is progressing – unevenly, as it always does under capitalism – at a very rapid rate under conditions of recession.

Of course, something can be done to reverse the trend of mass unemployment and deindustrialization. But, to be convincing, the short-term measures have to be credible and concrete, and the long-term strategy has frankly to acknowledge and address the structural problems. Labour has so far done neither convincingly. 'Jobs' and 'more welfare' are the pious hopes to which the so-called 'Alternative Economic Strategy' was reduced before it altogether disappeared – a paper tiger. In the long term – while microchips eat people's jobs, word processors themselves show secretaries the way to the local dole office and miners are forced to base their claims to a decent life on the strategy of mining pits until the sea begins to seep through the pit floor – Labour has nothing strategic to say about the strategy for economic revival.

This was clearly evident in the terrible strategic defeat which the miners suffered in March. To invite people in the tightest of economic squeezes to come out on strike when coal stocks are at record levels is to act, frankly, with the political nous of the leaders of the Charge of the Light Brigade. To imagine that people will sacrifice their livelihoods on the unevidenced assurances of their leadership and without an opportunity to argue through and express their commitment in a democratic form is to misread the relationship between leaders and troops and to misunderstand the rationality of working-class action.

To expect that the defensive position is enough on which to build a long-term alternative economic strategy, is profoundly to misread the current mood of the working class. Of course, Thatcherism's clear intention was indeed to savage and butcher the pits and destroy the mining communities. Of course, politically, the government meant to break the organized strength of the unions. Of course, the miners clearly perceived what was at issue. But to mistake the moment of 1983 for 1972 or 1974 was an unforgiveable error. Saltley Gates was a heroic moment: but there is no automatic button marked 'Destruct Mrs Thatcher'. To believe this is not to build on an understanding of, but to be transfixed by the past.

The miners were offered three reasons for supporting the strike: in memory of those who had built the union; for their families; and 'as men', who have a duty to stand up and fight. Glowing sentiments. And yet, in their backward trajectory, their familial and masculinist assumptions, those words fall on my ears as archaic. The cause is correct. The language is a dying one.

In an article which provoked much controversy on the left, Michael Ignatief argued that the miners' strike represented the end of class politics as we have known it. Raphael Samuel in reply argued, inter alia, that the defence of a class community was the essence of the issue. Both views seemed to me to be incorrect or, rather, each expressed only half the truth. The miners' strike certainly contained a powerful 'class' dimension. But politically it was not, as Arthur Scargill represented it, a 'class-versus-class' showdown because, far from 'the class' being united, it was deeply divided. The political task was not to fight a united heroic battle but to unify the miners, in order to unify the class, in order to unify a wider social bloc around the issues. The internal divisions within the miners' union had real, material and ideological conditions of existence, and were not simply attributable to the lack of some pre-existing and unproblematic class unity or solidarity. Seen in the light of the failure to address this critical and difficult political task, the absence of a ballot and the contempt which many showed for the very idea of the 'bourgeois' deviation of a vote when a 1917 'Winter Palace' scenario was unfolding before their eyes, was a gigantic tactical error, as well as a major error of principle. One result was that the strike was dominated, and ultimately defeated, precisely by the splits and divisions which our ritualistic commitment to the formulae of 'class politics' prevented us from understanding or addressing. There followed the police protecting the 'right' of one section of 'the class' to go to work against the interests of another section of 'the class', the media construction of the strike as 'about' law and order and violence, and the failure of one of the most strategic encounters of Mrs Thatcher's three terms.

The rational core in Ignatief's argument is that, though in a sense the very issue of class politics was at issue in the strike, it could not ultimately be won in the coalfields and mining communities alone, but only by generalizing the strike into a wider social struggle, projecting it on to the stage of national politics, in which various sectors of society far removed from any pit-head felt, not only (as millions clearly did) sympathy at a distance for the miners and their families, but understood that there was something directly at stake for them too. Around what issue could this building of a broad popular alliance have been developed? In part, around the question of the future of energy. But, much more crucially, what the miners' strike posed was whether, in making the painful transition from one stage of industrial development to another (as sooner or later Britain must) the 'cost' in human and social terms is going, as it was in previous transitions, to be borne by the sectors of the society who are most vulnerable to technological change, who are then simply thrown on the scrapheap of history, their communities and cultures offered up on the altar of efficiency and 'modernization': or whether, this time round, it is to be a social cost on all of us, on the society as a whole. We know what Thatcherism's answer is on this question. What is the left's?

The failure to see that an answer to this question was required, let alone to address, was (notwithstanding the crucial strategic mistakes committed, despite his great courage, by Arthur Scargill) ultimately a political one, and must be laid at the door of the Labour leadership. If Labour has no other function, it's role is surely to generalize the issues of the class it claims to represent on the stage of national politics and debate. Instead, its main aim seemed to be damage limitation. It wanted to be rid of the miners' strike (as, later, it wished to be rid of the GLC) instead of transforming that struggle.

The strike was thus doomed to be fought and lost as an old rather than as a new form of politics. To those of us who felt this from very early on, it was doubly unbearable because – in the solidarity it displayed, the gigantic levels of support it engendered, the unparalleled involvement of the women in the mining communities, the feminist presence in the strike, the breaking down of barriers between different social interests which it presaged – the miners' strike was in fact instinctually with the politics of the new, it was a major engagement with Thatcherism which should have marked the transition to the politics of the present and future, but which was fought and lost, imprisoned in the categories and strategies of the past.

In this climate of fatalism, a trace of the old recividism appears: 'what we need are more jobs but those can only be provided if industry becomes more competitive and more profitable. Therefore, do not rock the boat.' Of course, as long as capitalist imperatives prevail, there is a sort of logic in saying that more jobs will depend on the revival of capitalist industry. That is the logic in which reformism is always caught. In fact, of course, there is no historical evidence for the belief that recession produces an automatic turn to the left. Fascism has emerged as often out of such circumstances as socialism. Neither is inevitable. The outcome depends ultimately on how the struggle is conducted.

The problem about expecting unemployment to serve as an electoral conveyor belt is that Labour's alternatives run headlong into the brick wall of an ideological campaign which Thatcherism has already largely won. This has successfully imprisoned common sense thinking about the economy on the horns of the following dilemma: the only way to reduce unemployment is to increase public spending, but this will inevitably lead to inflation. We are trapped between the millstones of dislike of unemployment and fear of inflation. Thatcherism has effectively encapsulated all the economic alternatives within the terms of this brutal 'either/or'. It is part of a wider strategy, which it has also conducted with masterly effect. It has two prongs.

The first point in the 'new realism' consists of convincing people that the nation has been living beyond its means, paying itself too much, expecting perks and benefits it can't afford, and indulging in all that consumption, permissiveness, and pleasure. Very unBritish! Realities must be faced! Expectations are out of control and must be lowered. In that campaign, British masochism is a powerful ally. When the economy is not being represented in terms of the household budget ('you can't buy more at the shops this week than you have in the kitty'), then it is likened to the British weather. One good summer has to be paid for, in psychic currency, by at least five winters of discontent.

The second prong of the strategy is to disconnect, in the popular mind, the word 'public' from its association with anything that is good or positive, and to harness it instead to a chain of negative associations which automatically connect it with everything that is nasty, brutish, squalid and bureaucratic – and to exalt, in its place, the private market as the sole criterion of the Good Life.

This has been the strategic ideological project of the new right. It consists, first, of the struggle to disorganize the left; to interrupt the social-democratic consensus which has dominated and defined the political settlement between left and right since the war. Second, it aims to command popular conceptions of what is 'good for the country'. And third, it seeks to reverse every sign and signal pointing towards leftish or social-democratic solutions and move them in the opposite direction.

In 1945, it seemed that the only way to get less well-off people decent health care was to break the circuit of money and market in health and establish a public form of provision. In 1983, the aim is to make it seem inevitable that the only decent health service people can get is that which they pay for privately. This is much more than eroding the welfare state – a thing not wholly unknown to Labour governments. It is also, as the Social Affairs Unit (the Thatcherite 'think tank') pamphlet put it, 'breaking the spell of the welfare state' – dismantling it ideologically as a constant reference point, an inevitable fact of the political scene that is taken for granted.[2] The historical project of Thatcherism is to reconstruct and redefine the political terrain, to alter the balance of political forces and to create a new kind of popular common sense, in which the market, the private, possessive, competitive 'man' (*sic.*) are the only ways to measure the future.

'Hard-headed' Labour politicians dismiss all this as ideological window-dressing (and ideology is not serious politics), or as mere manipulation ('the Tories don't really believe it'). But the light that shines in Mr Tebbit's eye – or the one that has gone askew in Sir Keith's – is the light of the salvationist, the 'born again'. They regard the catechism of capitalism, so tarnished and discredited among the young in the 1960s and 1970s, as the Sermon on the Mount. It is a creed to live by, to bring up children by; a faith which will move capitalist mountains; the salvation of the civilized world – the 'free west'. For such things, Mr Heseltine is willing to commit nuclear suicide. Mrs Thatcher clearly commands the gift of translating this version into the homespun idioms of daily life. She has the populist touch. But the stake in the struggle remains the popular will. Why is Labour, then, politically illiterate about it?

On explanation is that Labour understands perfectly well, but is incapable of organizing a popular political and ideological struggle of this kind. It can mobilize the vote, provided it remains habitually solid. But it shows less and less capacity to connect with popular feelings and sentiments, let alone transform them or articulate them to the left. It gives the distinct impression of a political party living on the capital of past connections and imageries, but increasingly out of touch with what is going on in everyday life around it.

A second reason is that it has always been deeply suspicious of the self-activation of the working class. It is often the actual base for, but not the organizing centre of, local or national campaigns. It has become an electoral rather than a political machine. Extra parliamentary activity – politics and campaigning in any political space other than that directed to the House of Commons or within the confines of the formal electoral system – produces in its leadership the deepest traumas and the most sycophantic poems of praise for parliamentarism. Yet it is precisely the confinement within the parliamentary mould and Labour's containment within a formal definition of the 'political' which has been its undoing.

A further explanation is that it does not possess the material means with which to wage this kind of popular political/ideological struggle. Of course, it has to operate in the public terrain where the media are either entirely colonized by the populist right – like the popular press – or so solidly grounded in right-wing, neo-liberal assumptions that to start a conversation on radio or an interview on television from any other base-line is literally unthinkable these days.

But, even within the media as they currently exist, Labour commands no intellectual presence. It has never acquired a proper legitimacy. And that is partly because – apart from the handful of experts who advise its committees on policy matters – it has not organized a core of 'organic intellectuals'. Labour, then, still looks like a party which has never heard of the strategy of a 'war of position' – that is, struggling for leadership and mastery over a whole number of different fronts in the course of making itself the focal point of popular aspirations, the leading popular political force.

An even more worrying possibility is that Labour does not believe such a struggle to be necessary because it does not take mass political-ideological struggle seriously. Anti-Marxist as it is in its political culture, Labourism is profoundly 'economistic' in outlook and ideology. It really does suppose that economic facts transmit themselves directly into working-class heads, without passing through the real world. Working-class consciousness is as automatic as self-programming underground trains: once Labour, always Labour. And yet the clear signs are that political automatism is certainly at an end – if ever it existed.

Automatism was grounded on the assumption that Labour's political support is rooted in the material circumstances of the class Labour claims to represent: 'the culture of the working class is the culture of Labour'. But is it, in that obvious, immediate sense? The consequences of uneven economic restructuring, long-term economic change and short-term deindustrialization are bearing down directly on these tradi-tional Labour communities, whether occupational ones like mining, or ecological ones like Bermondsey. The heartland of the Labour vote, the backbone of its traditional support, the traditionalist roots of its loyalists have been profoundly disaggregated. The traditional vanguard sectors are also increasingly a dwindling proportion of the modern working class, though not for that reason insignificant or less important. The pattern of support in urban areas, where Labour has traditionally amassed giant majorities, is changing both in scale and political charac-ter. Unemployment is savaging the given structure of skills; technical developments are fragmenting occupational communities. The age, gender and ethnic structure of Labour's potential social support in the country is changing rapidly and profoundly and, so far we can see, permanently.

Changes of these kinds fragment the class culture of the party as a political formation. They give rise to new constituencies, new demands. They generate new tensions and demand new forms of organization, changing the social infrastructure of Labour politics. One has only to think of the profound shift in the character of industrial conflict from the private to the public sector, and add to that the social composition and charac-ter of social strata which, from this point of view, have represented the vanguard of the class in action against Thatcherism, to catch a glimpse of how out of date is the typical Labour view of the connections between party and class.

Far from guaranteeing Labour's inevitable return to popular ascen-dancy, the inevitability of Labourism – its automatism – is now Labour's most serious blockage to establishing a hegemony in these conditions.

What is at stake is no more and no less than 'the people': the popular will. Stuck at the end of the strategy of 'social democracy from above' for so long, 'the people' are taking a terrible revenge on Labour. Decades of blocked votes, things sewn up in backrooms, deals done in compositing meetings, localities where Labour mafias have ruled the roost like small-time Borgias, a view of politics which depends on mobilizing the respectability rather than the radicalism of the working class (and, in the actual contradictory nature of class consciousness, both do exist, to be mobilized by different political forces), the engineering or hydraulic view of electoral politics – these have become deeply ingrained in the culture of Labourism. But the times are changing.

As a consequence, some Labour voters, especially in the more prosperous south-east, are nodding at the canvassers when the knock on the door comes – but slipping, sliding, eroding, drifting into uncharted paths as soon as they go away, and they meet and talk in the pub, on the job, in families, with mates, hanging out the washing, calculating the pennies and the kids' chances in a microchip world of permanent unemployment. Are they really recidivist Tories at heart? No. Are they Labour's automatic electoral fodder? It would be unwise for Labour to bank on it.

Can they be won to a vision, not simply a programme, of the future? Here there is something to learn from Thatcherism, after all. Paradoxically, she does raise hearts and minds an inch or two because, vile, corrupt, awful as her vision of the future is, we *know* what it is. We can imagine what life according to the gospel of free enterprise, patriarchal respectability and authoritarian order would be like. We know how we would be expected to bring up our children, make them manage their pocket money; how women should live; who should have babies and under what circumstances; who should, and should not, go to bed with whom; how teachers in our classrooms should dress and what lessons are to be read in the religious education hour – as well as what the Public Sector Borrowing Requirement should be. It is an 'alternative future'. It is a philosophy of life.

The one thing nobody knows is what Labour conceives to be an 'alternative way of life'. It currently possesses no image of modernity. It provides no picture of life under socialism. It has failed so far to construct an alternative 'philosophy' of socialism for modern times. In its profound empiricism, it has mistaken adaptation to the present as progress towards the future. In fact, realistically, Labour can never adapt enough to become the 'natural inheritor' of capitalism. It has no alternative but to renew itself and its vision or to go out of business. Whether it is capable of that renewal or not remains an open question now – which is why the 'crisis of labourism' is not quite so exaggerated as it may at first have appeared.

1984

Notes

1. Eric Hobsbawm, 'Labour's Lost Millions', *Marxism Today*, October 1983.
2. Digby Anderson, June Lait, David Marsland, *Breaking the Spell of the Welfare State*, Centre for Policy Studies, London 1981.

13

The Culture Gap

Orwell was wrong about many things. But one thing he did get right was the general relationship between culture and social change. *1984* turns out, whatever its other faults, to be an uncanny anticipation of some major cultural trends in modern society. And the essay he wrote about 'Socialism and the English Genius' in the early years of the war – entitled *The Lion And The Unicorn* – was a brilliant attempt to ground the prospects for a genuinely indigenous British socialism in a reading of the tensions within British national popular culture. In the actual year, 1984, this is a theme worth returning to.

There are sectors of the left – especially those touched by the alternative currents of the 1960s – which do understand the relevance of cultural politics to the present conjuncture. They see the connection between cultural questions and the task which socialism has – to become part of everyday life, to make itself 'the common sense of the age'. But the left as a whole has not distinguished itself in this area. Indeed, one major but neglected factor in the crisis of renewal which facts the left today is the difficultly it has had keeping pace with the enormous cultural changes which have occurred since the 1950s. This has implications for the left's ability to relate itself to the society around it *as it is*. It also has consequences for the left's ability to renew its own vision and perspectives on the future – to imagine the future of socialism in ways which are in touch with the cultural categories the mass of ordinary people use to imagine theirs, as we approach the closing decades of the twentieth century.

There was a debate along these lines in the dark days of the 1950s when, face to face with the massive consumer boom which flourished under the aegis of Harold Macmillian (remember 'You've Never Had It So Good'?), and after a second defeat at the polls, Labour entered one of its earlier nights of travail. Could it be, Mr Gaitskell inquired at the Blackpool Conference, that the whole culture on which the labour movement rests – the 'cloth cap' communities of traditional working-class areas and occupations – was being eroded by the telly, the fridge, the new car, the washing machine and the glossy magazine?

It is instructive now to recall how that debate went. The Gaitskell view was part of the whole revisionist attack by the right – the attempt to shift the labour movement into more centrist, 'post-capitalist' paths. It was predicated on the 'embourgeoisement' thesis – the belief that, with affluence, the working class was becoming middle-class, and that class itself was a fast disappearing phenomenon. Put that way, the proposition was patently absurd, as well as politically dangerous. Class relations do not disappear because the particular historic cultural forms in which class is 'lived' and experienced at a particular period, change. On the other hand, because of its resistance to the political strategy and analysis in which the proposition was embedded, the left was largely driven into an equally untenable – but politically 'correct' – corner: the defence of 'Clause 4' of the Labour Party constitution and the denial that *anything* had changed or could change under capitalism. (Clause 4 remains enshrined; though that piece of formalism has actually contributed precious little to deepening the concept of *social* ownership: the statist form of nationalization has, meanwhile, continued to decline into widespread unpopularity, even amongst socialists).

Failing to think the thing through, because they did not accept the categories of analysis which the right provided, the left too found itself boxed in. For, in fact, as we all know now, the slow, uneven, contradictory impact of consumer capitalism *did* refashion and reshape social relations and cultural attitudes quite widely and irrevocably. Contrary to the popular view on the left, there is nothing 'unMarxist' about that proposition. Capitalism, throughout its history, has constantly restructured itself and the cultural relations in which we are all netted. The fact that it is a deeply exploitative system has never prevented it from continuing, even in the midst of crisis, to be a *dynamic* system, constantly revolutionizing the ground off which it lives – in Marx's famous phrase 'melting everything that is solid into air'.

British society – and thus the labour movement which is part of it – was extensively reshaped, culturally, by the long postwar boom, certainly the most sustained period of expansion this century. And, though the rhythm of capitalist development since then has been more uneven, the consequences of this reshaping have not disappeared. Nor, indeed, has its dynamic. The new technologies have not failed to emerge because the old technologies are falling apart. The growth in mass consumption, though it did not destroy or overturn the barriers of class divided society, did profoundly modify everyday life-patterns, the social experience and expectations and the lived universe of the majority of ordinary people. One can find evidence of this in a hundred everyday ways – in the new kinds of modern conveniences which found their way into ordinary homes; in the changes in patterns of leisure, entertainment and holidays; in shifts in patterns of drinking and entertainment, or food consumption. The areas most visible to public comment at the time – and impossible to deny – lay in the new youth culture: the revolution in musical tastes, styles of dress and modes of behaviour.

It is, of course, perfectly true that participation in the new mass consumer culture was and is very one-sided, and by no means a universal experience. Its distribution was highly skewed – often in predictable, class ways. Certainly, the system has not been able to sustain this level of popular consumption – though, as a result of the bargaining strength of the unions, money wages were maintained for a long period, into at least the early 1970s. The 'splurge' was one-sided in another, deeper sense. It was 'mass participation' *principally* through personal consumption in the mass market – a feature which undoubtedly strengthened the daily experience of 'the market as provider' running counter to, and often at the expense of, more socially responsible, welfare-oriented, common provision. This may well have also strengthened modern forms of 'possessive individualism' and privatization. That is certainly the negative side.

On the other hand – to take but one area – it transformed the immediate lives of many working-class (and other) women, who would never have come into the labour market or broken some of the leading-strings of domestic drudgery without modern appliances in the home; and who may therefore be forgiven for refusing to regret their appearance simply because they bought these applicances, when they could afford them, from Rumbelows rather than the Co-op. As an aside: there is, sometimes, in the reaction of the left to these matters, an inverted puritanism which hardly bears inspection. Middle-class socialists, heaving under the weight of their new hi-fis, their record collections, their videos and stripped pine shelving, cheap prints and Chinese lanterns sometimes seem to prefer 'their' working class poor but *pure*: unsullied by contact with the market. Yet the only tenable position for a true cultural materalist must be a deep sense of outrage that the fruits of modern industry, technology and knowhow which social labour itself has matured and developed, are still not available in sufficient amounts to the working people who produced them and need them!

The foundations of class society were not destroyed by the high wage, high spend, market-oriented consumer society which came into existence in this period – it would be absurd to overestimate the shifts which occurred. But it would also be quite wrong to imagine that its cultural effects have been totally eroded by the fact that the system is now in deep depression or that people can't afford all the new goods and services they would like to be able to buy. The new trends helped to remould habits, patterns, the models of everyday life: these have a profound impact on what people now expect; on the threshold of their aspirations and expectations, on how they lead their daily lives.

This underlying drift of cultural change, producing a more loosely textured, more diffuse and diverse daily experience (not, for that reason, a less exploited one), has never been properly analysed or drawn into the political calculations of the left. I believe, myself, that over time it made a considerable contribution to the resistance to the more *statist* features of welfare-state socialism. It strengthened what Ralph Miliband has called the trend towards 'de-subordination'.[1] I mean the loss of deference of an older and more paternalist kind which, in its modern form, was a strong feature of welfarism. Clients of the welfare state were expected, by Labour and Tory councils alike, not to push and shove for their rights, but to be grateful for what has been done for and to them. What did not change was the numbers of people who could not survive without the crutch of state welfare benefits. What did change in the 1960s and 1970s was this rhythm of gratitude and deference. There is nothing 'respectful' about Tesco's or Sainsbury's. If you want a trolley, you had better bustle on in there, pay your money and take your choice. Of course, if the consumer sharks or the bargain-today boys can rip you off, they will. No one could have any illusions – or require any monetarist instruction – about the character of trading in the mass market. But at least you aren't required to tug your forelock and look 'deserving' as you approach the till.

The resistance on the left arose in part from a failure to predict the possibility of capitalism's postwar recovery – against the background of the 1930s depression and the influence of a sort of Leninist law of inevitable capitalist crisis and decline; and partly from a failure to understand the double-sided and contradictory nature of the culture of mass capitalism. The left was not incorrect in seeing the massive manipulation, the advertising hype, the ballyhoo, the loss of quality, the up- and down-market division, which are intrinsic to commercial consumerism. The difficulty was that this manipulative side was *all* that was seen. But, of course, since the inception of commercial capitalism and the drawing of all relations into the net of market transactions, there has been little or no 'pure' culture of the people – no wholly separate folk realm of the authentic-popular, where 'the people' existed in their pure state, outside of the corrupting influences. The people have always had to make something out of the things the system was trying to make them into. People therefore used some of the opportunities opened up to widen their area of experience and choice, at the same time and in the same moment as their hard-earned wages circulated back through the tills and the ad markets into the coffers of the new entrepreneurs.

Consumer capitalism works by working the markets; but it cannot entirely determine what alternative uses people are able to make of the diversity of choices and the real advances in mass production which it also always brings. If 'people's capitalism' did not liberate the people, it nevertheless 'loosed' many individuals into a life somewhat less constrained, less puritanically regulated, less strictly imposed than it had been three or four decades before. Of course the market has not remained buoyant and expansive in this manner. But the contradictory capacity, for a time, of the system to pioneer expansion, to drive and develop new products and maximize new choices, while at the same time creaming off its profit margins, was seriously underestimated. Thus the left has never understood the capacity of the market to become identified in the minds of the mass of ordinary people, not as fair and decent and socially responsible (that it never was), but as an expansive popular system.

Another reason for the left's resistance to cultural change probably derives from the belief that the market has delivered most – as it usually does – only to those who already have the market advantages of wealth, power, status and influence: the sense that what we have been talking about is, for the majority of ordinary people beset by the harsh necessities of life, a minority experience. But is it? It certainly wasn't in the long boom. And while the recession prevents the mass of people from participating to the same degree on a regular or stable basis, it certainly does not prevent them, when they can, from wanting – and often having – not yesterday's but today's goods, both for themselves and their children. Television is now a majority interest and video could soon be. Britain is the largest market in Western Europe for the sale of personal computers, just as, for better or worse, the move to computer languages and thinking through video games is a mass, not a minority privileged interest, for children and young people. In part, of course, this is the product of a massively capitalized swamp advertising campaign. But, more importantly, it is also a perfectly correct perception that this is where modern technology is and that these are languages of calculation of the future.

We must not confuse the practical inability to afford the fruits of modern industry with the correct popular aspiration of modern people to learn how to use and master and bend to their needs and pleasures modern things. Not to recognize the dialectic in this is to fail to see where real people are in their heads. A labour movement which cannot identify with what is concrete and material in these popular aspirations, and expropriate them from identification with the private market and private appropriation, will look, increasingly, as if it is trapped nostalgically in ancient cultural modes, failing to imagine socialism in twentieth-century terms and images, and increasingly out of touch with where real people are at. What the left often sees only as minority trends have long since become majority aspirations. The question is, in what political environment are these aspirations to be developed and realized? Is it really only the capitalist market and consumerism as a way of life which can connect with popular pleasures and desires?

The left's resistance to cultural change is reflected in our everyday practices and languages. The style of propaganda, of party political broadcasts, of much educational and agitational material, locks us into very traditional and backward-looking associations. Our political imagery is even worse in this respect. We virtually fought the 1983 election on the political imagery of 1945. I am not suggesting that the left can survive without a sense of history: our own people know too little, not too much history. But developing a real popular historical consciousness on the left is not the same thing as thinking the present in the language and imagery of the past.

Of course, there are many exceptions to this – I am deliberately exaggerating. The alternative left currents of the 1960s were markedly different in their willingness to expropriate to the uses of the left the language, imagery and technologies of the present. And they did use these, with effect, to project, if not a hegemonic vision of the future, then certainly a powerfully alternative vision to what already existed. Many of those who pioneered these new modes of communication remain committed to the left, willing and anxious to put their talents and services at the disposal, not just of small campaigns and one-issue causes, but of the whole movement. They are a key sector of the modern intellectuals which the mass labour movement needs to bring over to its side and harness to a popular political project. Organizations pioneering a new relationship between power and the people, like the GLC, have demonstrated what can be achieved in the course of this kind of mobilization of new sectors and new skills for the construction of a new kind of cultural politics.

What is at issue here isn't a matter simply of goods, commodities, and technology. It is also a matter of attitudes and practices. Culture has never consisted of things – only of the particular pattern of relations established through the social use of things and techniques. Here again, it is a general failure of the left to see and make contact with the popular and democratic elements in daily life because of the forms in which they are presently packaged or observed. Take, for example, the current craze for body maintenance, the widening concern about questions of health, exercise, an unpolluted environment and the influence of ecological considerations. This appears as a spontaneous popular movement in civil society, ahead of rather than sponsored by 'the authorities'. It can look rather like a mere personalized fad – biological Do-It-Yourself: very apolitical and retreatist. And yet, they touch very popular attitudes indeed, and form part of a distinctively contemporary consciousness. These attitudes arise, in part, from an awareness that the ecological environment is as much of a social enterprise as other, more mundane aspects; that social irresponsibility arises as much in the exploitation of community health as it does in the exploitation of labour power. They may take a more personal form – and that, in itself, tells us something about the disillusionment with statism and the idea of the providing state as the bearer of socialism. But they belong to exactly the same complex which led to the foundation of the National Health Service in the 1940s and its massive popular defence in the 1980s. It represents an important ideological current: not the refusal of the welfare state as such but the correct view that state-provided social programmes only become part of a more democratic movement when matched by equivalent movements of self-activity in civil society itself. Raymond Williams once remarked that the 'long revolution' consisted in the slow reach for popular control.

The ecological and environmental impulse has, in addition to its own intrinsic democratic potential, links with much wider and more obviously 'political' trends. It has a powerful link with the pro-abortion movement, and with feminism and its commitment to enlarge the freedom of women to control their own bodies and pleasures. But it also has connections to the growth of health and safety legislation, a highly significant advance in trade-union work in recent years, and one where the unions can clearly be seen, not simply as defensive, but as advancing into and laying down the conditions of work and life in modern industry. To take another small example, it has links with the taking of responsibility for the public environment of others in the anti-smoking campaign. To take a very large instance, the whole thrust has clear links with the peace movement, the deepening sense of our interdependence in survival and the finite nature of 'Planet Earth'.

Yet – because of the more personalized and apolitical form of this ecological and environmental impulse – this is a cultural movement from which the left and the labour movement have remained, until now, largely insulated. But the forging of links is not inconceivable, especially against the background of other countries. Whatever one may say about the 'historic compromise' policies of the Italian Communist Party, it has remained a mass popular force – as compared, say, with the disastrous and understandable drop in popularity of the French party. And one of the reasons for this is that the PCI understands that it must maintain a popular cultural presence. That there is no popular occasion, no popular festival, no issue or cause about which the masses feel and no emergent movement in mass society where the left can afford not to be present. Why should socialism be a popular political force when it is not a force in the popular cultures and aspirations of the masses? Again, the fact that things can be done along these lines, even in more reticent Britain, is evidenced by the popular identifications which CND and to a lesser extent the GLC, have begun to forge. We need more not less; across a wider spectrum of activities; and as part of the building of a self-active, democratic popular force, not as mere fancy opportunism.

Horrendously, the right has been far more successful than the left in recent years, in connecting with some of these popular movements and trends in civil society. Of course, they have connected with them in their own populist way. Their strategy has been to align the positive aspirations of people *with* the market and the restoration of the capitalist ethic, and to present this as a natural alliance. Thatcherism has been remarkably successful at moving the counters around so as to forge a connection between the popular aspiration for greater freedom from constraining powers and the market definition of freedom. It has created a chain of equivalences between the reaction against state bureaucracy, so deeply inscribed in the Fabian version of social democracy, and the quite different passion for self-sufficiency, self-help and rampant individualism. But, like all ideological and political interventions – which is what Thatcherism is – these connections are neither 'natural' nor necessary. They represent an attempt to inflect and expropriate and absorb what are often democratic currents into free market channels. We have suggested already how and why in the earlier period the market came to be a popular mass experience. The right, after all, has no hang-ups about making money and stimulating the instinct for money-making as the driving force of society. In simple terms, that is what the capitalist system is. So to address itself to isolating and developing the competitive side of that contradictory experience was an obvious and natural way for the radical right to align itself with popular aspirations or, to put it another way, make itself populist. This is one feature of the wider phenomenon we have seen in this decade of the right showing itself once again capable of recuperating itself, renewing itself, taking on the challenge of the social democratic consensus and eroding its basis, and learning once again to address the people in accents which seem to groove more naturally with life as they live and experience it. This is the naturalization of the right which has provided the real changed ground on which the left in the 1980s has been forced to operate. It is part of the right's project to turn the tide on every front – in civil society and moral life as much as in economic habits and expectations. Its project, in short, is to become hegemonic, to address the common experience, to speak to and for 'the nation'.

The question is whether the left can also operate on the same ground and turn these popular experiences and emergent attitudes and aspirations to *its* advantage. Or whether its only alternative is to become aligned with important but increasingly minority and traditional constituencies which need defence in the face of the current onslaught, goodness knows, but which are no longer where the mass experience of the common people is at. This is not an argument for abandoning either the traditional Labour constituencies or those particularly hard-pressed and disadvantaged minorities with whom the labour movement now needs to forge real alliances in action at the grassroots level. But it is an argument for not seeing these existing constituencies in anachronistic cultural terms. Blacks, for example, in addition to being massively unemployed and socially oppressed, have constructed a whole culture of resistance around the appropriation of modern sounds and advanced technological equipment. It is patronizing to imagine them as if they have only just come down from the technological tree. Also, it is an argument for recognizing the complexity and diversity of cultural experience in Britain today and developing strategies which address the majorities and begin to conceive the future in ways which connect with the perspectives of the whole society. The approach which takes a rather patronizing tone to where ordinary people are at, and addresses them as if 'we' know better – by no means unknown in labour movement circles and, in sectarian form, in the left as a whole – only serves to marginalize the left from the parameters and circumstances of everyday life which ordinary people inhabit as a fact of daily modern existence. The democratization of the labour movement's own practices is the point from which this broader movement will stem. It would be fatal if the left became so disconnected from what that daily existence is really like – not just in Brixton or Clydeside but in less depressed areas of the south east or of London – that it appeared too out of touch to speak pertinently to anyone about how things might be for socialism *after* 1984.

1984

Notes

1. R. Miliband, 'A State of De-Subordination', *British Journal of Sociology* Vol. XXIX, No, 4. December 1978.

14

The State – Socialism's Old Caretaker

My aim here is to explore an issue which is central to the strategy for the renewal of the socialist project, but about which, however, I detect considerable confusion among socialists. This is the issue of *the state*. Now a great deal has been said about the role of the capitalist state by the left, especially in recent times. It has almost acquired the status of a fashionable political topic. My purpose is not to review this already complex literature, but to come at the problem from a slightly different angle. I believe that the status of the state in current thinking on the left is very problematic. Many socialists now stand in a very different place, on the question of the state, than they would have done ten or twenty years ago. And yet, I believe that we have not fully confronted or explained to ourselves why we have changed our minds or how this new thinking about the state is likely to influence strategies for the left.

I am well aware that this kind of exploration is a dangerous exercise. One of our present dilemmas on the left is the habit of thinking that we already know what the content and future of socialism is. We talk of socialism as if it were an already completed agenda: the script of a play which is already written and only waiting for someone to put it on stage. Of course, there is a tradition of socialist thought and struggle to draw on. But tradition is a tricky concept, especially for the left; a two-edged sword, more diverse and contradictory in reality than we make it appear when we construct it retrospectively. Our thinking about socialism must also reflect the history and experience of socialism as it actually exists – with all its vicissitudes. It must also ground itself in current realities, take the pressure of our time and reflect the world around us in order to transcend it. Paradoxically, socialism will perish unless it is able to grow out of the very soil of modern capitalism, which, despite everything, is still expanding, still revolutionizing the world in contradictory ways.

I do not, therefore, believe that 'what we have always thought about the state' on the left will necessarily *do* for the next ten decades; or that posing ourselves difficult questions is necessarily a sign of the weakening of faith. We should leave faith to the believers. Indeed, that other way – socialism as an already finished project – is one of the most powerful sources of, and an excuse for, that profound sectarianism which has always had a strong presence on the left and which I detect once again rising like the smog, as those who dare to put a question mark over our received wisdoms are instantly accused of treason, labelled as the enemy, or dismissed as 'pink professors misleading the left' (in Tariq Ali's recent, immortal phrase) and despatched into outer darkness.

So, braving the terrors of excommunication from the newly appointed guardians of orthodoxy, let us pose once more the question of where we stand on the question of the state. It is not difficult to see why the state has become problematic in recent years. This must reflect, on the one hand, our response to the whole experience of 'actual existing socialism' where, instead of progressively withering away, the state has become a gigantic, swollen, bureaucratic and directive force, swallowing up almost the whole of civil society, and imposing itself (sometimes with tanks), in the name of the people, on the backs of the people. Who, now, can swallow without a gigantic gulp the so-called temporary, passing nature of the 'dictatorship of the proletariat'? On the other hand, the very same period, since the end of the Second World War, has witnessed a parallel, gigantic expansion of the state complex within modern capitalism, especially in Western Europe, with the state playing an increasingly interventionist or regulative role in more and more areas of social life. It has become far and away the largest single employer of labour and acquired a dominant presence in every sector of daily existence. What are we to make of that unexpected development, never adequately predicted in the classical Marxist literature?

Even more difficult to work out is our attitude towards this development. On the one hand, we not only defend the welfare side of the state, we believe it should be massively expanded. And yet, on the other hand, we feel there is something deeply anti-socialist about how this welfare state functions. We know, indeed, that it is experienced by masses of ordinary people, in the very moment that they are benefiting from it, as an intrusive, managerial and bureaucratic force in their lives. However, if we go too far down that particular road, whom do we discover keeping us company but – of course – the Thatcherites, the new right, the free market 'hot gospellers', who *seem* (whisper it not too loud) to be saying rather similar things about the state. Only they are busy making capital against us on this very point, treating widespread popular dissatisfactions with the modes in which the beneficiary parts of the state function as fuel for an anti-left, 'roll back the state' crusade. And where, to be honest, do *we* stand on the issue? Are we for 'rolling back the state' – including the welfare state? Are we for or against the management of the whole of society by the state? Not for the first time, Thatcherism here catches the left on the hop – hopping from one uncertain position to the next, unsure of our ground.

Perhaps it might help if we knew how we got into this dilemma. This is a vast topic in its own right, and I propose to look at only four aspects here. First, how did the British left become so wedded to a particular conception of socialism through state management, the essence of what I want to call 'statism' or a 'statist' conception of socialism? Second, I want to sketch some of the reasons why the very expansion of the state, for which so many on the left worked so hard, turned out in practice to be a very contradictory experience. Third, I want to confront head on the confusion caused on the left by the 'libertarianism' of the right – the way Thatcherism has exploited the experience of welfare statism and turned it to the advantage of the new right. Finally, I want to consider some aspects of the changing social and economic relationships today which have influenced spontaneous attitudes on the left – what I call the growth of a left libertarianism. In conclusion, I can only roughly indicate some directions in which our thinking needs to be developed.

First, how did the British left get so deeply embedded in a statist conception of socialism? After all, it was not – as many people imagine – always like that. The state did not have a central, all-pervasive role in early socialist thinking. Marx and Engels understood the role of the capitalist state in developing a whole social and political order around a particular mode of exploitation and spoke briefly but vividly about the need to destroy it in its existing form. But their thinking about the future role of the state in the transition to socialism was extremely sketchy. Other radical currents of thought in British socialism were, if anything, more anti-state than pro-state in their general tendency. Even in the key period, between the revival of socialism in the 1880s right through to the 1920s and the emergence of the Labour Party in its modern constitutionalist form as *the* majority party politically representing the working classes, a statist-oriented brand of socialism within Labourism and the labour movement had to contend with many other currents, including of course the strong syndicalist currents before and after the First World War, and the ILP's ethical Marxism with their deep antipathy to Labour's top-downwards, statist orientation. One of the many tricks which the retrospective construction of tradition on the left has performed is to make the triumph of Labourism over these other socialist currents – the result of a massive political struggle in which the ruling classes played a key, educative role – appear as an act of natural and inevitable succession.

And yet, it was precisely in this critical period – between the 1880s and the 1920s, when the parameters of British politics for the following fifty years were set for the first time – that statism took root in British political culture. In those days, what we now call 'statism' went under the title of 'collectivism'. What is crucial for our analysis is the fact that there were many collectivisms. 'Collectivism' was a highly contradictory formation, composed of different strands supported in different ways by the right, the centre and the left – if, for convenience, we can use those somewhat anachronistic labels. Collectivism was regarded by many sections on the right, and by some influential sectors of the leading classes, as the answer to Britain's declining fortunes. The country – the new collectivists believed – required a programme of 'national regeneration'. This could only be undertaken if the old shibboleths of laissez faire were finally abandoned and the state came to assume a far greater role of organic leadership in society. They believed a 'populist' bloc of support could be won amongst the dominated classes for such a project, provided the latter were 'squared' by state pensions and other Bismarck-type benefits. This was the programme of both the 'social imperialist' and the 'national efficiency' schools, and of the highly authoritarian populist politics associated with them. And though they did not carry their programme in detail, they were extremely influential in pioneering the shift in the allegiance of British capital from its former commitment to laissez faire, to its newer link with a certain type of capitalist state interventionism.

There is no space to deal with the links between collectivism and the 'centre', but it is a critical link in the story to remember that it was also on this very question of 'the state' that the 'old' Liberalism transmuted itself into the 'new' Liberalism: and that the new Liberalism was, in its own time, the pioneer of the thinking which lay behind the early instalment of the welfare state (in the 1906–11 Liberal administration) and, in our time, is really the political force which created that space in British politics which we would now call 'social democracy'.

But the key factor for our purposes was the progress which collectivism made, under essentially Fabian inspiration, inside the labour movement and in the Labour Party. In this period Fabianism established its ascendancy as the philosophy of socialism for Labour. Collectivism became, to be blunt, what the Webbs and their many followers meant by socialism. That is, progressive legislation, social welfare, a measure of socialism. That is, progressive legislation, social welfare and a measure of redistributive justice, pioneered through the state by a political elite legislating on behalf of the working classes (who were required to elect on their own behalf); resulting in a gigantic state complex, administering more and more of society in the interest of social efficiency, where the experts and the bureaucrats would exercise a 'benevolent dictatorship' servicing society's many and complex needs. It was in this formative period that the statist conception of socialism became rivetted in place as the dominant current within Labourism and the British left.

We have no space to sketch the long, tortuous route which led from the emergence of this statist conception of socialism in the 1920s to the much-transformed reality of the modern state and state interventionism as we know it since 1945. Suffice it to say that the path from one to the other was by no means straightforward. Nevertheless, the welfare state was constructed after 1945 on those earlier foundations, and is rightly regarded as the crowning achievement of the postwar Labour government, the high tide of the spirit of popular 'war radicalism', and the most advanced achievement of the reformist tradition of British social democracy.

The logic behind this development in the second half of the twentieth century is not difficult to understand, even though we may not subscribe wholeheartedly to it nowadays. The argument ran as follows: capitalism has a thrust, a logic of its own – the logic of private property, capital accumulation, possessive individualism and the free market. This logic 'worked', in the sense that it created the modern capitalist world – with, of course, its necessary 'cost': exploitation, poverty, insecurity for the masses, class inequality, the many inevitable victims of its 'successes'. The left, it seemed, had only one alternative: to break the 'logic of the market' and construct society around an alternative logic – a socialist one. But to do this, it needed an alternative centre of power, an opposing rallying-point to that of capital and the market. This oppos- was the state. Either the state could be used to make inroads into the 'logic of the market', to modify its excesses, abate its extremes, graft alternative goals (e.g. needs not profits) on to the system, and impose a redistributive logic on the unequal ways in which capitalism 'naturally' distributes its goods and resources: this was the reformist alternative. Or else, the power of capital and the market, installed behind the capitalist state, had to be actively broken – 'smashed' – and the major social processes 'socialized' or made public by being progressively absorbed and taken over by the state: this was the revolutionary road. Both involved, to different degrees, massive inroads into the 'logic' of the market by expanding the role of the state.

I believe this crudely drawn political landscape, blocked out into its two, great, opposed 'continents' – the domain of capital and the market versus the domain of the logic of social needs, imposed through the state – is how the vast majority of us first entered into basic political thinking. It is only a slight exaggeration to say that these remain the two fundamental formations in British political culture – more inclusive, in a way, than the traditional division into left and right. They have helped to set the parameters within which British politics have fluctuated since the turn of the century. An essential part of the 'historic compromise' between the classes struck in the interwar period was the new balance established between public and private, state and 'civil society'. On this basic 'settling of the boundaries' much of the stability of Britain as a capitalist democracy has depended. It was the shifting of these boundaries, in some sectors, away from the free play of market forces, and closer to the reform-through-the-state pole, which constituted the 'revolution' of the Keynesian welfare state and the post-1945 settlement. This new consensus, basically, lasted up to the advent of Thatcherism in the mid-1970s. It is this 'settling of boundaries' which the new right challenged. Restoring the free-market principle to its former ascendancy is once again the fulcrum of politics, the key dividing line between right and left. That is why the question of the left's attitude to the state now matters so profoundly.

All this makes it sound as if the balance of forces on this question has been steadily moving in the reformist direction. Why, then, has this development of the state been so problematic for the left? One reason is that the state has gone on expanding and developing powered, so to speak, by *both* the right and the left. We still speak of the 'capitalist state'. But, infact, we no longer behave as if it had a single, monolithic class character. The left, despite its rhetoric, has its part of the state too: the welfare state, which distributes benefits to the needy; serves society's needs; redistributes resources to the less well-off; and provides amenities – and all on a universalistic basis, rather than on the market terms of 'ability to pay'. The NHS is the classic example. Despite its dependence one the private sector and the inroads made into it by private medicine, the NHS is still generally regarded and experienced as having broken the logic which connected health and medical care to wealth and the private ability to pay, and installed in its place the idea of medical need served by a universal provision. The history of Nye Bevan's struggles to install the NHS demonstrate not only how bitterly the market forces resisted this inroad into their territory, but how impossible it would have been without an alternative centre capable of organizing a materially different system of provision – the state.

How could anyone who understood the material difference which this has made in the lives of countless ordinary people regard this development as contrary to the logic of socialism? We – rightly – want to see more of this, not less: more aspects of life organized on a similar principle. This centrality of the state to the left is not confined to the area of welfare and benefits. We have tended to think that the nationalization measures of the 1940s and 1950s and the Keynesian interventions in economic life, which increased rapidly in the 1960s and 1970s, failed not because they went too far, but because they did not go far enough. The left is still basically wedded to a *positive* view of the state's role in socialist construction.

Matters are not quite so simple. Few areas of the welfare state are as clear cut in their positive image as the NHS. Also the welfare and benefit side is not the only form in which the state has expanded in post-war society. We have seen the parallel expansion of the warfare state too. And of the repressive, 'policing' aspects of the state: the state as coercive agent, defending the social order, punishing the deviant, extending its surveillance into civil society, disciplining the citizenry on to the straight and narrow, its operations increasingly shrouded in secrecy and beyond all normal forms of accountability. The 'Orwellian' state is alive and well, not only in Eastern European socialist democracies, but in Western European class democracies, alongside the welfare state. The state which gives out benefits also snoops on its recipients. Then there is the size and scale of the administrative side of the state, coupled with its bureaucratic mode of operation. People, when they are being 'done good to' by the state, increasingly *experience* it, in reality, as being 'put in their place' by the state: by 'experts' who always know better, or state servants who seem oblivious to the variety of actual needs on the other side of the counter. The feeling is very deep that the way the welfare state works makes people into passive, greedy, dependent clients much of the time, rather than people claiming rights from a state which is supposed to be their own, representing them against the logic of the market.

Then there is the awareness that welfare states have become general throughout capitalist systems, with levels of benefit which have long since outstripped ours and performing functions not only imposed on capital by the working class but necessary to the survival of capital. Free secondary education is, after all, a long standing radical demand and a reform imposed on the idea of an educational marketplace and the degree of training and skilling a modern capitalist system requires. The welfare-reformist and the reproductive aspects of the state are increasingly difficult to distinguish. As state functions multiply, so more of us are working in state-related jobs. The changing composition of the working class and the changing pattern of industrial conflict have moved increasingly to these contested sites within the state. Even there we are aware of the double-sided character of our work. The slogan which most accurately expresses our dilemma and captures this contradictory reality is 'In And Against The State'. Increasing numbers of us are, regularly, both.

This brings us to the 'libertarianism' of the new right. Because it is exactly this contradictory experience of the state on which Thatcherism capitalized. It rooted itself in these dissatisfactions, and inflected them into a whole broadside against the very principle of welfare as such. The new right harnessed these popular discontents to its cause, converted a dislike of the bureaucratic features of statism into a full-scale assault on the 'creeping tide of socialism' and the 'nanny state'. On these negative foundations it built the new positive gospel of the market as the universal provider of goods and of The Good; launched the savaging of public expenditure as a testament to Virtue; initiated the privatisation 'roll back'; and raised the war-cry of Freedom and identified it with the free market. The new right presented itself as the only party committed to oppose the exponential growth of the state, its penetration into every corner of life. This was one of the key ways in which Thatcherism cut into the territory of the traditional left, disorganized its base and made itself 'popular'.

The problem for the left is that the dissatisfactions with the state are real and authentic enough – even if Thatcherism then misdescribes and misexplains them. Thatcherism did not invent them – even if its remedies for the problem are fictitious. Further, it exposed a weakness, a critique, of the existing system which the left had made too little of: the deeply *undemocratic* character of state-administered socialism. Most disconcerting of all, this revealed that the left and the new right share, on this question, some of the same ground!

This was particularly disconcerting because the left believes that ideology marches in exclusive blocs of ideas, each bloc attached to its appropriate class or political position. It is therefore extremely odd to find the left sharing a critique of statism with 'the class enemy' – even if, when the conclusions from the critique are drawn, the two sides radically part company. Of course, the problem here lies in the fact that ideology does not function in blocs. The idea of liberty, on which the whole anti-state philosophy was predicated, does not belong exclusively to the right. They appropriated a certain version of it, linked it with other reactionary ideas to make a whole 'philosophy' and connected it into the programme and the forces of the right. They made the idea of freedom equivalent to and dependent on the 'freedom of the market' – and thus necessarily opposed to the idea of equality. But freedom or liberty – in the wider sense of social emancipation – has always been a key element in the philosophy of the left. Within this chain of ideas, emancipation depends on equality of condition. It is the equation with the market and possessive individualism which limits it. So what the left urgently needs is to reappropriate the concept of freedom and give it an alternative articulation within the context of a deepening of democratic life as a whole. The problem is that this socialist conception of freedom is not compatible with – is in fact deeply undermined by – the idea of a state which takes over everything, which absorbs all social life, all popular energies, all democratic initiatives, and which – however benevolently – governs society *in place of the people.*

Perhaps we can all agree about 'emancipation'. It has a resonant feel to it, and touches very deep chords – as the new right correctly understood. But what about another, trickier aspect of freedom: the question of choice? I am not sure the idea of 'choice' has so far played a very central role in thinking on the left. And yet the most widespread and basically correct 'image' of actual existing socialism among ordinary working people is the drab lack of diversity, the omnipresence of planned sameness and the absence of choice and variety. Our concept of socialism has been dominated by images of scarcity. The trouble is that on the question of choice, capitalism and the free market so far seem to have the best tunes. But *is* the idea of choice, which is intrinsic to the whole critique of statism, an essentially reactionary, right-wing capitalist idea?

I suspect this is partly a generational matter. Socially, culturally, in everyday economic life, younger people set enormous store by choice and diversity. They not only experience society as diverse, they positively welcome this proliferation of differences. And they see as the principal enemies of diversity both big, corporate capital and the big state. They know what Thatcherite economists do not seem to know – that the maximization of popular choice does not flourish in the storehouse of corporate capital, with its carefully calculated marketing and financing strategies. And they do not naturally associate it with the equally corporatist 'bureaucratic' modes of operation of the state. But, unfortunately for the left, they have found a measure of choice in what we can only call the interstices of the market. At the small end of the market, where the big battalions and competition to the death do not entirely dominate, small initiatives sometimes have a chance, and a degree of entrepreneurship can create openings, or recognize a new need, even a new social need, and experiment to a degree with satisfying it. I certainly don't mean to paint a rosy picture of the degree of openness which exists here: all markets are constrained above all by inequality. But most of the innovatory trends in everyday life with which younger people spontaneously identify – in music, clothes, styles, the things they read and listen to, the environments they feel comfortable in

- operate on what one can only call an 'artisan capitalism' basis. These things are in constant danger of being regulated out of existence by the state or ripped off by the big commercial providers.

Nevertheless, inevitably, the actual daily cultural experience of diversity has come to be identified with a certain conception, or rather a certain experience, of the market. And this is by no means confined to non-political people. Culturally, where would the left be today without initiatives like City Limits or a thousand other small, 'independent' publications; or Gay Sweatshop and hundreds of other little theatre groups; or Virago and History Workshop and Readers and Writers Cooperative and Compendium and Centreprise and Comedia and – you name it? Young people on the left or right do not expect to hear the new sounds which speak to them of their time on either BBC or ITV, though they might catch them from the 'independents' clustered around Channel Four, from Radio Laser or even, God help us, the dreaded, arch-commercial, 'pirate' Radio Caroline. Much of this is radical initiative operating precariously in the margins of the capitalist market. But even when you move from the margins of the market, the positive sentiments of younger people on the left, post-1968, instinctively gravitate to those local or 'grass roots' initiatives, where people, by their direct self-activity, can be persuaded to supplement or develop new struggles around the existing bureaucratic forms of provision of the state. The libertarianism of the right has been matched, I believe, by a steady and unstoppable, slow but strong current of 'libertarianism' on the left – mirroring in its own way many of the broader social and economic trends at work in society and transforming daily life and everyday attitudes, including those of the younger generations on the Left.

Does all this then add up to a covert invitation to give up another set of 'old' socialist ideas, lie back and learn to love the free market? Not at all. But it *is* an invitation to open our minds and fertilize our imaginations a little by direct infusions from the contradictory reality of what Marx, in his simple way, used to call 'real history'. For one thing, we know that wherever in Eastern Europe, under actual existing social-ism, the system of rigid economic planning of life, from steel factories to hatpins, has been relaxed a little, the first – though not necessarily the final – form which this has assumed is a return, within the framework of socialist planning, of some 'market mechanisms'. This is not a problem to be left to left economists and experts on Eastern Europe since the image and reality of actual existing socialism is a problem for *all* social-ists and has been a trump card in the right's struggle against the very appeal of socialism in the West. The second lesson we might draw is linked with this re-evaluation of a whole historical experience, though not in a directly organizational way. It is simply the re-examination of the new impetus towards choice, the new spirit of cultural pluralism and diversity, which has become such a driving force of the masses under advanced capitalism and which will have to be more centrally reflected in our thinking about socialism if we are ever to convince large numbers of people that socialism is a superior 'way of life' to that which, with all its ups and downs, they already know. Why else should the toiling masses under capitalism ever commit themselves to an alternative which offers them *less* than they can currently get?

I don't think we can afford to be naive about the state. Negatively, though the state is a contradictory force, it does have a systematic tendency to draw together the many lines of force and power in society and condense them into a particular 'system of rule'. In that sense, the state does continue to organize and orchestrate the space of capital accumulation in its broad societal aspects, and hold a particular, exploitative social order in place. This is not a neutral function – though it is not the state's only function, either. But insofar as this is its role, the state has to be dismantled, and another conception of the state put in its place. The lesson I think we can draw here is that we have as yet a wholly inadequate conception of how a socialist state would operate in ways which are radically different from that of the present version.

We can't afford to be naive about the market either. It is the principal exploitative mechanism of a capitalist social order when set to work in the context of private property and capitalist economic forms. I am not sufficient of an economic expert to know whether some aspects of the market can be combined with socialist economic forms but I am sure we need to ponder the idea more deeply. Certainly, I feel sure that socialism cannot exist without a conception of *the public.* We are right to regard the 'public sector', however little it represents a transfer of power to the powerless, as an arena constructed against the logic of capital. The concept of 'public health' *is* different from the idea of private medicine because it deals with the whole environment of health, which is more than the sum of individual healthy bodies – a *social* conception of health as a need, a right. 'Public transport' is not simply a practical alternative to private transport because it embodies conceptions of equal access to the means of mobility – to movement around one's environment as a publicly validated right. The idea of 'public space' signifies a construction of space not bounded by the rights of private property, a space for activities in common, the holding of space in trust as a social good. In each case the adjective *public* represents an advance in conception on the limits of possessive individualism, of liberal thought itself. In this conception of the public and the social, socialism is still ahead. And the public can only be carved out of market space, capital's space, by the engine of state action.

On the other hand, 'the public' cannot be identical with the state. Once the logic of capital, property and the market are broken, it is the diversity of social forms, the taking of popular initiatives, the recovery of popular control, *the passage of power from the state into society,* which marks out the advance towards socialism. We can envisage a 'partnership' between state and society, so long as the initiative is always passing to society, so long as the monopoly over the management of social life does not come to a dead halt with the state elite, so long as the state itself is rooted in, constantly draws energy from, and is pushed actively by popular forces. One of the reasons why some of the things which have developed around the GLC are so exciting, so prefigurative for the left, is precisely that one begins to see here and there a glimmer of a local state transforming the ways in which it 'represents' society politically; being more dependent on the passage of power, into the state from constituencies outside it than on monopolizing power; hence, of how a new principle, centralized through the instrumentality of the state, can then yield space to a wide variety of different forms, social movements and initiatives in civil society. What is no longer tenable or tolerable is the state-management of society in the name of socialism. Pluralism, in this sense, is not a temporary visitor to the socialist scene. It has come to stay.

We could put all this another way by reminding ourselves that what Marx spoke of when he referred to socialism was the *social* revolution. The democratization of civil society is as important as dismantling the bureaucracies of the state. Indeed, perhaps the most important lesson of all is the absolute centrality to all socialist thinking today of the deepening of democracy. Democracy is not, of course, a formal matter of electoral politics or constitutionalism. It is the real passage of power to the powerless, the empowerment of the excluded. The state cannot do this for the powerless, though it can enable it to happen. They have to do it for themselves by finding the forms in which they can take on the control over an increasingly complex society. Certainly, it does not happen all at once, through one centre – by simply 'smashing the state', as the sort of socialist thinking which is fixated on the state would have it. It has to happen across a multiplicity of sites in social life, on many different fronts, including, of course, the state itself, whose tendency to concentrate power is precisely what constitutes it as a barrier to socialism. Gramsci advanced the profound idea that hegemony is not constituted only by the state, but also by the multiple centres of civil society. It follows that an alternative conception of socialism must embrace this struggle to democratize power across all the centres of social activity – in private as well as public life, in personal associations as well as in compulsory obligations, in the family and the neighbourhood and the nursery and the shopping centre as well as in the public office or at the point of production. If the struggle for socialism in modern societies is a war of position, then our conception of socialism must be of a *society of positions* – different places from which we can all begin the reconstruction of society for which the state is only the anachronistic caretaker.

1984

15

Face the Future

The question of the GLC and local authorities – and not just the campaign to save them – has become the most important front in the struggle against Thatcherism.

It is strategic, first, because of its impact on the popular classes – that very wide section of the population, cutting across many internal social divisions – who are affected by what happens because they are citizens of some of the largest urban complexes of the westeren world.

Second, because here we have the two essential conflicting principles of English political life in direct confrontation. This refers not so much to the formed political ideologies of left and right, as to the essential dividing line which cuts the whole nation in its fundamental political culture into two camps: the camp of the profit motive and possessive liberalism, which Thatcherism represents; and the camp of collective social need and the public interest, which the labour movement, even in its most degenerate form, has always represented. Thatcherism put that fundamental divide squarely on the political agenda. The local authorities are contesting it on that very ground. It cuts through to the roots: a question of and for all the people.

Further, the Thatcher government's decision to abolish the GLC and other municipal authorities because it does not like their political complexion, and to abolish the democratic process on the way to that larger goal, has rendered visible the essential 'authoritarian populist' character of Thatcherism. It is essentially the anti-democratic character of Thatcherism which has turned the popular tide in recent months.

The defiant local authorities represent a direct obstacle in the path of reconstructing British society on which Thatcherism embarked in 1979. Public expenditure cuts are the 'cutting edge' of the whole monetarist doctrine. Privatization is a key instrument of 'radical' social and economic reconstruction. Both have bitten deep and directly into local democracy because local authority spending parallels and overlaps with the structure of welfare support. 'Breaking the spell' (ideologically), as well as dismantling the patchy reality of the welfare state (materially), is a central plank in Thatcherism's project to deconstruct the postwar settlement.

That is why the local authority question has emerged as a key front of political struggle and why 'the rates' – the petty-bourgeois essence of Mrs Thatcher's larger vision on behalf of the capitalist order – have become so pivotal. The people had to think of themselves as 'ratepayers' – as opposed to citizens needing housing, public transport, clean streets, their children educated, their roads repaired, and a thousand other essential collective 'needs.' Thus was the world to be reconstructed, ideologically, in possessive individualist terms.

So it has not been enough to struggle to prevent the further erosion of services and support. Those interdependent collective human needs on which life in the city depends must be made visible. My favourite GLC slogan, plastered across a most unprepossessing corner of a sliproad on to the Brent Cross roundabout, is 'GLC WASTE DISPOSAL UNIT WORKING FOR YOU.' And a good thing, too, or by now the rubbish would be up to our ears.

The struggle around the GLC and local authorities elsewhere is therefore not local and peripheral but strategic and organic. It would be premature to attempt any general assessment, but it is not, in my opinion, premature to ask what pointers we can extract from this experience as to future strategies of renewal on the left.

First, I would put the demonstration effect of a Labour administration in office which not only maintains, but deepens, its radical momentum. This is something of a nine days' wonder. Our lifetimes have been dominated by the experience of Labour administrations, national and local, being tamed by forces they do not understand, being ruthlessly 'adapted' to terrain they are trying to fight on or being re-educated by the realities of the system they are trying to operate. Worst of all, they have even become the really 'conserving' social force, deeply enmeshed in the structures of power, interest and patronage.

There have been many honest local Labour administrations and even more devoted local councillors. But for every one of those there have been twenty suffering from a serious and advanced political ossification. These have contributed more than anything to substantiate Mrs

Thatcher's claim that the state under Labour was bureaucratic and dictatorial.

Closely allied with that is the atrophied relationship between the political representatives and the people, groups and interests they claim to represent. The GLC and other councils where 'local socialism' has emerged as a renovated political force have attempted to move the 'relations of representation' in the direction of local activism and partnership with the people in government, even if the reality is patchier than the ideal. Labour's advance to government in the postwar period has been predicated on the passive character of that relationship of party to class and people. Here, Fabianism has everything to answer for, having installed the image of the passive client class and its professional politician-engineers at the heart of Labourism. A passive, or pacified working class has been integral to Labour's smooth succession to power – and to its signal loss of momentum once in office.

Atrophied political relationships of that kind are not remodelled in a week. But the GLC has gone some way in the attempt to build on, rather than substitute for, the activism of people at the grassroots.

Labour-in-government is not an alternative to the activity of 'making mass politics' in civil society! Instead, the GLC had to recognize that activism outside the state is the source from which a radical administration in power draws its political energies. It has therefore had to acknowledge the necessary autonomy of the different social movements – blacks, women, neighbourhood groups, welfare rights organizations, gay people, the unhoused, the urban disabled, etc. In its more inspired moments, the GLC has looked for means to draw the energies of these movements into the vortex of power, to associate the movements with their 'representatives,' and thus to fertilize and pressure those in power and inside, to deliver to those without power and outside.

Inevitably, the tensions remain. The fatal mistake would be to try to seal some bargain which would guarantee those in office a free ride from criticism and 'trouble,' or alternatively to stitch up the constituencies on the ground as silent partners in the great 'experiment in government' up above. When the contradictions are resolved, you may be sure they have been resolved in a bureaucratic, conformist, statist direction. The ding-dong, complaint, pressure, pushing-and-response, the negotiation in public forums between the movements and the politicians is the positive sound of a real, as opposed to a phoney and pacified, democracy at work. It is also a positive recognition of the necessary tension in the contradictory relations between civil society and the state. That is what socialist pluralism in a real democracy will be like.

The GLC has also attracted into political administration – by the very same movement which has 'politicized' it – a range of talent of the nonprofessional political classes: that cadre of activists who have normally been obliged to choose between the harsh alternatives of being 'in politics' (and therefore staying out of politics in the conventional sense) or going into politics and thus being politically neutered. The narrowness of Labour's intellectual support, the poverty of its ideas generally, its inability to connect with the vast range of ideas simmering and bubbling among, especially, radical young people today, is one of the most compelling signs of its distance from the real forces for change and innovation in society at large. By contrast, the GLC has mobilized some of the most innovative political talent in radical politics and unleashed a stream of new political thinking, even though it has not always known what to do with it.

Then there is the larger issue of how to construct a social base for the new politics. London has always been different from the other large labour and trade-union heartlands in its industrial structure and class composition. However, it is also possibly closer to emerging patterns of occupations and culture. It is therefore something of a test-bed for any political strategy which seeks to build a broad popular base for radical change and to integrate the great diversity of needs, conditions and demands which now form the social basis of a possible socialist politics. No one would pretend that it is easy to develop such a politics, or to find those political themes and issues which genuinely unite the disparate, sometimes conflicting, demands of a series of social movements into a more organic social bloc or, indeed, to bridge the gap between the offensive thrust of the new politics and the necessarily defensive strategies of service and support which still define the primary needs of many of the traditional class constituencies.

The GLC has not resolved this fundamental issue in the building of a new historic bloc in the politics of socialism. But it has recognized it as *the* issue of contemporary politics, and addressed it directly.

A detailed examination of the successes and failures of this strategy would take more space than I have, but I offer three indicators. This is the only political administration to date with which black community groups and black activists have had anything but the most cynical and opportunist relationship: which only means that, for the first time, they have been prioritized in the political agenda, recognized for what they are, seen themselves more accurately reflected and not totally distorted in the political mirror.

This is one of the few Labour administrations with which active feminists are working without seriously compromising their commitments to feminism (which is far from suggesting that this relationship is smooth, settled or unproblematic).

Finally, the GLC has courageously challenged the conventional structure of social ideas in the labour movement by giving some open and genuine support to gay politics. Nowhere is it more clear than in the arena of sexual politics how the left can be systematically undercut and undermined by being held in place by conventional commonsense ideas. Nowhere is it clearer that we cannot build a politics which corresponds to the actual diversity and radicalism of the new social movements transforming society unless these aspects are given a leading position in the agenda of new demands.

Another important aspect of the GLC's activity is the investment in the production of positive alternative programmes. Socialism has been so long on the defensive in Britain that it has by now acquired a permanent negative posture. But the hard truth is that simply saying 'we will turn the clock back to where it was before the Tories came in,' does not now convince anybody. And rightly so. There are serious economic and social problems confronting the country, which stem from the whole structure of industry, the economy and the disaster of Britain's historic place in the world capitalist system which, far from resolving themselves overnight at the touch of a socialist administration, would be immediately and infinitely exacerbated by its very appearance.

These problems cannot be solved at the level of the local state. Yet this is often where and how they first bite into people's experience – and hence where conceptions of the political alternatives are first formed. In several areas, not least the challenging one of employment and the structure of industry and investment, the GLC has tried to intervent positively, and to generate concrete alternative strategies. This 'making concrete' of the problems and alternatives is one of the few available ways to break the stranglehold of the fatal idea, on which Thatcherism so depends, that 'There is No Alternative.'

Finally, I want to consider the terrain on which the GLC political initiative has been working. To put it crudely, it has operated right across the spectrum, politicizing sites of daily life and drawing them into the orbit of politics in ways unthinkable to most conventional Labour councils – which have tended to adopt a narrow view of 'the political.'

The case which the GLC helped to make, not only for cheaper fares, but for greater mobility as a contribution to the quality of life of ordinary people in a modern city; its opening of local authority venues to new kinds of activity, stressing the 'public' character of their point and purpose; its subsidizing of popular entertainment and public occasions on the open access principle; its use of sites and hoardings in the city to publicize radical themes and demands; its opening up of the Festival Gardens, and use of the parks as active centres linked with the general renovation of cultural life; its free concerts, even the diversity of musics sponsored by this public authority – classical music, jazz, advanced rock, black gospel music – these and many other examples could be quoted to show how cultural life can be reconstituted as a site of politics; to show how a radical left administration can positively identify itself with popular cultural life, and feed into itself some of the energy generated.

This transformation of the spaces of the city – a modern entity in which greater and greater numbers of ordinary people live the whole of their lives but which has become, under the domination of capital and commerce and the banalization of everyday civic life which they engender, a tawdry and ugly place of alienation and loneliness – is one of the most innovatory, most 'transformatory' aspects of the politics of the GLC.

It is one of the aspects of GLC politics – rooting itself in the everyday experience of popular urban society and culture, and becoming the leading force in moral and cultural life – which most holds out the promise (not everywhere much in evidence) that socialism could become the politics and culture of the future, and has something to say about living in the twenty-first century.

1984

16

Realignment – for What?

In recent weeks, the process of realignment on the left has been rapidly gathering steam. By realignment, I mean a fundamental regrouping of people and ideas across the existing boundaries, initiating a process by which the left slowly and painfully acquires the capacity to address its own crisis. It seems now as if what the left could not achieve on its own may yet happen as a result of combined pressure from two different directions at once. The first is from 'Thatcherism' – weaker now, but still, after the riots, very much 'in place' – which has brought the crisis of the left to a head by disorganizing it and effectively rewriting the political agenda. Second, as the result of a series of strategic reversals – amongst which I would list the defeat of the miners' strike (despite the heroic struggle); the subsequent emergence of the UDM breakaway union in Nottingham and elsewhere; the crisis about ballot money which the TUC seems too paralysed to resolve; the debacle around ratecapping and the sluggish quality of Labour's recovery in the polls.

It seems an opportune moment then to ask what realignment is really about? Why does the left need it, and is what it needs what it is getting? Some things can be definitively said at this point on what realignment is not about. It was never about getting quick popularity in the opinion polls by an opportunistic move to the centre or by subordinating everything to winning the next election. It was never principally 'about' – and cannot therefore be measured in terms of – greater loyalty to, or 'rallying around', the Labour leadership. There is nothing new about this type of loyalism. It has consolidated a variety of past Labour leaderships, of varying political complexions, without setting in motion any fundamental reappraisal or forging any new strategies for change. On the contrary, loyalism has most often been associated with a tactical closing of ranks, a surge of electoral opportunism and the taming of the left within the confines of a narrowly conceived parliamentary 'realism'. Whatever else realignment is about, it is certainly not about that.

The relevant questions remain: what new political positions are being staked out? Is the process addressed to the fundamental issues of the crisis of the left? Where, in all this, is the renewal of the meaning, content, perspectives and languages of the left?

The failure to grasp this brings in its wake all sorts of shortcircuits and false stopping points. Realignment is not an event but a process which has to be continuously negotiated. If realignment is defined exclusively in organizational terms, then it is perfectly possible to assume that, once a few extremists have left or some new alliances forged, the process has been completed. Another false ending is to be found in the belief that swearing at the 'hard left' is really what it is all about and is, in itself, sufficient. Nothing could be further from the truth. It is one thing to expose the disastrous consequences of the one-eyed militancy espoused by the Liverpool council under Hatton's leadership, whose constancy in the issue of the rates is having to be bought at the price of sacking thousands of council workers whose jobs the strategy was in part devised to protect in the first place.

But it is not enough. It is Mrs Thatcher's government, not Derek Hatton, who chose local authority spending as a strategic front of struggle. The Liverpool crisis flows directly from the application of monetarist doctrine to local authority spending, the general attempt to restore market criteria at the expense of public need, the attack on the living standards of the less well-off and the government's authoritarian and anti-democratic character. It is an offensive aimed explicitly at Labour and its constituents and its political base in the large urban conurbations. What is more, it is precisely along this very front that, in some places – most notably in the GLC, but also in South Yorkshire – the left has made the most imaginative and innovative political response, in the form of the new 'municipal socialism'. Yet, if you listened carefully to Mr Kinnock's conference speech, you would have caught everywhere the whiff of grapeshot directed at the Hatton 'extremists', but you would have searched in vain for the slightest hint of how significant, in Labour's thinking, the strategy of the GLC should have become, and the political lessons which should be drawn.

Realignment, then, is only a means to a larger end. In this context, the attempt to isolate the 'hard left', which has become the cutting-edge of the process, does not mean trying to get rid of this or that grouping whose political position (on, say, nationalization or council housing or the state or the Soviet Union or Poland) we don't happen to share. There are differences of this kind on the left, the product of different traditions, outlooks and formations, which are likely to persist for the foreseeable future. Indeed, the whole idea of a 'monolithic left' now seems to be a contradiction in terms and against the grain of contemporary experience.

Rather, it is the 'hard left' as a peculiar and distinctive political style, a set of habits, a political-cultural tradition, stretching right across the actual organizational subdivisions of the left, which is at issue. It is the 'hard left' as keeper of left consciences, as political guarantor, as the litmus paper of orthodoxy, which is the problem. That is why realignment turns out to be a lengthy process with all sorts of stopping-points, and why it keeps running into the sand. It is because there is a tiny bit of the 'hard left' inside all of us – patrolling the frontiers of consciousness, repressing from memory certain profound but awkward facts, ruling certain questions 'out of court', keeping us all on the straight and narrow and thus helping to hold in place certain automatic and unquestioning responses.

Ken Livingstone is a good case in point. In the political areas where he moves and initiates, his instincts are totally opposite to those of the 'hard left'. He listens – where they don't. He engages, where they tend to retreat to the bunker of left orthodoxy. He contests opposing positions whereas the tendency of the 'hard left' is simply to swear at them. Livingstone could never have fought the miners' strike as Scargill did. He would never have regarded the question of the ballot as unimportant, especially when entering so strategic a battle. And yet, the way the 'hard left' has distanced itself from him since ratecapping, far from freeing him to transport the lessons of his GLC strategy on to a wider, national canvas, appears to have immobilized him, rendering him virtually silent.

It needs to be clearly said, then, that the ritual expurgation of the 'hard left' is not what realignment is about. It is the 'hard left' as a blockage to a long, difficult but necessary process, which concerns us. Gradually, the renewal of the socialist project and the generation of new strategic perspectives for the left has come to have, as one of its necessary preconditions, the erosion of many of the political positions and habits of the 'hard left'. It is this political fact which has forged the link between 'rethinking' and 'realignment'.

The 'hard left' in this sense is to be found as much in the economism of 'mainstream' Labourism – the belief that being economically of the working class automatically guarantees you a certain political and ideological position – as in the unquestioning support for the Soviet model of socialism to be found in the more vocal sections of the *Morning Star*. The 'hard left' is present in that tendency not to analyse the new configurations of class forces but to affirm, ritualistically, a belief in 'class politics', whatever that means, which you can find in some of Labour's most fiercely loyal constituency sectors. It is the commitment to the programme, demands and forms of organization associated with the days of a trade unionism shaped by the experience of the white, skilled, organized, male labour force in heavy productive industry which continues to dominate trade-union thinking and strategy long after the actual social composition of its membership has been transformed. It is to be found in what I can only call the untheorized 'neo-Trotskyism' which shapes some of the unthinking responses of the independent left. For example, the nostalgia for an undefined 'class politics' recently to be heard from some sections of the feminist movement, when the very term was clearly a coded way of launching an attack on the political relevance of feminist experience and struggle. Realignment has had the unexpected outcome of forcing to the surface some of these bizarre convergences.

What is wrong with the habits and positions – or model – which have shaped the 'hard left', as I have been defining it? Basically, that model has committed us over the years to an analysis which no longer has at its centre an accurate description of contemporary social, economic or cultural realities. Second, it has attached us to a definition of how change occurs in society which in no way adequately reflects the actual social composition of the class forces and social movements necessary to produce it or the democratic realities of our society. Third, it is no longer able to politicize and develop the majority experiences and dispositions of the popular forces which the left must enlist. Fourth, it is wedded to an automatic conception of class, whereby the economic conditions can be transposed directly on to the political and ideological stage. Marx's formidable distinction between a class 'in itself' and one which has developed sufficient political, cultural and strategic unity to become an active force in history – 'for itself' – is wholly foreign to it, though 'Marxism' as a sort of magic invocation is constantly on its lips.

It is deeply linked to a politics of gesture, whereby it is better to lose heroically than to win. It blackmails everyone into the leapfrog game of 'lefter-than-thou' which is so often the main if not the only business actually conducted at meetings of the left. Its conception of socialism remains profoundly statist – Fabian or Soviet style. It has never really squared up to the profound damage done to the left by the experience of actual existing socialism. It has lost the capacity to advance a convincing political vision of a more egalitarian, more open, more diverse, more libertarian, more democratic, more self-organizing type of socialism conceived in relation to the actual historic trends at work in the world today. This is what is really meant by the 'hard left'.

The need to erode these positions and habits on the left is what is meant by 'rethinking'. Regrouping the old forms and forces into a new historic bloc linked with that process of rethinking is the key task of 'realignment'. Seen in this way, realignment really touches the fundamental structures of left politics in Britain and is only the first step along a lengthy, hazardous and painful road. It involves remaking the very language of socialism itself. It means opening up the structures of the left to a deep process of democratization. It means remaking the politics of the labour movement in the light of the struggle for feminism – the 'feminization' of the left, which is so far only nodding opportunistically in feminism's direction. At the same time it involves drawing the feminist movement directly on to the terrain of the struggle for general social, economic and cultural change – the 'socialization' of feminism. It implies the recognition of the irreversible way in which British politics and society has become imprinted by the ethnic factor. It involves the construction of new kinds of political linkages between representatives and their constituencies, between old and new class forces, between the skilled and the unemployed, between the older dispossessed and the new social movements: in short, between the grand old cause and the brand new times ...

These problems must be seen in a wider context. They represent a fundamental dislocation of both socialism and the left from contemporary society. Though this dislocation may appear far advanced in Britain, it is by no means confined to it. It has a clear, international dimension. One has only to observe how, across the globe, the policy and thinking of the new right has undergone a steady revival, destroying an older Keynesian and welfarist consensus: how the global market forces have come once again to be acknowledged – by left governments, who took power on quite different terms – as setting the parameters of manoeuvre.

In part, this is a question of the renewed political vitality and self-confidence of the new right and its success in actually shifting the balance of forces in different societies. But it is also something else – something more indefinable. For the time being, the new right looks like the historic force which is capable of harnessing the contradictory new currents abroad in the world. It is the right which has the confidence ruthlessly to clear the way for a re-energized world capitalist market which 'naturally' speaks the language of the new computer-men, the marketing whiz-kids, the hard-selling merchants in the fast lane. Historically, for the moment, the initiative is not with us. The left is being daily shaped by those forces, rather than harnessing and shaping them.

What, then, has triggered off such a profound historical transition? Why do people on the left feel not only that they have lost the tactical initiative for a time, but that their very language is collapsing on them? Everyone on the left will probably have his or her favourite reason. But it may be worthwhile taking the risk of setting them out, not only as a way of stimulating debate, but also because, since we do not know yet precisely what we think, we might begin to make some headway towards that by identifying what we ought to be thinking about. We badly need just now to identify a limited number of strategic issues around which we should initiate a wide-ranging debate on the left.

Debates, in this sense, are not a polite way of referring to 'policy documents'. They are more – as Peter Glotz, general secretary of the West German SDP, wrote recently, initiating a very similar discussion there – 'collective learning processes'. One precondition of this learning process is that we clearly understand that such strategic topics do not necessarily 'belong' to the left. They are not 'our' property. For example, one such strategic topic is 'democracy'. Far from 'belonging' exclusively to the left, we have mercilessly neglected its force as a revolutionary idea over the years. The left and the right do not live in sealed universes. They have to contest ideas and engage realities which are simply the common determinations of our lives today. Of course, the left ought to have something fundamental to say about these ideas and have a fundamentally different strategic perspective from that of the right. But we don't live in a totally different world from which the right is somehow excluded.

Our critics are sometimes correct when they observe that 'realism' is often simply a codename for giving in, for settling for whatever already exists because there is no alternative. On the other hand, the left has rarely been in such need as it is now of a healthy, solid dose of 'realism' – in the sense proper to any Marxist perspective, of understanding the determining limits, the inescapable lines of tendency and direction established by the real world. No amount of prayer will make the British economy – capitalist or socialist – prosperous overnight. No government – left or right – can dramatically lower Britain's structural rate of unemployment overnight. What sets these necessary limits to political and economic strategies is not simply political 'will', important as that is. It is what Marx, in his old-fashioned way, used to call 'the real movement of history', which is an exceedingly hard taskmaster.

The first major cause of this historic dislocation of the left is the failure of the latter to move on to the ground of the new industrial revolution and to locate the arguments for socialism on the terrain of a new phase of Western economic development. Of course, there is no planned or rational shape to this epochal development but we should not lose sight for a moment of the fact that it is, in the usual uneven and contradictory way, in process and transforming everything in its wake. It isn't by chance that the Marxist conception of socialism was grounded in an earlier grasp of the historic tendencies of capitalist development, which is why the key work was called not socialism but *Capital.* It could never be said that Marx elaborated a conception of socialism which simply amounted to accepting and working within the parameters of industrial capitalism at the stage which it had reached when he undertook his labours. But there is no way in which a socialism for our own times can evade the terms of reference of the forms of social, economic and cultural organization which currently dominate the centres of advanced production in the modern world.

The failure of the left to refract these new realities within its own perspective on the future is the result of a series of interlocking developments. There are the new technologies, which are rapidly reshaping skills and social identities, regrouping the workforce into new divisions and destroyin the older patterns of work. On these older forms of material labour the social and political disciplines of the working class and the labour movement in the past fundamentally depended. Then, there are the new forms of capitalist production. These occur both at the level of the multinationals, coordinating processes across the globe, between fragmented labour forces, through the integrating mechanisms of the information revolution and rapidly advancing the new international division of labour; and at the level of national production, where the large-scale, on line factory processes, characteristic of that era of development in which the classic models of a socialist future were devised, are being rapidly eroded through the new impetus towards 'flexible specialization'. The whole imagery of socialist production was dominated by the modern flow-process of the Fordist factory, the object of a revolutionary iconography as well as an industrial sociology which underpinned the aesthetic of socialism at the time of the Russian Revolution. This aesthetic may appeal to our revolutionary sensibilities, but fewer and fewer of those who actually work in any kind of industrial production in the future – in any case, a decreasing proportion of the whole workforce – will work in places like that, under that sort of labour regime. Hence, the economic programmes and demands formulated with this type of industrial economic organization at their heart, are becoming unevenly obsolete. With them, what we might call the older socialist imagery is collapsing.

At the same time, the character of the world market is being refashioned by a new dynamic. It now enters directly into the production and distribution cycles of national economies, disorganizing their rhythms, undermining the classic Keynesian strategies of control and making the whole idea of 'socialism in one country', to which the mainstream thinking of the British left is instinctively committed, increasingly out of date. What hope is there for a 'socialist Britain' escaping the consequences of this global revolution of production, perched as it is on the outer edge of Western Europe and held at the centre of a worldwide financial network, when the much more autarchic structures of the East European economies have not been sufficiently 'closed' to protect them against the wind of change?

Of course, the new industrial revolution is occurring in fundamentally lopsided and distorted ways. The 'globalization' of capitalist production has produced mainly recession, deindustrialisation and unemployment at home. But a politics of redistributing wealth from within the limits of the existing economic cake cannot any longer do the trick. Some regions of production, central to the whole history of the labour movement, have gone forever. The new international division of labour is here to stay. The smaller, more dispersed scale of capitalist production – decentralizing component stages into independent specialized units – is the rational core underlying the drive towards privatization, with which any socialist conception of modern production will need to come to terms. It provides the basis for more refined controls over demand and supply in keeping with modern markets and greater flxibility of choice, which are not only 'capitalist' virtues. Certainly, at the moment, these elements, like those of the new technologies, are being imposed piecemeal, and in ways deliberately designed to weaken collective rights and labour organization, fragment the workforce, deskill jobs and impose new market criteria of value and worth. Socialist thinking will need to transform these in the light of a quite different scale of social priorities. But, like it or not, this is the world in which socialism must now survive or disappear.

The second, closely related factor in this historic dislocation of socialism and the left is the recomposition of the working classes of modern industrial societies – the historic agents of change in the socialist scenario. It was difficult enough when, against the classic predictions, this class failed to realize its historically appointed role. That, in itself, was no mere contingency. It arose from many factors, one of which was certainly a too automatic conception of class, which failed to recognize how the capitalist labour process divided, fragmented and segmented the labour force at the same time as it provided the potential conditions of its political unification. But what we face now is not merely the failure of a certain revolutionary scenario to unfold but the actual recomposition of class itself. Recent contributors to this debate have mischievously tried to resolve this problem by posing it in terms of who does and who does not 'believe' in the class struggle. This is wilful distortion. The question is not whether we 'believe' in class politics but what, in the here and now, it concretely *is.*

Again, the process of recomposition and restructuring of the working class is neither even or uniform. But gradually changes are overtaking the way labour is organized due to the expansion in the types of activities which now constitute 'work', the new social divisions which flow from it and the new places in the society where the exploitation takes place. The old distinctions between 'productive' and 'unproductive' labour, or between production and reproduction, which imprinted the sexual division of labour so deeply and powerfully into the very centre of socialism itself are breaking down. These factors are reshaping the very agendas of socialism and redefining the culture of those who might one day make socialism. Its whole material basis is being slowly but inexorably transformed. In the era of flexi-time and part-time work, with women and blacks constituting a growing proportion of those at work, with work in the service sectors rapidly overtaking those in so-called 'productive industry', with the preponderance of women in the deskilled echelons of modern technology and with such a large preponderance of the workforce in some local or national state-related activity, the whole masculine imagery of the proletariat – the 'vanguard class of production' – simply doesn't make any sense, except as a historic recall. What we are referring to here is therefore more than the collapse of the traditional historic agencies of change. It is the erosion of the cultures of work, economic organization, social and sexual identities in which the left, in an earlier era, was unreflectively rooted. It is therefore necessary to ask on what new, actual forms of social life is socialism's conception of the future rooted or grounded today? The answer is by no means obvious.

The third factor in this historic dislocation is that aspect of the crisis of the left which arises from the dissolution of the models based on forms of 'actual existing socialism' in the world today. Little needs to be said in detail at this point about the radical failure of the Soviet model of socialism to constitute a real alternative for the left and there is no need to fall into a simple-minded anti-communism to carry the argument. Nevertheless, it is not at all clear that the left has squared up to this historical fact and rigorously rethought its own conceptions of a more democratic model in the light of that experience. The left, after all, has no cause to feel easily superior. There is a world of difference between the regimes of Eastern Europe and the Fabian models of social democracy for which the left in the West has largely settled. But, despite these differences, which have to be openly and plainly stated, there are also some surprisingly similarities to contend with.

In both these systems, socialism has assumed 'statist' forms. In both, things have been imposed on or given to the masses – but the latter have not been empowered or politicized by the process. One knows the terrible costs for socialism when, as in the Soviet Union, the party has become a substitute for the people. But let us not forget that, in the Fabian conception of social engineering, the people are also the objects not the subjects of political practice. Humane as the impulse behind the welfare state may have been (and that was not the only motive behind its appearance as a feature of all postwar advanced capitalist societies), there is little doubt that the establishment of beneficient welfare bureaucracies has effectively demobilized popular power.

Both systems, in their radically different circumstances, have neglected the connection between socialism and the expansion of social freedom – tending, mistakenly, to regard that concept as exclusively 'liberal' in its reference. We are only just beginning to come to terms with the degree to which statism – a system in which the state expands to become coterminous with the whole of society – is a historic tendency now shared by both 'actual existing' socialist and capitalist class democracies: and how, in both, it represents a deformation of the original emancipatory socialist impulse.

The fourth and potentially explosive area of debate is around what is sometimes called the 'fiscal crisis of the welfare state'. The Thatcher government much exaggerates the extent of this for its own purposes, but it did not invent the problem. Of course, the left would like to immediately restore the cuts and expand the welfare state. And the more complex are the forms of social and industrial organization, the older the average age of the population, the greater the range of social needs we ought to care for and support, the greater is the scale of expansion envisaged. An expanded welfare state commensurate with the range and depth of social problems in modern industrial life may not be beyond our means. But equally, it is inconceivable that it could be sustained, on exponential rates of population growth, without real and sustained economic expansion. The problem is, incidentally, not restricted to Western capitalist welfare states. It is beginning to make itself felt in the 'actual socialist' countries too, as slower rates of growth set in.

Of course, what the left must do is to find ways of prioritizing social need over 'value for money'. But the days when socialism was predicated on the idea of infinitely expanding social needs and infinitely expanding resources are over, if they ever existed. If you are providing for people's social wants and needs with their money, there is nothing 'essentially capitalist' about asking what the comparative costs are, what are the constraints on different types of expenditure at different times and how one will arrive in a more public or collective way at the choices and priorities which will have to be made in the 'real world'. A world in which vast numbers of people die daily of starvation does not 'owe' Britain a welfare state. It is true that the language of technocratic efficiency and 'value for money' which is sweeping through the managing committee rooms of all large-scale institutions in Britain is explicitly aimed at extolling the free-market and privatized greed. But I have yet to see a convincing argument in favour of inefficiency and waste 'for socialism's sake'. Many people, however, are still in the age of 'Before Planet Earth' – i.e., before the ecological consciousness of the finite character of global resources dawned.

The fifth and final area I want to mention here concerns feminism and sexual politics. The demands of the women's movement on such issues as abortion and contraception, legal rights, equal pay, work organization and protection against domestic violence are slowly but surely beginning to unravel women's traditional role – and not only for those women active within the feminist movement. It is hard to understand how a left, whose explicit purpose is to 'refashion society', could so persistently exclude itself from this new, socially revolutionary force. The growing self-consciousness of women is only just beginning to transform the whole of our social thinking.

But the connection I am pointing to here is of another kind. I mean the uncompromising assault, spearheaded by feminism and the revolution in gay and sexual politics, on patriarchalism and patriarchal forms of masculinity. The reason why this development is not an unqualified gain in strength for the left but also an element in its dislocation, is that the culture of patriarchalism is nowhere so deeply embedded as within the left itself. The left has always tended to maintain a very narrow definition of 'the political'. When one says that the British left can be strong in corporate defence but is not 'hegemonic', one is drawing attention to precisely this failure to understand that the struggle to 'remake society' has to be fought as a war of position, conducted on many different fronts at once. It is a struggle to realize the interconnectedness of things which in our prevailing commonsense are kept separate. Hence the view that moral, social, familial, sexual, cultural questions have nothing to do with the 'struggle for socialism' – a view which is inscribed through and through by a masculine conception of the world. Somehow, it is imagined, the left will bring into existence a freer, more emancipatory kind of life – while the forms of familial and sexual life, where our instincts for authority are first formed and our desires and pleasures are regulated, remain untouched. Socialism will be introduced – by revolution or the ballot box – while somehow culture remains unchanged.

The question of the possible forms of social life under any conceivable socialist society is the real time bomb which feminism, the gay movement and sexual politics generally has delivered to the 'patriarcha-lism' of the traditional left. The harsh truth is that the political move-ment for socialism and the left has often been stabilized and disciplined by the very social and cultural forms which help to preserve its sub-ordination. Patriarchalism, the uncritical forms of the modern family, the patterns of sexual dominance, the disciplining of pleasure, the reinforcement of the habits of social conformity are some of the key ways in which the political movements of the left have remained deeply conservative and traditionalist at their cultural core. The tiny 'family man' is still hiding away in the heads of many of our most illustrious 'street-fighting' militants.

It is not possible for the left to reshape its own culture overnight. What is, however, inconceivable is that the left could ever become again a hegemonic historical force without undergoing a cultural revolution of some kind.

Is realignment is about anything it must be about confronting these strategic areas of debate. Those outlined here do not exhaust the problem. Others can be added. Together they represent a profound challenge. No imminent policy document will resolve them. Rethinking and renewal, given the size of the problems we face, will take a long time.

1985

17

People Aid – A New Politics Sweeps the Land

with Martin Jacques

Politics is certainly unpredictable. Who would ever have thought of Bob Geldof – a Boomtown Rat who had seen better days – as one of the key political actors of Thatcherite Britain? More to the point, who would have guessed in 1979, or even perhaps in 1983, that the plight of the Third World would generate one of the great popular movements of our time?

The triumph of Thatcherism represented the triumph of an ideology of selfishness and scapegoats. National failure was believed to be the result of individual profligacy. The road to salvation lay through people pulling themselves up by their bootstraps. The only acceptable motive for action was self-interest. What the unemployed needed was not handouts but initiative. In this view of the world, there was little sympathy for the casualties of the crisis at home, and no concern at all for less fortunate nations. People – and countries – were expected to put their own houses in order.

For some months now a sort of running battle has been going on between this creed of selfishness and the attempt to put together a broad, alternative vision around the notion of a 'caring society'. Some of the recent turning-points in the fortunes of Thatcherism are related to this struggle to polarize the field of social ideologies. Now, with the rise of the Band Aid/Live Aid/Sport Aid phenomenon, the ideology of selfishness – and thus one of the main ideological underpinnings of Thatcherism – has been dealt a further, severe blow.

Thatcherism arose partly as a way of thinking about recession. Its account of recession is, however, one-sided. Recession is not only about tightening belts. It is also about structural change and who is to carry the costs. It is about change and its consequences: within industry, as between declining and emergent technologies and communities of skill; within countries, as between the rise of some regions and the decline of others; and, internationally, in terms of the reordering of relationships within and between the so-called 'three worlds'. It is precisely these structural aspects of recession which have assumed increasing political importance.

The first, structural industrial change, is a growing area of political conflict, of which the miners' strike, Wapping and the shift of the tide against Thatcherism on unemployment and the unemployed are all manifestations. The most obvious expression of the second is the growing division between the declining north and the more prosperous south. So far as the third strand is concerned, though the reassertion of US power under Reagan has stimulated a flowering of the peace movement, the questions of Third World poverty, underdevelopment and the vicious circle of debt have stubbornly refused to assume a popular political character. However, the groundswell of political resistance in South Africa coupled with the rise of the 'famine movement' has begun to turn the tide here, too.

Thatcherism's account of recession – and, with it, a certain Thatcherite vision of the world order and Britain's role in it – has taken a drubbing. Selfishness and greed have been, if not eclipsed, then to some extent displaced by altruism and conscience.

Band Aid/Live Aid/Sport Aid encapsulates this shift more dramatically than anything else. One effect of a Thatcherite-dominated recession was to reinforce a narrow nationalism, helping to breed a reactionary mood of 'Little Englandism' and to nourish the roots of popular racism. A lifting of the popular horizons beyond our own shores, beyond even the boundaries of Europe, to Africa thus represents a crucial turning point in the erosion of Thatcherite hegemony.

The political significance and power of the 'famine movement' was enhanced rather than weakened by its origin and authorship. It came from outside the Left, however widely you define it. Its mobilizing reach was quite different even from CND's. Sport Aid, while resembling CND's age profile, attracted a youth constituency which, for the great part, had never previously been on any kind of demonstration. It reached the previously unreached. The famine movement's capacity to mobilize new forces has thus helped to shift the political centre of gravity. In 1979, a majority of young voters identified with Thatcherism and saw it as a vision for the future. In 1986, there is a new mood amongst contemporary youth. A sea-change has taken place.

This capacity to mobilize new constituencies is bound up with its character as a movement, the way it has evolved and, above all, its deep roots in contemporary popular culture, especially the culture of rock music.

Geldof's former career as a rock star was in no way coincidental to the movement's success – his rock connections were his political credentials (a guarantee to the fans that, at least from him, they were unlikely to hear a replay of the old-style lyrics of the professional politicians). The famine movement only really took off with the coming together of some of the biggest of the contemporary British pop stars for the Band Aid single, 'Do They Know It's Christmas?'. Since every fan knows how much it costs a star to give a free performance, this gesture helped to put 'caring for others' on the map as a value that belonged to the world of rock culture.

This was followed in July of last year with Live Aid, the one-day, open-air pop extravaganza in London and Philadelphia with global television coverage. The garnering of such a broad cross-section of pop stars for such a universal cause had enormous pulling power. The rock music connection gave the cause a national – indeed international – stage which it otherwise could not possibly have enjoyed. The combination of culture and politics, altruism and fun, was irresistible. The link between rock culture and politics is not, of course, new – it was a powerful element in the politics of the 1960s. Rock against Racism, the GLC's cultural politics and Red Wedge are more recent examples from the left. But the sheer scale and ambition of Live Aid was unprecedented. Never before had 'pop politics' created and shaped a whole social movement in this way.

No other cultural form could have played the political role that rock did in the Band Aid/Live Aid phenomenon. Its ubiquitous presence in the lives of young people gives it an unparalleled mobilizing power. When politics makes contact with this culture, it finds itself in touch with the cultural language which, for the majority of young people today (and for many not-so-young people, too), most authentically expresses how they experience the world. The rise of Geldof as the representative figure of the movement is a good illustration of this point. It's not just that he is a very talented politican: he became its cultural representative. He symbolized the fusion of two worlds usually kept well segregated.

Nothing more graphically illustrates this than Geldof's visit to the European parliament and his meeting with leading EEC figures. His dress and appearance was of the street not the committee room. His language was direct and uncomplicated. His demand was uncompromising. He was the representative of something new, a political movement born of a youth culture. This has enabled him to polarize the politics of aid in a new way: direct democracy versus bureaucracy. The nearest parallel to this mobilization was the 1960s, when the fact that youth stood so massively on the side of radicalism was due, above all, to a rare and powerful crossover between politics and culture.

Sport Aid, like Live Aid, also built on a popular cultural form. Unlike Live Aid, however, Sport Aid used a form which placed a premium not on spectatorship but on participation – that is, in the doing (i.e. running) as well as the giving. 'Run the World' was an appeal to everyone, if somewhat utopian. The growing popularity in recent years of jogging, fun runs, ten-kilometre races, half-marathons, marathons and what have you offered an ideal participatory form. It drew on one of the most progressive sporting and cultural traditions of the last few years, and through it, also on a growing ecological environmental consciousness connected to the 'politics of health.'

The London marathon, for instance, is an event of the people: anyone can run (not only the 'professionals'). It goes right through the city. Communities as well as groups of friends and individual runners of friends and individual runners of all kinds and ages turn out for the occasion (allowing for a variety of forms of participation not a feature of demonstrations, the left's preferred mass cultural form). The emphasis in Sport Aid, moreover, was no longer on a single national event, but rather on doing it where you are: 'let a hundred runs run' as it were (even if it was only across your own living room).

Another key feature of the Band Aid/Live Aid/Sport Aid phenomenon has been its capacity to transcend national frontiers. Live Aid was staged on both sides of the Atlantic: the stars belong to a highly internationalized market and audience: the concerts were beamed by satellite to many countries. By using the global networks of rock music and television, the movement was able to be, at once, both national and international. For a movement where the key issue is about the relationship between the First and the Third Worlds, this was not only appropriate but added significantly to the power of the appeal.

Sport Aid built on this international dimension in a number of different ways. It was sponsored by Sport Aid and Unicef. It was timed to have maximum impact on the UN Assembly debate of Africa, which immediately followed it. It was preceded by a week of activities across the globe, in the West, in the East and in Africa itself. The main focus of the event was the Sudanese runner, Omar Khalifi. The ten-kilometre run itself was staged at the same time in over 270 cities in 78 countries. Brisbane, Budapest, Leningrad, Paris, London, Ougadougou, New York, Nairobi, Rome and many more. And, like Live Aid, it was televised across the world. Unlike Live Aid, however, which at the end of the day was primarily focussed on London and Philadelphia, Sport Aid engaged in a more direct and active manner with the Third World, and with Africa in particular. Africa was not just an object of a movement in the developed world, it was also, at last, one of the subjects.

So what has the Band Aid/Live Aid/Sport Aid movement achieved? Its greatest success has been to change the national and, to a rather lesser extent, the international political agenda. The plight of the Third World has never been a national political priority. Nothing has symbolized this more clearly than the low priority which has always been accorded to expenditure on aid, the patronizing and forked-tongue way in which it is usually discussed. Britain's aid contribution – as a proportion of national income – has always been miserable, especially when her past contribution to undeveloping the underdeveloped world is borne in mind. And when the era of paring down public expenditure arrived, aid was high on the list of sacrificial lambs. Under Thatcher it has been ruthlessly pruned back. Now, for the first time, expenditure on aid is a big political issue.

Of course, it isn't simply a question of aid. 'Aid', in fact, is a very inadequate way of thinking about the relationship between the developed and the underdeveloped worlds or the causes of world poverty and famine. Some genuine reservations have been expressed about the limitations of the kind of 'famine consciousness' which has developed in the wake of Live Aid/Sport Aid. It certainly cannot yet be said that the majority of people in Britain, or even the majority of the participants in 'Run the World', have properly grasped the dynamic relationship between 'us' and 'them' across the North/South divide.

The largest chunk of 'aid' imaginable in any one year will not create the conditions in which Africa can feed itself if world commodity prices, the terms of trade, interest rates and Third World indebtedness to the international banking system remain unchanged. No act of charity can heal the breach within poor nations when the superpowers are exploiting those divisions in the attempt to recruit them into their side in the cold war which is being conducted on a worldwide scale.

However, the record of the famine movement on this aspect is not as inadequate as it is sometimes depicted and is manifestly improving. In highlighting the causes of African poverty, Geldof and co. have drawn attention to the underlying economic relationships between the First World and the Third World, questioning not only the levels but also the forms of aid, singling out the squeeze in which the Third World is caught by the debt problem, and ridiculing the absurdity of grain and butter mountains in Europe and famine in Africa.

It has been argued that, although the famine movement is beginning to highlight these deeper aspects of the problem, it has, like the older aid and emergency agencies, portrayed Africa simply as victim, linked to the charity of the West in what is essentially a paternalistic relationship. Again, there is something in this: it could hardly be otherwise, given the way our imperial history has shaped our political and cultural traditions. But the Third World as victim no longer seems the dominant image. Sport Aid did indeed talk about the responsibilities of the First World to the Third World, and Africa was, as we have seen, a participant. Aid is moving from the realm of charity to the world of politics. In generating a popular movement around this, it has given internationalism a new content.

It's worth adding too that, although the UN debate yielded little tangible result, international neo-liberalism was exposed to quite new pressures. Not only has the Thatcherite 'put your own house in order' attitude towards the African crisis been shaken dramatically, but it has been placed on the defensive internationally. Shultz's lecture to Africa on privatization and more initiative by private enterprise and less by the state was revealed for the hollow, cynical sham it certainly was, an excuse to do little or nothing.

Another achievement of the Sport Aid movement is the way it has combined charity with politics. Again, this has been a controversial aspect of Sport Aid on the left. The traditional left has long regarded charity as a sop, which eases the conscience but does not tackle the problem at the root, and which moreover makes such matters appear to be the responsibity of private individuals rather than of the state. Of course, it is true that famine cannot be permanently averted in Africa by charity alone.

But this partly misses the point. For Third World poverty is the responsibility of people and governments. Politically, the state is not likely to do much unless the people are pushing it. But for the people to mount an attack on the current set of national priorities and to engage in the enormous task of moblizing public opinion so as to create a new political agenda, they must find ways of identifying with and committing themselves to the cause in some public and socially validated way. Personal giving is one important way of relating to an issue, though it may not be enough to constitute a whole politics. But it implies commitment. We must not underestimate the role of movements, which have their base within civil society, in creating a current or movement of opinion which has a shift in state policy as one of its ultimate objectives.

Sport Aid was essentially a civil society movement, arising outside the state and formal politics. That was a major part of its attraction. It was therefore participatory in its whole thrust – getting ordinary people to do something, to give directly, themselves. But, in addition to raising a great deal of money, it also placed new and quite dramatic pressures on the government to take the aid question seriously and to act. Far from being simply a sop, charity in this context has become a powerful political weapon. It seems unlikely that a broad-based, anti-Thatcherite popular politics can be built without politicizing the charitable impulse.

In this context, it is worth noting the story of the government's attitude towards Geldof and the famine movement. At the time of Live Aid, the government simply ignored it. But such has been the success of the famine movement, and the changed popular mood, that when it came to Sport Aid, the Tories were no longer able to remain so aloof. Now, grudgingly, a knighthood has been found. Meanwhile, the hectic search is on for a megastar of the pop world more politically acceptable, more amenable to the Leader's whim – and preferably, no doubt, English rather than Irish. Richard Branson, of the Virgin record and travel empire and 'Litter Aid', is the latest candidate for this role.

This brings us, finally, to the attitude of the left. Sadly, the left's attitude has been, at best, praise from the sidelines; more usually, grudging support, with a good supply of sectarian sniping. By and large the organized left has been almost totally absent from the whole movement and process. The left has sought no popular points of entry into it. To cite just two examples of what might have been. Following Live Aid, there was a series of initiatives such as Fashion Aid, Food Aid and Art Aid. But no Union Aid. A popular initiative from the unions last year with Live Aid et al., could have raised large sums of money from within the unions, increased awareness amongst union members about Third World issues, created new links between popular cultural figures and the unions, enhanced their public image, and enabled new forms of mobilization and creativity within the unions themselves. And when it came to Sport Aid, everybody seemed to be falling over themselves to join it except the labour movement. True, Denis Healey was seen on the TV screens in his 'I Ran the World' teeshirt, limbering up on the House of Commons grass with other MPs. But where was the Labour party NEC or the TUC general council?

This absence is not accidental. The continuing suspicion about 'charity' and about youth culture amongst sections of the left is no doubt one reason. Another is reservations about the way Africa is portrayed. But the most important reason is surely a profound cultural sectarianism which still pervades the left. The real reason, one suspects, why there has been no relationship with Band Aid/Live Aid/Sport Aid is because the initiative came from *outside* the left. It was not 'ours'. If it had been Nicaragua, Chile or South Africa, it would no doubt have been different. But here was an initiative which came from quite new quarters *and* on an issue on which the left has traditionally had precious little to say beyond slogans.

Yet the capacity of the left to act as a national force cannot only be about its own creations, its own capacity to initiate. It must also be about its ability to relate positively to others, and the initiatives of other forces. That is what hegemony is about. Otherwise our model of society is that the only things worth getting involved in are our own things; others are not capable of creating movements and currents which deserve our support, enthusiasm and intervention. This is a very patronizing view of the world.

By absenting itself from a popular movement like Sport Aid, the left thereby also largely deprived itself of a voice in the direction of that movement and of the debate which has inevitably followed, and thus once again isolated itself from the mainstream of national popular life which, on this occasion, seems -- like the great swarm of anonymous runners – to have passed us by somewhere along the way.

This is inexcusable for another reason. The famine movement has asserted at a popular level the need for a new relationship between Britain and the Third World. The peace movement of the 1980s has been more internationalist and less parochial than that of the 1960s. Taken together with the reassertion of a more traditional strength of the left – solidarity movements with Third World struggles, now dramatically expressed in the context of South Africa – we can now detect the emergence of something new, a number of parallel popular movements all of which are about a different post-imperial role for Britain.

1986

18

Blue Election, Election Blues

Thatcherism's third term was not unexpected, but the reality of it is devastating and will take some time to think through properly. It is all the more depressing because, in the event, Labour had a relatively good campaign. For three weeks it looked like a party that could actually win and hold power. Kinnock's self-confidence, though overplayed, proved infectious. Organizationally, the party looked for once as if it belonged to the twentieth century. The manifesto was muddled; but, once the campaign got off the ground, it found an image and acquired political definition. Labour managed to 'stage' a broad political choice for the nation between the party of greed, privilege and self-interest and the party of caring, collective provision and the underprivileged. This was the only chance Labour had, and it went for it with surprising energy.

However, though Labour's 'good' campaign put heart into party activists and the committed left, it did not in the end shift the overall disposition of the vote. Some voters may have changed their minds but the swings cancelled one another out. There was no massive change of heart in the final three weeks. Few voters, for instance, seem to have been swayed by the famous party election television broadcasts, which caused such excitement amongst media pundits and so much heart-searching amongst the Labour faithful. The election, in short, was won (i.e. lost) in those terrible months and years since 1983. Thatcherism's victory was rooted not in any temporary fluctuations of support, but in the deep movements and tendencies which have been reshaping the British political map. The problem the left now faces is structural and organic.

One clue to this may lie in a persistent trend over the past five years. Asked what policies they supported, significant majorities consistently preferred Labour on unemployment, health, housing and education – the 'welfare' issues. During the campaign, these remained the most important issues for the majority of voters polled. In fact, Labour actually had some success in pushing them up the political agenda. However, both before and during the election, if asked about image – who was 'doing a good job', 'giving the country a lead', making people 'feel good to be British again' – a majority consistently said 'Maggie'. The same thing has been going on in America, where no majorities could be found for specific policies like winding up welfare programmes, yet, when it came to 'making you feel good to be American', people said Ronnie was their baby.

One way of interpreting this trend is that, increasingly, the electorate is thinking politically not in terms of policies but of images. This doesn't mean that policies don't matter. It does mean that policies don't capture people's political imaginations unless constructed into an image with which they can identify. Far from this being a sign of voter irrationality, there are a number of quite 'rational' reasons why there should be a trend in this direction in the advanced 'class democracies' like Britain and the US.

First, we live in a world where decisions are both complex and remote, and the big bureaucracies of state and market control a great deal of social life. So people are quite 'rational' to believe that they can't intervene with much hope of success, in detail, into policy matters, nor can they affect the fine tuning of the economic or policy machines.

Second, the electorate is now mercilessly exposed to ceaseless massaging by the media and to 'disinformation' from the politicians. It isn't surprising that politics, too, is being absorbed into this game of impression-management.

Third, voters know perfectly well that, these days, a five-year mandate will be interpreted any way the party in power likes. The abolition of the GLC was never 'popular' but that didn't stop Mrs Thatcher from doing what was politically expedient. Democracy, even in the narrow sense of 'government by popular consent', didn't once sully the lips of a single Tory spokesperson, and is a concept altogether foreign to Thatcherism's universe. 'Choice' was counterposed to 'democracy' precisely because, whereas the latter is public and social, the former can be defined in wholly private and individual (i.e. 'familial') terms.

In all these circumstances, people aren't wrong to imagine that what is required of them as citizens is simply to express a broad, undefined 'preference' for one scenario or another, this image or that. Some people regard this as a trivialization of politics. But images are not trivial things.

In and through images, fundamental political questions are being posed and argued through. We need to take them more seriously than we do. Mrs Thatcher claimed she was excited to be not just fighting for power, but helping to 'set the agenda for the twenty-first century'. But, how else can you discuss what Britain and the British people are to become, except in terms of broad images? The future has to be imagined – 'imaged', to coin a word.

The question of political imagery is not a matter of presentation, but of ideology and representation which is a different and altogether more serious matter. One reason why Labour did better than most of us expected is that, this time, it did engage in ideological struggle. One reason why the campaign failed to shift minds, hearts and votes, was that it lost that struggle, despite its efforts. And part of the reason why Labour lost it is that, while it has only just begun to take these questions seriously, Thatcherism has been intervening ideologically with consummate skill ever since 1979.

Why has it taken Labour, and the left more generally, so long to appreciate the strategic importance of the ideological arena? In part, the answer lies in the way the left normally thinks about 'politics'. Electoral politics – in fact, every kind of politics – depends on political identities and identifications. People make identifications symbolically: through social imagery, in their political imaginations. They 'see themselves' as one sort of person or another. They 'imagine their future' within this scenario or that. They don't just think about voting in terms of how much they have, their so-called 'material interests'. Material interests matter profoundly. But they are always ideologically defined.

Contrary to a certain version of Marxism, which has as strong a hold over the Labour 'centre' as it does on the so-called 'hard left', material interests, on their own, have no necessary class belongingness. They influence us. But they are not escalators which automatically deliver people to their appointed destinations, 'in place', within the political ideological spectrum.

One reason why they don't is because people have conflicting social interests, sometimes reflecting conflicting identities. As a worker a person might put 'wages' first: in a period of high unemployment, 'job security' may come higher; a woman might prioritize 'child care'. But what does a 'working woman' put first? Which of her identities is the one that determines her political choices? Take another example. I am a socialist and therefore passionately in favour of state education. But I am also a parent with a child who is taking O levels in a hard-pressed local education authority. Do I stick by my political principles or squeeze her into a 'better' school?

In fact, the harder things get in Thatcher's Britain and the more competitive they become, the more divided society is. And the more divided it is, the more these ideological conflicts bear down on people's actual lives, cutting their 'natural' social and political identifications in two. Appealing to the 'real experience' of poverty or unemployment or underprivilege won't do the trick. Even poverty and unemployment have to be ideologically defined. A young unemployed person may interpret this experience to mean that you should work and vote to change the system. But it could equally be defined as a sign that you should throw your fortune in with the winners, climb on the bandwagon, earn a fast buck and look after 'number one'. Material interests did not, on their own, guarantee an automatic majority for Labour in the working class this time, and it won't necessarily do so in the future because it never has.

This does not mean that ideology determines everything. If nobody was prospering under Thatcherism, ideology alone could not parachute such an 'illusion' into the heads of the majority. However, if some people are doing well – as they are, especially, in personal terms, in the 'South' – and the ideological climate is right, and the alternative ways of measuring how 'well' you are doing are effectively silenced or stigmatized, then the small number who define themselves as 'doing well' will be swelled by a much larger number who identify with this way of 'getting on'. Elections are won or lost not just on so-called 'real' majorities, but on (equally real) 'symbolic majorities'. Mrs Thatcher's 'symbolic majority' includes all who identify ideologically with the enterprise culture as the way of the future, who see themselves in their political imagination as likely to be lucky in the next round. They form an 'imaginary community' around Thatcherism's political project.

The whole point of Thatcherism as a form of politics has been to construct a new social bloc, and in this project ideology is critical. A social bloc is, by definition, not homogeneous. It does not consist of one whole class or even part of one class. It has to be constructed out of groups which are very different in terms of their material interests and social positions. The question is, can these differences of position and interest be constructed into a 'unity'? (It never is a unity, in the strict sense.) Can these diverse identities be welded together into a 'collective will'?

In the second term, Thatcherism did not make a single move which was not also carefully calculated in terms of this hegemonic strategy. It stepped up the pace of privatization. But it took care, at every step, to harness new social constituencies to it, to 'construct' an image of the new, share-owning working class, and to expand the bloc, symbolically, around the image of 'choice'. It has not only attacked state education and the health service. It has created, side by side and in competition with them, among the majority of users and right in the heart of the working class, an alternative image: quicker service via private health and a better chance for kids in a deregulated education system – the 'fast-lane' schools and inner-city technology colleges.

Don't for a moment underestimate the resonance which a slogan like 'power to the people' carries in our overbureaucratized, overmanaged, underresourced society. Of course, only a few can actually choose to be better off in these ways. But, for the time being, a lot of people think this is the only way open to them to advance in a society where competition and selectivity have become the name of the game. If that's the only game in town, some of them will play it!

Building a new social bloc means not only 'symbolically' including as many different groups as you can in your project, but also symbolically excluding the enemy. The 'loony left' image was one powerful example. Once the one-liner was launched, the deep symbiosis between Thatcherism and the press guaranteed it an uninterrupted flight. It locked together in a single image high rates and political extremism with those powerful subliminal themes of race and sex. The discourse of the 'loony left' was a code. In London it made it possible to expunge the legacy of the GLC, and to bring into the election, race (the anti-anti-racism backlash) and sex (the anti-feminism, anti-gay, anti-permissive, post-Aids backlash – Thatcherism's hidden 'moral agenda') without a word having to be explicitly spoken. So successful was it that the Labour leadership, the party machine, much of the traditional 'hard left' and the slick *New Statesmen* and all, could also make a heavy investment in it without having to reveal their hand about race, feminism or sexual politics.

Instead of engaging with the 'loony left' image, Labour in effect colluded with it. In the weeks before the election, the leadership cast its vote unflinchingly for the 'traditional' image, in search of the 'traditional Labour voter'. Again, everybody understood that this, too, was a code. It is a code for 'back to the respectable, moderate, trade-unionist, male-dominated working class'. Mr Kinnock appeared as a manly 'likely lad' who owed everything to the welfare state. His 'familial' image carried not a single echo or trace of feminist struggles over two decades. The investment in 'strong leadership' and in 'ordinariness' carried its own message. It signalled the distancing of Labour from all those 'fringe issues' and a commitment to rooting Labour political loyalties exclusively through an identification with the traditional culture of the left.

This was the image with which Labour chose to engage, ideologically, with Thatcherism. The key question is, can Labour win with it? Can it harness the fragmented experiences of living in Great Britain Limited to a new, radical political will? Can it construct around Labour a new social bloc?

Of course, millions of people desperately need the welfare state. And identification with parts of it remains strong. So, in some areas, the traditionalist appeal did lend conviction to Labour's programme. It also contained an element of forward-projection – in the form of the question 'what sort of society would you prefer to live in?'

On the other hand, it was also fatally narrow and backward-looking. It does not have roots in the things which are transforming social and economic life and it lacks a convincing strategy for, or image of, modernization. Labour may have carried conviction on the 'fair shares', redistribution, front; but it lacked credibility on the 'wealth-creating' front. It could not construct a picture of what a wealthy society might be like or how it could be created. And since many identifications were made, not in terms of social wealth but in 'family fortunes', it had no image to set against Thatcherism's image of personalized and privatized 'prosperity'.

The sober truth is that Labour probably did as well with this traditionalist image as it was possible to do. It does not and cannot carry majority support. It appeals to some sectors of, but cannot unify, the working class. And it certainly is not hegemonic enough to construct out of our increasingly fragmented and divided society a new social bloc or collective political will for the future.

In the aftermath of the election, many people have been seeking consolation in the belief that the appeal to the 'traditional Labour voter' could, at least, carry half the country – the 'North'. The 'North' has become a sort of geographical metaphor for where the traditional Labour voter now resides. If only things were so neatly divided, Labour's traditionalist appeal would make more sense. But, unfortunately, that story is deceptively neat.

The 'North' is not just a geographical entity: it is also a state of mind. Looked at in this way, the picture becomes a good deal bleaker.

First, the 'North' is not as solid as it looks. There are plenty of 'Southerners' living in the 'North'.

Second, the disaster which Labour suffered in London and the southeast suggests that many people there who may be 'North' in their living standards, conditions and even origins have, nevertheless, become 'Southerners' in their heads. The 'new' working class in the geographical 'South' now identify and vote in a majority for Thatcherism. They no longer identify themselves with Labour's traditional working-class Labour voter. What is more, many people in the underclasses – the unskilled, part-timers, young unemployed, women living alone, black people, the homeless, inner-city casualties – don't see themselves or identify with this traditionalist image either. Looked at not so much in terms of economic class, but as ideological identification, Labour could not and cannot for the foreseeable future make any inroads into the social landscape of the 'South' on the narrow basis of the image they chose.

Third, the 'North' is not impervious to Thatcherite inroads, as we shall see in the coming months. The inner-cities strategy will not bring about long-term sustained growth in the 'North', but it is going to erode Labour's political base in the great industrial urban areas. Thatcherism in the 'South' has already had considerable success in targeting the big-spending Labour councils, the comprehensive schools and council housing – three major pillars of Labour's political base. In the next months we are going to witness a similar assault, economically and ideologically, on Labour's base in the 'North' with blistering effects.

There will be a flood of small businesses, pump-primed, by industrialists who know on which side their political bread is buttered. The press will trumpet its immediate 'success' and Lord Young will be 'economical' with more statistics. Labour authorities will be sidelined by 'alternative' private channels of growth, and isolated for attack (some version of the London 'loony left' ideological missile is at this very moment cruising up the M1). Thatcherism can't 'restore' Britain's old industrial base – but that is not the project. It may not be able to positively win over everybody – but that is not necessary either. It has never had an overwhelming social majority on anything. But it can mobilize the crucial two-thirds, which is enough. Not all of them are, as yet, Tory voters, but many who still vote Labour or Alliance have begun to benefit from Thatcherism, or are making pragmatic adjustments to it.

What's more, not all the two-thirds need to be in any real sense 'prosperous'. All Thatcherism has to do to erode Labour's 'Northern' bastions is to lay a base for just enough people to put their feet, tentatively, on the new Thatcherite ladders of success. Firstly, it has to convince them that, concretely, this is a more likely way to a better, more prosperous life than any other alternative on offer. Secondly, it has to convince others who have not yet begun to do well, to cast their lot in with the free-market society. Once this threshold has been crossed, a much larger number – a strategic majority, the necessary two-thirds – move in their heads. The balance shifts. The 'North' has begun its symbolic journey 'Southwards' ...

What, then, about the possibility of constructing the different social constituencies into a new social bloc around Labour's traditionalist appeal? Clearly, few modernizing industrialists can be harnessed to Labour's current strategy. Big business is now pro-Thatcher, not simply in pragmatic but in ideological terms. They 'believe'. They understand that Thatcherism is not just a strategy which favours capital; it must also be a strategy for the whole society, 'for capital'. The middle classes are interestingly split. The self-made middle classes – numerically, the overwhelming majority – who inhabit the culture of the private sector, are Mrs Thatcher's ideological vanguard. They have talked their way into an impregnable philosophy of 'number one'. The 'public sector' middle classes in education, local government or the social services are not so directly in touch with the new prosperity and are more inclined to seek rewards from socially useful and personally rewarding forms of work which have been brutally savaged by the new criteria of 'value for money' and 'efficiency'. They are more detached from Thatcherism. But this does not help Labour as much as it might, since the Alliance now soaks up their disenchantment with Thatcherism – it's a 'nicer' option.

In the aftermath of the election, many people on the left are arguing that Labour's only hope lies in the working class. However, Thatcherism's electoral hegemony continues to rest precisely on certain parts of the working-class vote. Where Labour commands a majority, that majority is overwhelmingly working class. But the working class is not overwhelmingly Labour. Indeed, there is no such thing as 'the' working-class vote any more. Divisions, not solidarities, of class identification are the rule. There are large and significant sectors of the 'working class' as it really is today – the unemployed, semi-skilled and unskilled, part-time workers, male and female, the low-paid, black people, the 'underclasses' of Thatcherite Britain – who no longer see themselves in a traditional Labour way. In Greater London and the south-east, Labour failed to connect with the forces that are remaking the working class. Skilled workers in the new industries, and the expanding clerical and office workforce, are, in their majority, voters for Thatcherism. There are more of them in the south-east than in the north, but the balance is changing and will continue, unevenly, to do so. The sectors of this vote who are home owners or new shareholders are even more committed.

What then of the new social constituencies which, in any case, have less of a clearcut class identity? Women, whether in or out of full-time work, did not vote overwhelmingly for Thatcherism and have not done so since 1979. But Labour made absolutely no direct, strategic or distinctive investment in what, from any point of view, is a historic shift of political identification. Presumably, on the analogy with 'black sections', to do so would be 'sexist'! By the same token the 'ethnic' vote is less and less a Labour possession – and after the disastrous handling of the black sections issue, who can blame them? More owners of Asian small businesses are beginning to vote by class rather than by race. A proportion of Afro-Caribbean people will not be far behind.

None of this augurs well for the future. Politics does not reflect majorities, it constructs them. And there is no evidence that Labour's commitment to traditionalism can construct such a majority. Certainly, the consequences of Thatcherite restructuring are horrendous. But larger and larger numbers of people no longer experience all this as 'traditional Labour voters'. Even less can they articulate their aspirations through the traditional Labour image. The question of Labour becoming in a deep sense the majority party of society is therefore not whether it can rally and mobilize its past, but whether it has a convincing alternative scenario to Thatcherism for the future. It cannot build such an alternative by, however honourably, replaying '1945' in 1987. It can only honour its past by aiming to move forwards. But to do so it needs a strategy for modernization and an image of modernity. What the election suggests is that Labour, far from opening the hard road to renewal, has largely turned its back on it. It is therefore not surprising that – despite the good feelings and high morale – its historic decline continues.

1987

PART FOUR

◆

Conclusion

19

Learning from Thatcherism

'Ten lessons from madame LaZonga;
She does the rhumba, and she does the conga'

The process of 'rethinking' has begun – many would say, not before time. Admittedly, it is taking some peculiar forms – the 'Labour Listens' campaign being one of the most bizarre. Is it really useful to listen to all and sundry about the future of socialism without, at least, first formulating some themes or propositions of your own? Are there no policy directions or tendencies already emerging inside Walworth Road? No matter. Even this muddled exercise should be seen as part of a wider process – painful, contorted, but an absolute prerequisite to any possible renewal of the project of the left.

The issue, now, is not whether but how to rethink. The temptations for the left will be either to fall back on The Faith as we know it or to race forward to embrace the new Thatcherite 'consensus'. Another, more radical, proposal is that we could do worse than to start the process of rethinking with a little thought. What the 'Thatcher revolution' suggests is that good ideas, or what the political commentators were calling, in the aftermath of the election, some 'Big Themes', don't fall off the shelf without an ideological framework to give those ideas coherence. By framework, we mean a perspective on what is happening to society now, a vision of the future, a capacity to articulate these vividly through a few clearly-enunciated themes or principles, a new conception of politics. In short, a political strategy. In this, as in much else, the left could do worse than begin by 'learning from Thatcherism'.

Now, nothing is more calculated to drive the left into a tizzy than this scandalous proposition – especially when advanced by *Marxism Today*.

The very idea of Thatcherism is anathema to the left. Decent people everywhere hate and revile it. Where Thatcherism is, there the left cannot be. They inhabit two, not only different and hostile, but mutually-exclusive worlds. What on earth could the left possibly learn? Besides, isn't this slogan simply a cover-up for the attempt to shift Labour irrevocably to the right – an injunction to cuddle up to the 'enterprise culture' on the if-you-can't-beat-them-join-them principle?

It is a sign both of the defensiveness and the residual sectarianism afflicting many parts of the left that it misreads an injunction to analyse 'Thatcherism' for a recommendation to swallow it whole. It is time to correct this fatal confusion, most of all because it is now so politically disabling. Unless the left can understand Thatcherism – what it is, why it arose, what its historical specificity is, the reasons for its success in redrawing the political map and disorganizing the left – it cannot renew itself because it cannot understand the world it must live in if it is not to be 'disappeared' into permanent marginality. It is time, therefore, in the context of rethinking, to make clear exactly what is meant by 'learning from Thatcherism'. And we can do this, not only in general terms, but in relation to a concrete example: the current crisis surrounding the NHS.

The first thing Thatcherism teaches us about the NHS is that crises always present opportunities as well as problems. The problem here is not only how to reorganize the NHS but how to turn the crisis to our political advantage. It is not only a chance to defend the NHS but an opportunity to construct a majoritarian politics of the left. If the left cannot develop an alternative long-term political strategy it cannot save the NHS. What most distinguishes Thatcherism's wide-ranging conduct of ideological politics from Labour's narrow, tactical parliamentarianism, is exactly this unremitting attention to the long-term, strategic, political 'payoff' of apparently short-term crises.

The present uproar around the NHS is, after all, the most protracted crisis affecting the welfare state of Mrs Thatcher's reign. We always knew – and she always knew – that it was her Achilles heel: the area where popular opinion would be most stubbornly resistant to the project of 'breaking the spell of the welfare state'. What we have now is a crisis that refuses to go away, unremitting (and often critical) media coverage, widespread and varied popular support for a change, and the government temporarily on the ropes. How could the left and the Labour Party fail to profit, politically, from such a conjuncture?

And yet, the more the crisis unfolds, the more the left's political and ideological gains seem, at best, 'passive' ones. Mrs Thatcher has personally taken charge of the crisis – always an ominous sign. 'The impression which the prime minister was trying to create was that she was pleased that talk of crisis by the opposition and health professionals had opened up the NHS to her radicalism. Her spokesman countered the impression of government panic by stressing that she was "seizing the tide of public perception"' (*The Guardian* Jan 27). The talk is now exclusively about 'alternative ways of funding' (which every post-Thatcherite child of nine knows is a code-phrase for the massive expansion of private medicine and privatisation within the NHS) and 'breaking the barriers to greater efficiency' (which we know is a code-phrase for destroying COHSE and NUPE).

Haven't we been here before? A great, thundering crisis – and then, inexorably, as it unfolds, the tide beginning to turn, the ideological advantage shifting to the other side, victory snatched from the jaws of defeat ...? Politics, waged by Thatcherism as a relentless 'war of positions'? Crisis as a God-sent opportunity to radically restructure society (or, as Gramsci put it, 'reconstruction already under way in the very moment of destruction')? Why do we still find it impossible to believe that this could happen, when it has been happening to us, steadily, since 1979?

There are several reasons for this reluctance. The left keeps telling itself that 'the postwar settlement is over': but we still find it difficult to think politically in a world where its terms can no longer be taken for granted. We find it easier to be righteously moralistic about Thatcherism ('isn't she a cow?'): harder to grasp its logic as a political strategy. Another reason is the left's defensiveness. It is as though the moment we stray, even for a moment, from the straight-and-narrow path of conventional left wisdom, the big, bad wolf of Thatcherite revisionism is waiting to gobble us up. Our sectarianism is often a product of fear – the changing world is seen as a strange and threatening place without signposts. It is also symptomatic of the way our thinking has become stuck in a particular historic groove, of how our agendas are fixed by the circumstances (the 1930s, 1945) in which they were originally formed.

It is also due to a certain notion of politics, inhabited not so much as a theory, more as a habit of mind. We go on thinking a unilinear and irreversible political logic, driven by some abstract entity we call 'the economic' or 'capital', unfolding to its preordained end. Whereas, as Thatcherism clearly shows, politics actually works more like the logic of language: you can always put it another way if you try hard enough. Current campaigning on cuts in the NHS could lead to a leap in public spending. Alternatively, it could lead to the argument that – since the NHS is underfunded but the demand is potentially limitless, since taxpayers are looking to pay less in taxation and there is money swilling around in the private sector – the only solution is value for money and privatization. The difference between the first and the second scenarios is not determined by some inexorable 'law of history' but by the effectiveness of our political-ideological intervention, above all in the 'theatre' of popular politics and popular conceptions.

Let us stay with the question of 'popular conceptions' for a moment. The popular defence of the NHS is genuine. But so is the demand for lower taxation. (In the same way, the commitment to the state education system is widespread. But so is the sense that, in some places, it is beginning to fall apart). These interests genuinely conflict. They collide inside the heads and hearts of many ordinary folk who aren't one hundred-and-one-per-cent committed 'Thatcherites' – people who we will have to win over if the principles underlying the NHS or state education are ever to prevail again in a new form. This conflict of loyalties and desires is what precipitates chaos and unpredictability in the ideological field: precisely the rupture on which Thatcherism capitalizes.

So, the balance of ideological advantage slowly turns Thatcherism's way, because the specific issue of the NHS is secured for the right by a deeper set of articulations which the left has not begun to shift. These include such propositions as: the public sector is bureaucratic and inefficient; the private sector is efficient and gives 'value for money'; efficiency is inextricably linked with 'competition' and 'market forces'; the 'dependency culture' makes growing demands on the state – unless ruthlessly disciplined – a 'bottomless pit' (the spectre of the endlessly desiring consumer); public sector institutions, protected by public sector unions, are always 'overmanned' (*sic.*); 'freedom' would be enhanced by giving the money back to the punters and letting them choose the form and level of health care they want; if there is money to spare, it is the direct result of Thatcherite 'prosperity'; and so on. In short, the familiar Thatcherite litany which is indelibly imprinted on the public mind and imposed on public and private discourse everywhere.

The unpalatable fact is that, despite the crisis, Thatcherism continues to hold the high ground because, among large sections of the population (including Labour voters), the political ideological thematics of Thatcherism remain in place.

So, one thing we can learn from Thatcherism is that, in this day and age, in our kind of society, politics is either conducted ideologically, or not at all. Thatcherism has put in play a range of different social and economic strategies. But it has never for a moment neglected the ideological dimension. Privatization, for example, has many economic and social payoffs. But it is never advanced by Thatcherism without also being constructed ideologically ('Sid', the 'share-owning democracy' etc). There is no point giving people tax cuts unless you also sell it to them as part of the 'freedom' package. In this sense, Thatcherism is always, and consistently, multifaceted. It always moves on several fronts at once. It moulds people's conceptions as it restructures their lives as it shifts the disposition of forces to its side.

This is what is sometimes called a 'hegemonic political project'. A simpler way of putting it would be thinking and acting strategically. This word is constantly bandied about by the left. But do we know what it means in practice? In his recent pamphlet on *The Politics Of Prosperity* Charles Leadbeater argued that 'thinking strategically' implied

'recognizing the enormity and significance of the changes which have taken place in the last decade. It must not simply modernize past policies ... There must be some vision of what kind of society this strategy would create ... It must be built up from the foundations of the cultural identities and lifestyles it sanctions and approves ... through the institutional mechanisms which promote and maintain these ... to the higher political ideology.[1]

These aspects need to be spelt out more.

The 'enormity and significance of change' does not only refer to the consequences of Thatcherite cuts and restructuring. There are deep-seated underlying, economic, sociological and cultural trends which are profoundly reshaping Britain. Thatcherism did not create these, though it appropriates them politically and harnesses them to its own strategies. But any left-of-centre government will have to deal with them too. In that sense, whether we like it or not, we exist in the same universe, and are subject to some of the same conditions of existence. This is not the place to elaborate on what these trends are. But, broadly speaking, organized capitalism, the industrial proletariat, the labour movement and the very idea of socialism itself were all brought to their mature modern forms alongside and in conditions (around the turn of the century) associated with the 'Fordist revolution' in the organization of modern production. 'Fordism' stands for the large-scale, flow processes of the modern factory, the skilled factory proletariat, the intensification of management, the rise of the corporate giants, the spread of mass consumption, the concentration of capital, the forward march of the technical division of labour, the intensification of world competition and the further spread of capitalism as a 'global system'. This was never only an 'economic' revolution. It was always a cultural and social revolution as well (as Gramsci, who discussed the connection of 'Fordism' with the reorganization of sexual life in his classic essay, 'American and Fordism' perfectly understood).[2]

Now we are beginning, in the usual highly uneven and contradictory way, to move into a 'post-Fordist' society – what some theorists call disorganized capitalism, the era of 'flexible specialisation'.[3] One way of reading present developments is that 'privatization' is Thatcherism's way of harnessing and appropriating this underlying movement within a specific economic and political strategy and constructing it within the terms of a specific philosophy. It has succeeded, to some degree, in aligning its historical, political, cultural and sexual 'logics' with some of the most powerful tendencies in the contemporary logics of capitalist development. And this, in part, is what gives it its supreme confidence, its air of ideological complacency: what makes it appear to 'have history on its side', to be coterminous with the inevitable course of the future. The left, however, instead of rethinking *its* economic, political and cultural strategies in the light of this deeper, underlying 'logic' of dispersal and diversification (which, after all, need not necessarily be an enemy of greater democratization), simply resists it. If Thatcherism can lay claim to it, then we must have nothing to do with it. Is there any more certain way of rendering yourself historically anachronistic?

'The significance of change' also has a more practical meaning in relation to *this* crisis. We cannot simply defend the NHS as it is, as if nothing has happened since it was first introduced in 1947. In practice, the Left can only seize the political advantage by mounting its own critique of the NHS – since as everybody quietly recognizes, things were not hunky-dory in the NHS long before the advent of Thatcherism; and not all the problems are of Thatcherism's making. Steve Iliffe long ago convincingly argued that, in fact, there is not one, but 'two interconnected crises within the health service. One is a direct consequence of the economic recession and Conservative attempts to escape from it' (coupled, we would add with Thatcherism's project to restructure the welfare state). 'The second is a long-term structural crisis of medicine itself running over decades and common to the industralized world.'4

There is a deeper side to this as well. We may have to acknowledge that there is often a rational core to Thatcherism's critique, which reflects some real substantive issues, which Thatcherism did not create but addresses in its own way. And since, in this sense, we both inhabit the same world, the left will have to address them too. However, squaring up to them means confronting some extremely awkward issues. One example is the fiscal crisis of the welfare state – the ever-rising relative costs in the NHS as the average age of the population rises, medical technology leaps ahead, health needs diversify, the awareness of environmental factors and preventive medicine deepens and the patterns of disease shift. The fiscal crisis of the welfare state is not simply a Thatcherite plot, though of course Thatcherism exaggerates it for its own political ends.

The left's answer is that there is more to spend if we choose; and this is certainly correct, given Britain's pitiful comparative showing in terms of the proportion of GDP spent on health amongst the industrialized countries. But only up to a point. At the end of this road, there are limits, which are not those set by Thatcherism's artificial 'cap' on spending but those limits set by the productivity of the economy itself. What the right argues is that, once this limit is reached (even at the USA's 10.7 per cent rather than the UK's miserable 5.9 per cent), there is then not much to choose between rationing by price (which they would prefer) and rationing by queue (which is what has been going on in the NHS for decades). Naturally, they prefer rationing by price, since it increases the incentive to the patient to save on costs and puts pressure on the 'health market' to become more efficient. We have rooted objections to this path: but this must be because we have a different game-plan, not because we are playing in a different ball-park. But have we spelt it out? Do our supporters and the public know what it is?

One thing for certain, then, that we mean by 'strategic' is thinking in a sustained, interconnected way – right through to that painful point where one policy crosscuts another. The point, for example, on the one hand, where simply 'spending more on the NHS' comes up against the barrier of the failure of the left so far to elaborate a strategy for an expanding economy. On the other hand, where it hits the road block of the unpopularity of higher taxation in the form of that entrenched figure (which, at the moment, belongs exclusively to the right) – the 'sovereign taxpayer'. Thatcherism is also held in place by this ideological figure of 'economic man', the measure of all things, who only understands cash-in-hand, readies-in-the-pocket, and who apparently never gets ill, doesn't need his streets cleaned or his children educated or to breathe oxygen occasionally. Clearly, the NHS issue cannot be won in terms of the NHS alone. If Thatcherism wins the argument about 'wealth creation', 'prosperity' and 'taxpayer freedom', it will, sooner or later, win the argument about privatizing the NHS.

Of course, you only get a clear sense of strategy going among the people you are trying to win over to your side, if they can see clearly how it is counterposed to the strategy of the other side, what the underlying organizing principles are, and the perspective, the 'philosophical themes', which distinguish them. Successive encounters at the dispatch box are small beer when compared with a systematic form of ideological contestation which polarizes every topic between 'their' way of conceptualizing it and 'ours', and drives home in popular consciousness the clear distinction of principle between them. (Mrs Thatcher 'set the scene' for her ascendancy in exactly this way in the late 1970s, remorselessly punctuating the world into a series of vividly contrasting images – Labour's 'statism' against her 'freedom' – making the flat earth of consensus politics into a contested battle-zone.) We have to find ways of dramatizing the difference between the public and the private definition of social need, between medical care by income or by need, between a first-rate service for the few and a second-rate one for the majority, between paying for health by universal standard contribution and paying for it by privatized insurance. These are organizing principles, pertinent to but not restricted to the NHS (they apply, *pari passu* to education) because they are the bare bones of a social philosophy we are attempting to unfold by articulating it.

Contestation, however, is not enough, because by itself it is too negative. Thatcherism did not simply mount a principled critique of 'statism'. It unfolded a positive conception of the 'enterprise culture', which has taken root, despite the left's scepticism, to an astonishing degree. This suggests that, whilst much of it is political hype, some of it connects with real issues in the popular mind (its 'rational core'?). For example, Britain's relative 'backwardness', its sluggish performance even as compared with other capitalist countries, its suffocating traditionalism, which is linked with one of Mrs Thatcher's favourite targets – the power of entrenched vested interest.

To develop this more positive perspective, means thematizing the NHS crisis in terms of wider ideological debates: for example, around 'the politics of choice' or the question of the market versus the state. The popular theme of 'choice' has no 'necessary belongingness' to Thatcherism. It can just as well be understood as belonging to an older, deeper, complex of attitudes: 'Why shouldn't ordinary people have a piece of the action too?' Put this way, 'choice' is as much part of the political repertoire of popular radicalism as it is of the populist radical right. The problem is that Thatcherism articulated this popular desire to the 'free market' and the very powerful idea of 'freedom' – which in reality can only satisfy it in a certain form, at a certain price: and the left, having accepted this linkage (secured not by nature but by the politics of Thatcherism) consequently abandoned choice. It nevertheless remains possible to recontruct the idea of 'choice' in relation to such themes as the growing diversity of society, the widening of access, the empowerment of ordinary people through their 'right to choose' (even if it is only, to start with, choosing their GP, or having a wider range of therapies and community support services available at health centres or simply the right to know what is wrong with you or see your own medical records); or in terms of the contrast between negative and positive freedom. In short, dramatizing the NHS crisis in relation to the concepts Thatcherism has not managed to appropriate: democratization, rights and the expansion of social citizenship.

However, the left should not expect to get very far on this issue until it has clarified its mind on the underlying issue of strategic principle – that of 'market or state'. The left had a critique of 'statism' – whether of the stalinist or Fabianist varieties – long before the neo-libertarianism of the new right. But, in part because of Labourism's complicity with the latter variant, we never pushed that thinking past the point where the free-marketeers could hijack it. The so-called 'rediscovery of the market' is not a phenomenon exclusively of the right (as any Hungarian, Soviet or Chinese economist will soon tell you). And the greater flexibility, flow of information and maximization of choice which the market signals is part of that 'dynamics of change' which we identified earlier.

However, 'the market' in this generic sense is quite different from the 'free play of capitalist market forces' (another Thatcherite elision). And both are different again from the 'religion of the market' – 'value-for-money' as the sole criterion of the good life or of social need. In their unregulated forms, 'market forces', now as always, create wealth and dynamic at one end, and gross inequalities and deprivation at the other. As for value for money as the only measure of the social good, and Mrs Thatcher's 'new Benthamites' who 'take the modern shopkeeper, especially the English shopkeeper, as the normal man' and apply 'this yard measure to past, present and future', surely Marx said the last word on Mr Tebbit, Mr Baker, Lord Young, Mr Ridley and this tribe of philistines: 'geniuses in the way of bourgeois stupidity'. In a proper conception of modernity, they are cultural primitives. They have hardly come down from the trees.

Just as we have not thought through what the left 'appropriation' of the market means – what forms it can take, how far it should go, what are its necessary limits – so our critique of 'statism' remains at an extremely primitive level. If 'the state' is no longer to be the monolithic caretaker of socialism, what is it? What are the institutional forms of a responsive (rather than a prescriptive) state? Or a regulative (rather than a centralizing) state? Of a state whose function is not to curtail but to expand civil society and the democratic character of social life? And (the joker in the pack) how, if not through the state in some form, is the 'social interest' to be formulated and represented? Can the left abandon the ideas of the rational planning of resources and the rational choice between priorities in a society of scarcity, together with the 'grand narratives' of reason and progress? Can we combine a greater use of the market mechanism with greater regulation (rather than with 'deregulation')? We raise these awkward thoughts to drive home the point that a left in quest of a strategic position in political life must launch this debate and take command of this agenda itself, rather than be dragged along in the slipstream of the Adam Smith Institute.

The move from a monolithic 'state', the omnipresent provider, to a pluralized 'civil society' also entails giving value in our thinking to areas of social life and arenas where we put in play new social identities which classically the left has much neglected. For example, in relation to the NHS, the role of consumers of health care in defining needs and how they are met; or our 'rights' as citizens of an increasingly 'well' society, alongside our place as producers and suppliers. This marks the coming into play, within the discourses of a contemporary socialism, of the politics of the private as well as the public; of domestic, familial and sexual life as well as the life of the republic; 'the personal as political'. Where better to see how in modern society, these so-called 'separate spheres' increasingly interpenetrate than by looking at the arena of health, medical care, illness and the body? Where better to open up the exciting challenge of trying, in the context of the NHS debate, to think them together? This is one of the elements which anyone who has listened attentively to the radio phone-ins on the NHS will have heard being enunciated with remarkable clarity.

This shift in the postwar period from the ever-expanding state to a more diverse democratized 'civil society' state (and a 'withering' state) is one of the most profound advances to have taken place in the thinking of the left this century. It transforms the very meaning and image of socialism. It is to begin to think socialism anew from the perspective of some of the major themes of the agenda of feminism and sexual politics. (Is anybody in Walworth Road ready for that?) And it is startingly new (allowing us therefore to appropriate many themes which our commitment to 'statism' precluded) because it has taken on and been transformed by the modern experience of contemporary society. The whole 'experience' of the deformations of both Stalinism and Fabian social democracy are inscribed in that shift.

We have been concentrating, so far, on question of 'popular conceptions'. However, 'strategy' cannot be a matter of ideological politics alone. It is also a question of how to construct around those conceptions, a popular politics or, to put it more simply, the difficult business of constructing alliances. The left needs to build a majority around the NHS, not passively reflect the fragile consensus which is already there. Since this is composed of such heterogeneous social interests as are those represented by the BMA, senior consultants, junior doctors, nurses and ancillary health workers, it is an extremely unlikely alliance, destined to fall apart at the first touch of Thatcherism's magic wand if not consolidated around some common points of unity and welded into a 'bloc'. Any broader alliance in favour of some form of free, universal health care will have to be constructed across classes. That is, it will have self-consciously to be the result of a politics dedicated to speaking to people in quite different social positions. The great majorities of the dispossessed, for whom a publicly funded NHS is a life-line; the low-wage, unemployed and single-parent families who could not manage without it; the overwhelming bulk of working people, whom Edwina Currie invited to forgo their fortnight's holiday in order to be able to afford 'adequate' private health insurance; but also teachers and public sector workers and people in the service economy and those in the middle class, who might be able to afford some sort of medical premium but who value a service within the 'enterprise culture' where the best goes to those who need it most rather than to those who earn or possess the most. This is a politics which is at last face to face with, and knows how to address, the great diversity of contemporary society.

The idea of using the crisis to construct a majority means giving up the illusion of a built-in, permanent, automatic majority for the welfare state. It is better to start by assuming that there are no 'natural majorities' for anything. Class, the great backstop of the left, has certainly not disappeared. Indeed, nowhere is it so powerfully etched as in the class distribution of illness, types of health care, and death. But the underlying social, economic and cultural forces which are bringing the era of 'organized capitalism' to a close, coupled with the vigour of Thatcherite restructuring, have decomposed and fragmented class as a unified political force, fracturing any so-called automatic linkages between economics and politics: if, indeed, any such 'unity' or 'automatic linkage' ever existed (which I beg leave to doubt). The multiplication of new points of antagonism, which is also characteristic of our emerging 'post-industrial' societies, while making available new potential sites of intervention, further fragments the political field, dispersing rather than unifying the different social constituencies. These processes have unpacked the old majorities (which were, of course, never 'natural' but politically constructed) and eroded the old agendas of the left.

The stubborn truth is that social interests are contradictory. There is no automatic correspondence between class location, political position and ideological inclination. Majorities have to be 'made' and 'won' – not passively reflected. They will be composed of heterogeneous social interests, represented through conflicting social identities – like the ones emerging around the NHS. Unless they are unified by some larger political project which overrides, without obliterating, their real differences, they will fall apart (more likely, Mrs Thatcher, who does know how to recognize and exploit differences, will blow them apart).

As well as trying to unify the existing social interests and identities, the left also has to put itself 'on the side of' the new constituencies. For example, the greater involvement of mothers in the hospital care of children; the social movements for a healthier diet, for better care of the body, for greater control by women over their fertility and reproduction; for a less unequal relationship between patients and the medical profession; for more preventive medicine, a healthier environment, a programme of health education that is not at the mercy of the industrial lobbies, the pharmaceutical companies or the homophobic and anti-abortionist bigots of the 'moral monority'. If it knew how to articulate these new forces within the great levelling experience of illness, which hits everyone sooner or later irrespective of wealth or class or sexual preference, it would soon discover that society, looked at in a more diversified way, is not at all 'passive' about new needs in the field of health and medical care. People think the NHS needs more funds. But they are also willing to do something about it, as the public health movement, 'Health Alert' or the Terrence Higgins Trust suggest. The link, so often forged willy-nilly by the left, between welfare and passivity has been disastrous. But it is not inevitable.

If this is to be part of a wider, popular political strategy, it has to be fought in the end as 'a struggle for popular identities'. That is, it must draw to itself the widest range of popular aspirations about health and enable different sorts of people to see themselves reflected in this emerging conception of health and thus come increasingly to identify with it. Once you give up the idea of an automatic identification with the welfare state which is guaranteed by class position, you are obliged to address the subjective moment in politics because, unless people identify with and become the subjects of a new conception of society, it cannot materialise. Thatcherism has a perfectly focused conception of who its ideal subjects are, those who best personify its sacred values. It has used its moral agenda as one of the principal areas where these identities are defined – the respectable normal folk who people the fantasies of the new right in relation to current debates around abortion, child abuse, sex education, gay rights and Aids. It is above all through this moral agenda that the new right has become a cultural force. Significantly, all these issues of 'moral hygiene' explode directly into an expanded definition of social health

Labour has no moral agenda of its own except an inherited, conservative one. Consequently, it is not a force that is actively shaping the culture and educating desire. The paradox is that, banished by the front door, the politics of identity and desire return by the back door to exact a terrible, regressive revenge ('the London effect').

It should, by now, be crystal clear that 'learning from Thatcherism' is neither an easy nor simple task and is light years away from trying to do what Thatcherism does, only with a bit more 'caring'. It is a painful exercise since it plainly involves the left squaring up to its own past in a radical way and confronting head-on the forces which are undermining the very ground on which it has traditionally stood.

1988

Notes

1. Charles Leadbeater, *The Politics of Prosperity* (Fabian Tract 523), London 1987, p. 3.
2. A. Gramsci, 'Americanism and Fordism' in *Prison Notebooks*, London, 1971, pp. 279–316.
3. See Robin Murray, 'Bennetton Britain', in *Marxism Today*, November 1985.
4. Steve Iliffe, 'The Painful Path to Health', in *Marxism Today*, October 1986.